How to
Quit Golf
AND GET YOUR
LIFE BACK

How to
Quit Golf

AND GET YOUR
LIFE BACK

DANNY CAHILL

GREENLEAF
BOOK GROUP PRESS

Persons referenced in this book may be composites or entirely fictitious, thus references to any real persons, living or dead, are not implied.

Published by Greenleaf Book Group Press
Austin, Texas
www.gbgpress.com

Distributed by Greenleaf Book Group

For ordering information or special discounts for bulk purchases, please contact Greenleaf Book Group at PO Box 91869, Austin, TX 78709, 512.891.6100.

Design and composition by Greenleaf Book Group
Cover design by Greenleaf Book Group
Cover Images by Jake Nackos, Önder Örtel, and Miki Fath from Unsplash.com

Publisher's Cataloging-in-Publication data is available.

Print ISBN: 979-8-88645-144-3

eBook ISBN: 979-8-88645-145-0

To offset the number of trees consumed in the printing of our books, Greenleaf donates a portion of the proceeds from each printing to the Arbor Day Foundation. Greenleaf Book Group has replaced over 50,000 trees since 2007.

Printed in the United States of America on acid-free paper

24 25 26 27 28 29 30 31   10 9 8 7 6 5 4 3 2 1

First Edition

Contents

For Dale and Todd, who were the first to convince me to
"spoil a good walk," and for Brian,
who helps make it just a little less maddening

"If I ever find the guy who talked me into taking up this game, I'm going to drag him out back of the snack shack and shoot him like a rabid dog. If I get a golfer on the jury, I'm pretty sure I'll walk."

—Seventy-five-year-old starter of a Myrtle Beach semi-private club

Prologue

Y ou know you have to quit golf. You bought this book, after all. That was a good first step, but you're probably still in denial. You latch on to pathetic signs that you don't have to quit. Maybe you were at a business conference with a resort course, and you didn't play. Maybe you didn't pay $9.95 for WiFi on your flight just to check the PGA leaderboard. (It wasn't a major, just the John Deere Open.) Maybe you tell yourself you're fine because you haven't played in a month, even though it's February and you live in New Hampshire. Or worse, maybe you just hit a hybrid high-and-soft 205 yards over a water hazard and it rolled to 2 feet on the hardest par 3 on your home course (pick it up, you know you can miss that putt) and you see this as a sign that you not only don't need to quit golf, but that at fifty-four you are about to unlock your potential.

No. No, you're not. You need to quit golf and get your life back.

But that's a big ask, and I get it. And hell, I don't know you—maybe I'm wrong. (I'm not. You really, really need to quit.) Maybe you're not in denial. (You are.) Let's take a test, and then you can decide whether it's worth reading the rest of this book.

The test:

Answer honestly. No one is going to see this, unless you show it to someone, which you probably will because . . .

1. Do you show your golf scorecards to, well, anyone?

2. At dinner, do you find yourself practicing your grip on your utensils? (The Vs of the fork's first tine, for the righthander, should point to the right shoulder.)

3. Look above you. Are there marks on the ceilings of your house because you can't help but try to "bust one" even when you're indoors and there is no ball?

4. Have you lied to your boss about having to leave early so you can sneak in nine holes before dinner?

5. Have you lied to your spouse about having to work late so you can sneak in nine holes before dinner?

6. Do you stop and hit a range ten minutes from the course, but then tell your buddies you haven't picked up a club since the week before and request a breakfast ball on the first tee despite the fact that you've sweated through your shirt?

7. Have you taken to reflexively calling your children "pards"?

8. Do other golf aphorisms make their way into your personal life? (Examples include finding your lost car keys and with a shrug saying, "Even a blind squirrel finds a nut now and again," or feeding your actual dog and exhorting, "Time to let the big dog eat!")

9. Are there more clubs in your garage than at Golfer's Warehouse?

10. Despite your inventory, are you planning on buying new clubs soon?

11. Do you refer to your putter as "my Scotty Cameron"? Did you pay full price for it?

12. Do you actually know your MOI (moment of inertia)? Your club head speed? Your launch angle? How about your smash factor? Considering your double-digit handicap, is this a good use of your mental energy?

13. When someone in the office pool for the Masters says, "I'll take Tiger," do you find yourself rolling your eyes dismissively while secretly being pleased that Xander Schauffele is still available?

14. Do you watch so much Golf Channel that when Brandel Chamblee starts ranting, you find yourself yelling, "That's the exact opposite of what you said last week! Have you no shame?"

15. Do you watch so much Golf Channel that you find yourself, in a sentimental mood, wondering what happened to Peter Kessler?

16. Do you watch so much Golf Channel that in the evening you watch the "encore" replay of the golf you watched this afternoon (justifying it by saying you napped through some of the key holes when it was first broadcast)?

17. Do you watch so much Golf Channel that, during those naps, you find yourself sexually fantasizing about Win McMurray and Cara Banks?

18. When you sexually fantasize about Golf Channel women, is there part of you that feels that you are cheating on Holly Sonders and Paige Spiranac?

19. Does your dry cleaner, never having seen your swing but processing your bill, assume you are a golf pro?

20. Do you think of all spatial relationships in the real world in terms of golfing distance? (When, while parking at the mall, your wife suggests you are too far away, do you say, "What? It's like a stock gap wedge to Panera from here." When she disagrees, do you break out the Bushnell and shoot the store's signage?)

How's the test going? Are you downplaying? Getting defensive?

You're probably thinking, "I might be investing a little too much energy in the game, but I'm not going to apologize for being passionate. I'm not home sitting on the couch, I'm doing something I like to do. I work hard, I deserve golf!"

Or maybe you're thinking, "It's very healthy, I'm outdoors, eighteen holes of golf burns five thousand calories." (That's if you walk and if you don't drink two beers and down two hot dogs at the turn. You get exhausted if it's cart paths only.)

Then again, you might say to yourself, "It's social! All the data says middle-aged men have higher rates of depression and suicide because they don't form or keep friendships the way women do. Golf is the ultimate social sport!"

And you might have a point when you argue, "So what, then? Crossfit? Head to a park and see if I can get into a pick-up basketball game with my knee pads and compression stockings? My Achilles gets sore from bunker practice! Golf is the one game I can still play! It's the only game where improvement is possible, where I can still hope I haven't peaked!"

Hope! Ah, yes, golf's default setting. Its fallback position allows it to survive when you reach the point—and you will—where you realize:

It's too hard.

It's too expensive.

There are other ways to be miserable.

And most important, in a fallen world where 100 percent of the non-divine among us will die . . .

It takes too long to play.

Look, I know. I know! You're thinking, "Can't I just cut back?" No more stopping at the club on the way home to chip and putt. Just show up and play. And I'll delete all golf apps and unfollow Rory on X (formerly known as Twitter), and I'll cancel my Revolution Golf subscription. Would that work?

Look, I know that sounds reasonable, but let me ask you this: Can you not only remember every shot you have hit but also every shot your buddies have hit? Do your conversations go something like this?

"Remember that time, I don't know where we were. . ."

"It was the sixth hole at Richter Park, you double crossed a six iron, you found it but you had to take an unplayable and you punched it to the fringe and made the putt for 6. It was 2012, the week after the Open."

Thought so. No, you can't cut back, you have to quit!

You suggest transitioning over time. You'll just play charity scrambles while you take up yoga or chess. You'll stop Zillowing Myrtle Beach real estate that you can't afford. And you'll budget. You'll start playing Maxflis or even those stupid yellow matte balls! You'll quit your league—well, you'll quit it next year, you'll just sub this year!

Dude, you're not hearing me. Aren't you the guy who used to go to church on Sundays? Remember the inexplicably liquid feeling you would get when you would look down the row of that pew and see your family, and know that there was no other place in the world you should be other than where you were? Remember how clean that felt? But last year you pretended to be sick for your niece's First Communion because you had the qualifier for the club championship. The C flight, for God's sake.

You need to quit!

You argue that you're not as bad as Carl, who plays like six times a week. You and your buddies call him The Velvet Hammer because he can get up and down from anywhere. You've literally never been to the club and not seen him there.

And how would you know he plays that often unless you're there at least as often as he is?

Okay, maybe you hadn't realized how much you've been playing. But you've been under a lot of pressure at work. Golf is how you relieve stress!

Think about the panic attacks you have when you have to carry a water hazard. Think about your Tarantino-influenced stream of profanity when you hit one OB. Think about the fact that you went to a cardiologist last year to get beta blockers to help you fight the yips. Golf *is* your stress!

But not always! Sometimes it's amazing! The weather is perfect, the ball is going where you aim it, your buddies are in a good mood, the match is tight, there's not a concern in the world, not a thought in your head besides golf.

Speaking of which—and please be precise—while all this is going on, every weekend, what is your wife doing with her day?

You stutter for a moment. "Umm, well, It depends. I mean, I'm sure she's glad to have some alone time, we've been married a long time, she's got a lot of stuff to catch up on."

So you have no idea?

Not the slightest.

Other than near the end of the round, when you wonder how pissed she is going to be about how long you've been gone, do you ever wonder how she feels? About golf? About you? About how she's spending all those hours alone?

"Okay, okay, I get it . . . But do I have to quit cold turkey? Nothing in the middle? No golfing, even on vacation?"

You have to be as all out as you've been all in.

"I can do it. I know I can. It's just a game, right?"

Exactly. So, you're ready to quit golf and get your life back? What's the matter?

"I can't believe how scary this is. How did I get here?"

Great question.

CHAPTER ONE

How Did You Get Here?

There was a time when you wouldn't even have considered playing golf. Golf was something old men played. You'd see it on TV and think, "They don't even sweat, how is that a game?" And it vaguely annoyed you when people referred to golf as a sport. You put golf in the category of bowling or billiards or darts. In fact, for a long time, all during your twenties, golf had two distinct functions in your life. Mini golf was a great, non-threatening summer activity with any new girl you were dating. No one is any good at mini golf, and everyone plays loose with the rules because no one cares who wins. Golf's only other function for you was as part of your hangover cure. The morning after a night out, where two weeks after you last vowed to never, ever do tequila shots again, you in fact had three such shots and chased it with the remnants of the evening's twelfth beer and you generally found yourself on the couch in a world of hurt. You knew you had to sleep it off, but your pounding head and post-vomit dehydration made the task difficult. So you turned on the TV, located the week's PGA event, and closed your eyes as the announcers sang their lullaby of birdies and doglegs and undulating greens. The building "ooh" of the crowd as a long putt rolled toward the hole was particularly comforting, but the ensuing cheer if the putt dropped could snap you out of your trance. The days the putts weren't falling provided some deep REM just when you needed it most.

But other than as a way to kill time during the infatuation stage of a relationship and a crucial part of your rest and recovery protocol after drinking, golf meant nothing to you. It was something your friends' fathers did. In fact, one of them—a purist, apparently—could no longer take your ignorance: "Stop asking me if I am 'going golfing.' I am going to play golf. You don't 'go golfing.'"

You thought he was being a jerk, but now you can tell the difference between a fade swing and a draw swing without Toptracer technology. When did this all start?

Every golfer's story is different. Some got to the point where they realized they not only didn't like cycling for fifty miles on Saturday mornings anymore, but the tight spandex biking shorts were starting to look ridiculous. Others reached the point in the gym where they were maxing out with the weights they used to warm up with. For some other guy, at some point during his ongoing denial of his evaporating youth, someone took him to a driving range. Maybe he rode along with a buddy for nine holes and he let him drive the cart. Then he asked if he wanted to try taking a swing. "I'm an athlete," this guy told himself, "How hard could it be?" Maybe he was thirty-five, or forty . . . It happens a lot when people turn forty and start to panic.

For you it was a tennis tournament. You had been playing tournament tennis for twenty-five years, and had reached the 4.0 level, which is similar to a single digit handicap in golf. You won your share of tournaments and nearly always reached the semifinals or finals. In club tennis, they have singles ladders, and your name was on your club's top rungs for two decades. Someone might beat you, but you were a tough out, and through the magic of Kevlar racquets and synthetic strings, you could still compete in the "open" division.

Until the day you decided it was time to take up golf. You had reached the finals of your club's singles championships. You were forty-two years old. You strode on to the court, and a man about your age with a Fila warm-up suit and the obligatory overstuffed racquet bag introduced himself. You assumed he was your opponent, and you liked your chances. He was clearly overweight, so you instantly assumed he got to the finals because he still had a big serve. You ran down your checklist of how to play him: take a step back to return the first serve, hit to big targets and keep it in play, run this guy into the ground, attack short balls. Your strategy session got interrupted when his son, who turned out to be your actual opponent, casually sauntered over with his water bottle and apologized for being a little late. He said he was twenty-one. Half your age. His dad wished him luck and went upstairs to watch from the spectator's veranda.

We'll spare the audience the full story of your tactical guile, your ability to counter his power with slice and moonballs. Let's move on past your decision not to correct him when he called some shots "in" that were clearly "out," and nothing really needs to be said about how he seemed to be trying to impress his father by overhitting. All that we need to know is that you refused to lose. And two hours later, you sat in the locker room with your tiny, plastic trophy, feeling like you had been overcome by the flu. Beyond exhausted, you were unable to take your drenched clothes off to shower. Your knees, hips, and shoulders were throbbing, and you took 1600 mg of Motrin to match the dose you took before the match. You knew you should drink water, but grasping the bottle two feet away from you seemed impossible. And out of the showers popped sonny boy. He waved to you and said, "That was a blast, right?" He took his phone out of his locker, and over the next couple of minutes of eavesdropping, you gathered that he would be at a party within the hour, and of course he knew how to tap a keg. The tournament was the least of his day, just a way to get a little exercise and burn some calories. For you, it wasn't as much "do or die" as "do and then die." You wanted to go home and nap, wake up, and then go to bed.

The next day, you asked your employee Dale, an inveterate golfer, how one might go about learning to play golf. His eyes lit up. And not with the humanistic light of a born teacher who lives for the satisfaction of helping others. No, Dale realized instantly that if he got the boss hooked on golf, 1) sneaking out on Fridays to play would soon become sanctioned, and 2) the boss would join a country club and then he would get to play a nicer course for free! You agreed to meet at a driving range the next day, and Dale volunteered to show you the basics. "You've been an athlete your whole life, you'll be a natural," he said.

Dale was habitually late for every work meeting and all appointments in life except his tee time. You got to the driving range first, bought an extra-large bucket of balls that you had to bend your knees and deadlift in order to get it out to the hitting area, and rented an ancient, dinged up driver, because it had the logical number 1 embossed on the underside of the club head. While you waited for Dale, you sat back and observed the group hitting balls on the mats. Some things were clear.

One guy had to be a pro. Everything seemed to go long and high, in a pretty, right-to-left trajectory that had to be on purpose because each ball landed near one of the various targets with numbers like 100, 150, 175 and 250. You assumed these were yards. He wore golf shoes and slacks that matched his golf shirt. You noticed that before every swing, he did the exact same things, sort of like a basketball player at the free-throw line who always bounces the ball twice, breathes, and shoots. This guy would look at the target, waggle his hips, set the club down, and pull the trigger. Every time. You knew nothing about golf, but you knew he was good.

Everyone else sucked. Their shots were so poorly struck they would roll only a few feet. Some of them would run out to get the ball so they could try it again. Most hit the ball in a wild, banana-shaped slice. Once in a while, a ball would go toward the target, and their faces would beam, but by the next swing the magic was gone.

There were a few couples on the range, and you could tell by the shorts and flip-flops this was a date, a lazy alternative to a hike. The woman would tee a wedge up on a 4-inch tee, predictably scoop the club under it, and the man would tell her she "moved her head." Then he would offer to illustrate and do no better.

Everyone seemed frustrated, some seemed miserable, and some glass-half-full types would adjust their shirt sleeves to remind themselves they were at least getting a tan.

Suddenly the guy you thought was a pro inexplicably lost his mojo and started smothering the ball low and left. He became enraged and slammed his club into his bag, pulled out another club, and did the same thing. He asked someone, I assume the golf gods, "Are you joking?" And now it was unanimous—everyone on the range, there in their leisure time and using their hard-earned disposable income, was somewhere on the spectrum from flustered to furious.

But you saw Dale's car pull up and you knew this wouldn't be your fate. Dale could teach you, and as he had said, you had been an athlete forever. You had great hand-eye coordination from a very young age, and the sports you played all involved balls moving—tennis serves, baseballs coming at you at high speeds, basketballs several feet over your head that you had to leap to procure. Whereas in golf, the ball is stationary. You said to yourself, "I got this!" Golf was going to be a breeze.

Dale laughed when he saw your extra-large bucket and extra-small-headed driver. He said he didn't hit that many balls in an entire season and stated one simple goal for the day: "Our goal is to get the ball in the air. Once we do that, we're done for the first lesson."

You didn't know what you had expected, but Dale's idea of teaching was to hit balls while you watched. He was every bit as good as the pseudo-pro at the far end of the range who had left nearly in tears. He hit one he particularly liked and that indeed landed right on the 100-yard marker. Then he handed you his club and said, "I can't hit it any better than that, you try."

The first few swings, you were unable to make contact. You blamed the defective club. Then you somehow managed to hit the wooden wall of your cubicle. You blamed the limited space. Then you shanked one so horribly it nearly hit the woman in the next cubicle.

Dale decided a short tutorial was in order. He showed you the correct grip. Whatever you were doing before was too "weak." He turned your left hand clockwise until you could see three knuckles and told you to turn your shoulder until it was under your chin—that would complete the backswing. Then he said to hit the ball, "from the ground up." You nodded without any understanding of how that could be possible. He told you to keep your left arm straight, to keep your head still, and to grip the club lightly, as if you were holding a bird in your hand, which was not helpful given that you had never held a bird before, and if you had, you reasoned it would try to get away and you would have to squeeze the little sucker tight. Dale told you to keep all these things in mind and "swing like an athlete!"

You didn't know it then, but being an athlete was exactly the problem.

Give a pro golf coach a choice of which forty-something they would rather teach. Option one: someone who learned the game at twelve, taking lessons at their parent's club, but gave it up when they got caught up in other high school sports, and is now returning to the game after a twenty-five-year absence. Or option two: a forty-something weekend warrior who lettered in baseball, still plays pick-up basketball, and does CrossFit twice a week but who has never touched a golf club in his life. Notice how fast they ask you for the contact info for the former, and how they refer the latter to the junior pro.

Why? Because everything you learned about other sports hurts you in golf. Let's look at the ways—

- In other sports, the harder you try, the better you do. In golf, you have to try to not try.

- In other sports, you play by instinct and muscle memory. In golf, you have the luxury of overanalyzing. When you react to a tennis serve, you don't have time to think about whether your racquet face is square to the target or if you're rolling your wrist to create topspin, you just know you want to hit the serve deep to the deuce court, and you trust your brain and body to somehow make that happen in a split second. In golf, you have a ton of time (which is why it takes so long) to consider which physical mistake you will make on this particular shot.

- Stick with any other sport long enough and you'll get a feel for it, even as an adult. Not so with golf. If you played golf as a child and have muscle memory, you can golf as an adult. If you didn't, you will spend your life playing "golf swing," where the true objective of the game— getting the ball in the hole in as few strokes as possible—is lost, and only your golf swing mechanics matter to you.

- Unlike other sports you have mastered, golf is about opposites. If you swim, various strokes propel you forward in different ways, but always forward. Likewise, you never hurl a Frisbee to the ground in order to make it go up. And if you swing up at a baseball, the ball will always go up. But in golf, you swing down to make the ball go up, you swing to the right to make the ball go left, and vice versa. When you want the ball to go a short distance, you swing hard (after you've opened the club and changed your stance), and if you want it to go a long distance you swing easy.

- In golf, what you are doing is not what you think you are doing. If you miss a spike in volleyball, you don't ask your teammates what you did wrong. You hit the damn ball into the net, probably because you didn't jump anywhere near as high as you thought you would. But in golf, if you miss your drive so badly the ball rolls to the women's tee, you will be told 1) you lifted your head, 2) you swayed, 3) you "came off that one, bud," 4) you teed it up too high. (And one guy will point out you didn't clear the women's tee and so it's time to unzip. Forget about him.)

- In other sports, practice is invaluable. But because "feel isn't real" and you're not doing what you think you're doing in your swing (and you won't even believe it when you see it on video), practice at golf just makes you worse. This is the unkindest cut of all for an athlete. In all your other athletic endeavors, if you learned enough from others who are good and you committed the time to the task, you improved quickly, soon became very adept, and eventually mastered the sport. In golf, this sort of commitment all but guarantees failure.

Here's the evil, insidious part: The golf gods are like crack dealers in a new neighborhood. Give everything away for free, let them get hooked on the high, and then extract your price. And crack dealers don't even have mats! Driving range mats give the illusion of skill. You bounce your club into the mat and the ball still goes 130 yards. Little do you know that on the course, that same swing gets you a face full of divot dirt. And you get Driving Range Amnesia, where you hit 40 percent of all your shots off-line, but because you managed to catch a few in the middle of the clubface, you leave feeling like you did pretty good, only to be humiliated when you realize missing 40 percent of all shots on the course means you pretty much suck.

Dale had to know all of this, of course. Or maybe he had been playing so long he forgot. But because of all the tennis, or because of an innate understanding of shifting weight and swinging an object meant to propel a ball, or because your weightlifting regimen enabled you to strong-arm the ball, or maybe just from beginner's luck, about thirty balls in, you got the ball in the air with the wedge. Dale then gave you a 6 iron, and you were able to hit it 120 yards and straight. He handed you a 3 wood, adjusted your ball position, and told you to imagine, "If the ball was at noon and there was a line straight behind it, that would represent six p.m. Now swing from seven to one p.m. And stop being a wimp and swing the freaking club—hard."

The first one you sliced badly.

The second one you topped.

Then it happened. The ball jumped off the club head, soared into the air, and carried nearly 200 yards before bouncing into the 200-yard marker. It was amazing! Dale asked you later what it felt like, and you told him you really didn't feel anything, and he smiled and nodded.

You hurried to put another ball down, to get another fix, but Dale wouldn't have it. He said, "Always go home on a good one. End of lesson, boss man. You're a natural."

No, no, you're not. No one is.

Well, let's not blame Dale. If it wasn't him, it would have been someone else. But that was helpful, because now you know how this all started. It's the same for every beginning golfer—you got hooked the moment you got the ball in the air.

And now, God save your soul, you have been bitten by the Golf Bug!

CHAPTER TWO

The Golf Bug Bites

You are a golfer so, by definition, you are hard on yourself. What kind of worthless specimen of a human would top a tee shot in front of "everyone" on the first tee? You tell yourself a child could tap in the 16-inch putt you missed to push the last hole—no one abuses you like you abuse yourself when you are playing badly, and no one is less convinced than you that you are playing well when you are, in fact, playing well.

You abuse yourself, so let's clarify: You didn't set out to recklessly abandon most of what you thought you valued in life in the name of playing golf. You were bitten by the Golf Bug.

No, you say? You certainly enjoy golf, and you absolutely try your best to improve your game, but hey, that's just who you are. It's how you approach everything in life. It's how you got to the point in life where you could fund your golf hobby. But it is very much just a hobby. Something you can do as a family, a great way to meet people, a tax-deductible way to entertain clients. But it's strictly a weekend pursuit, done only in good weather, and you never go out early, when all the hardcore golfers are out. You have it all in perspective.

Uh huh.

Let me help you determine if you are smitten or bitten. Let's break this down.

First, let's talk about your golf lessons. A casual golfer, just smitten, might not get lessons at all. They might just take some pointers from their neighbor's son, who is on the high school team and launches balls into the woods that abut both your properties. A smitten golfer might go to the range a couple times before the season starts and then just show up and play the rest of the season. Let's be really charitable and say a smitten golfer might even go to their local PGA pro and take actual lessons.

You signed up for a package of five lessons. The plan was to start with the full swing, practice in between lessons, and then dial in the short game in lessons four and five. You left the first session with a video your pro downloaded for you, and you even looked at it a few times, with its dizzying blur of lines intersecting your shoulders and your club. You were over some plane, he said, and you were not shifting your weight correctly, but he was impressed with your address position and felt you had potential.

You were supposed to practice for a week or two and then schedule your second lesson, but in this hypothetical, it's been a month and you just haven't had time. You coach your daughter's lacrosse team, and you wouldn't be able to make dinner on time if you stopped at the range on the way home during the week. Okay, you might be smitten.

But, if you moved on from your local pro after four packages of five lessons each, Googled *Golf Digest*'s Top 100 pros, flew to PGA national, and took a private lesson with him or her for $800 (only to be told the same thing your local pro told you about casting the club), then you've been bitten.

If you went from shooting 100 to shooting in the low 90s and decided it was time for genuine commitment, so you used the three remaining personal days you had at work to attend a three-day golf school (rather than taking that getaway to a bed-and-breakfast in Maine with your spouse), and not only spent five grand but found that seven hours of lessons in the Florida sun left you exhausted and so sunburned you stuck to your sheets each night, and left completely confused by the amount of information you were getting, to the point where on the last day, when everyone got to play the Champions Course, your reward for your diligence and your newfound knowledge was to shoot 109, then you've been bitten.

If at your local driving range, you get irritated when someone has "your spot," and you pound buckets during your lunch hours, often returning to work drenched and smelly and wondering alternately why you can't hit the ball like that on the course and why the swing-thought that served you so well yesterday is futile today, then you've been bitten.

Still don't believe me? Let's move to your garage. Do you have a variety of golf training aids that you saw endorsed by a cavalcade of has-been pros from yesteryear? Do you have the club with the orange for a head that is supposed to increase your mobility? Do you have the club that makes a clicking sound at the point of impact that is supposed to increase your swing speed by 20 mph in just ten swings? Do you have an impact bag that costs $100 but is functionally no different from hitting a pillow or cushion? How about the swing contraption that is supposed to create width but is nothing more than a clothes hanger stuck under your arms? What about the sand wedge with a leading edge the size of your driver that is guaranteed to hit it out of the sand every time? The putter that looks like you could rake your leaves with it in the autumn? Don't be ashamed if you have all these things and don't use them. Now your ab roller doesn't feel so lonely!

And what about in the trunk of your car? Do you have TrackMan? Dude, you don't even have your phone synced to your car and you're a 13 handicap with Trackman?

Guess what, my friend? You've been bitten by the Golf Bug.

"Are you *sure*? What if I'm just passionate? I mean, is that a problem?"

Good question. Well, businesspeople (you used to be one on a full-time basis before you were bitten) often refer to lost opportunity costs—the potential benefits foregone by choosing one course of action over another. It's not just that you are playing golf and talking about playing golf and thinking about playing golf. What could you be doing, discussing, and thinking about if you didn't have the Golf Bug? Think of how much time and mental energy that would free up!

But okay, I'll indulge your delusion for a moment. What are the associated lost opportunity costs of having the Golf Bug? Let's start with a literal interpretation. The Golf Bug is expensive!

The average golfer spends between $2,700 and $3,000 a year on the sport. They play 45–50 rounds at public courses at an average cost of $36–$40 per round, and that includes a cart. Most golfers have one set of clubs that they've had for many years. Every half decade or so, a loved one gives them a new driver for Christmas. (The gift giver wraps the head in colored paper and puts a bow on the shaft, and when the golfer says, "Gee, what is this?" everyone rolls their eyes.) They buy a bag of recycled balls from Walmart each spring, and those Nitros and Noodles you toss when you're looking for your ball in the fescue? They're picking up those suckers and hitting them next Saturday off the first tee.

They play courses that are having specials on greens fees, and while you stand behind them in the fairway they dredge the water hazard in front of the green with an extender retriever rod in search of wayward premium balls. They have one pair of black golf shoes, and they spend hours attempting to replace the soft spikes with a tool ill-suited for the task. When they inevitably fail, they play in sneakers. They search the par 3 teeing grounds like a sniffer dog in an airport security line, looking for broken tees they can salvage for their shot. When the minimum-wage kids looking for tips offer to clean their clubs at the cart return, they say, "No, thanks" and schlep their clubs to the car. They don't clean their clubs, or buy new grips, or even worry about what else they throw on top of their clubs in the trunk. Once they hit the $3,000 mark, they stop playing, and it's usually about the time of year when they've gotten kind of bored with it or the weather is turning. They put their clubs away, and the next April, it takes a while to find them in the cellar. Most importantly, if they are planning on playing, and someone suggests doing something else—going on a picnic, a trip to a water park, a concert—they're in and think nothing of committing the cardinal sin of canceling on the rest of their foursome via text.

But while most work to live, you work to play golf. And if there's any disposable income left over, you're happy to share it with your family to buy staples like food and shelter.

Let's run your numbers from last year.

You pay $1,800 a month for your country club membership, not counting the quarterly charges for food at the restaurant where you hardly ever eat, or the $350 a year for the locker you store nothing in, or the $10–$50 a week you spend on beverages and snacks from the cart girl, or the $20 you give the kid who cleans your clubs. Then there are the charges for the men's club where you play every Saturday, and the money you lose not only by opting to get in on the closest-to-the-pin contest you have no chance of winning, but by agreeing to play in a match with your foursome that you don't quite understand. ("So, simple Nassau gentlemen, greenies, sandies, press on each side, $20 a man?") Then there are your guests. It's $75 a round and $25 for their cart rental. This really isn't like spending money though, because they belong to their own clubs and when they reciprocate, it's a push. (But don't waste any energy wondering why they never seem to reciprocate. Thinking that way will only upend your economic model.)

Next, there's your clubs. Despite logic and your double-digit handicap, you play forged blades for irons. No cavity backs for you—forgiveness is for church, not your golf bag. You prefer the feel of Pings, but your favorite players on tour play Callaway, so for that idiotic reason, you do too. Your irons cost $1,199. You replace them every two to three years, even though it is fair to say the sweet spot in the middle of each club remains chaste.

Your driver is new every year. You're a man of science, and who are you to question the increased ball speed you get from the ultra-thin face that is made from artificial intelligence or the lighter triaxial carbon that increases MOI and allows you to hit it straight and far even on off-center hits, even though you have never hit it straight or far even on dead-center hits? Now they include a screwdriver-ish looking implement to adjust your settings and promote a draw or a fade on demand. I mean, the whole world is about changing settings and getting things on demand; why learn how to work the ball if they have technology that will do it for you? How is that not worth $599 every year? True, the same club will be in the used drivers bin at the back of the store in ninety days for $219, but the season, like life itself, is short! You can hit a lot of big drives in ninety days.

Your golf balls are another thing you don't scrimp on. The last time you restocked, you ran into the A flight champion at Golfer's Warehouse. He was there because spring was blossoming and it was time to buy the season's supply of golf balls. You bonded over the fact that you were there for the same purpose. But he bought a single sleeve of Titleist Pro Vs that would last him through the season, while you not only brought your SUV and put the back seats down to make room, you also rented a small U-Haul in case it took a while to get the rust off your swing and you lost some balls. The Taylor Made TP-5s you play costs $49.99 a box, and due to the ravages of cart path damage, water hazards, your penchant for poison ivy which keeps you from venturing into the woods, and the irrational but genuine feeling of having "never liked that ball anyway," you make this trip quite often. Lately you have added to the expense by ordering mono-grammed TP-5s online. You put your kids' names on them, which you thought would endear you to your wife, until she asked if you are harboring a deep-seated wish to hit them as hard as you can with a club.

Now let's take a tour through your walk-in closet and talk about your golf clothes. Even having been bitten by the Golf Bug, you only play two or three times a week due to the cosmic inhumanity of daily employment. Your spouse is kind enough to do laundry during the week, and yet you have sixty-one different polo-style golf shirts, and each one averages around $79.99. (We're going to forget your regrettable experiment with trying to wear the super tight Tiger Woods "blade" shirts that made your abdomen scream for mercy, and I don't think anyone has to know about your short-lived Tommy Bahama untucked period where you looked like a bouncer at Bada Bing! circa *The Sopranos* 2002.)

Pants are a bit more complicated, because you wear shorts and slacks. Now, you live in the Northeast, so one would expect a 2:1 ratio of slacks to shorts, but it doesn't work that way. Today's golf pants are so nice they can be worn as biz casual to work, and one has to have heavier wool pants for the beginning and end of the golf year, as well as lightweight pants for the season. And, being a purist, you won't wear shorts for a tournament or serious match. So an approximate count of golf pants, including shorts, comes to around a hundred pairs, with an average price of $98 each.

Not to mention, you have to keep the decorum at the club and wear a belt, and you've now taken to matching your belt with your shoes and your golf hat and maybe some accented color in your shirt. Your wife has taken to calling this "ridiculous," but that's because her own walk-in closet is full and she wants in on your space. You will concede that you favor certain golf hats and seem to ignore the others, so maybe you don't need all fifty-seven your wife says are stacked in your closet.

The weather gear—the rain suits, the rain gloves, the rain hat, the extra wide golf umbrella—is all kept in the garage. They cost around $600 altogether, and you replace them each year for no apparent reason. But since they are not in the house proper, we're not going to add that to your total. However, even though they have their own shelf in the garage, it only seems fair to include your golf shoes. You have twenty-two pairs. (That doesn't count the Puma Ignites you just ordered because you saw them on a guy at the club last week and they looked amazing and he said they helped with his balance, since those haven't arrived yet.) You no longer replace spikes, you just buy new shoes. Due to the aforementioned desire to match outfits, you need an array of colors and styles. You have low-key Skechers, serious golf Foot Joys, and $1,200 Treccani Milanos custom cobbled from ostriches that you only wear . . . well you haven't actually found the heart yet to wear them on the course and get them all dirty, so you weirdly play in your Eccos and then change into your Treccanis before going into the grill room.

Next category: your technology. No one ever said golf was fair, so while it may not seem fair that you said no when your daughter wanted a brand new laptop, or that you rolled your eyes when your wife wanted the Apple Watch to monitor her heart rate in spin class ("You know what, if you can talk to the woman on the next bike, your heart rate isn't high enough!"), but bought yourself a new SkyCaddie for $399, it's just as fair as when you hit a perfectly struck 7 iron and come up 5 yards short. Or when your lay-up goes into the drink because you didn't know the yardage. Your wife's argument that she doesn't understand why you need a GPS device when you play the same course week in and week out and know all the yardages because you hit the ball in the same place every time you play, is a sign of her lack of understanding of the nuances and complexities of the game. And while it's true that your new five-inch touchscreen with a multicore processor and rotating views has not seemed to improve your scores one bit, your wife doesn't appreciate how selfless a gift it truly was. She doesn't see you practically bound out of your cart to say to your partner, "Let me shoot that for you, Bill!" Your GPS device makes you a giver. Can she offer to read someone else's heartbeat in spin class? Exactly!

On the topic of technology, it's just occurred to you that you might want to delete your browser history, since last Sunday your wife spent the afternoon reviewing student loan applications while you were shopping for home golf simulators. She probably would be understanding if she saw that OptiShot sale for $499, but that's just software and a mat with a net. Kid stuff. But if she finds out you watched a YouTube demo for a $65,000 full swing golf simulator that will take up most of your garage, meaning one of your cars (hers, since you leave first in the morning) will have to sit outside at night during the winter months, she might go on one of those rants about impulse control and therapy.

Are the dollar signs starting to add up yet? But wait—we haven't even gotten to the big-ticket items yet: your golf trips. Even for those bitten by the Golf Bug, the expenditure here exists on a spectrum. On one end of the spectrum, usually during the winter months or early spring, a group of guys invite you to go to Myrtle Beach for a long weekend. You stay in crappy hotels where the word "courtyard" is code for "we have no room service, there is no free WiFi, our gym used to be just another hotel room but we took out the furniture and put in a treadmill and a stationary bike, and breakfast is ironically complimentary even though it has never, ever received a compliment, given that it is a buffet of dried scrambled eggs, grits, and greasy bacon; refills on the watery coffee are free but no one ever takes them up on the offer."

But it's all good, because you and your crew are there for the impossibly low-priced but pristine golf courses that seem to be around every corner. You play eighteen holes, drink way too much at lunch, and then play another eighteen holes before downing NSAIDs, showering, and going out to Myrtle Beach's dizzying array of practically-fast-food restaurants and hybrid sports bars/strip clubs. (You knew you were getting old when you politely offered the girl on stage several dollars to bend over, but only because you wanted to see the Tiger Tracker on the TV screen she was blocking.) By day three of this junket, you are tired of hangovers, you are so sore you can barely swing the club, and you have gained four pounds you are unlikely to do anything about once you get home. Worse, you miss your kids, your wife, your dog, the way the sun seems almost purple as it goes down over your deck. You say nothing of this to your friends. You nod furiously when they insist it was "the best trip ever!"

On the other end of the spectrum, no one needs to ask the true, hard-bitten golfer about his bucket list. All one needs to do is Google *Golf Digest*'s top 100 courses. Your goal is to knock them off one by one. Luckily, your honeymoon was long ago, you have dispensed of the obligatory kids' trip to Disneyworld, and now vacations and long holiday weekends exist solely for you to choose a new elite golf resort destination. With the same guile you use to get up and down from a short-sided downhill lie, you sell these trips to your wife as a couple's weekend. The resorts are always beautiful, they always have a world-class spa where you can, for a few hundred dollars, have hot stones placed on your back or seaweed and mud caked all over your body, and a salon where you can get your hair blown out or, treat your skin to a collagen resurrection. And once all that is done, you can enjoy the coed steam sauna, or drink champagne and eat candied apricots presented in glass vases while they blast New Age music, or sit in your $500 robe in the "meditation and silence" area, where no one meditates and everyone chats. Take your time, meet a new friend, and go to lunch.

Because while she's doing all of that, you're on the course you actually came here for. Standing on the same tees as the pros (well, okay, 50 yards up), playing the exact same holes they play, running your approach up at Pinehurst #2, staring over the cliff on #8 at Pebble, watching the sheep graze in the middle of the fairway at Whistling Straits (knowing they're safe from your errant tee ball). Sure, the round costs $500–$600, and that doesn't count the caddy, but you're playing one of the finest golf courses in the world.

Golf is spiritual, but there isn't just one Mecca, no one-and-done pilgrimage to Rome. There are a hundred trips to be had. You will keep the scorecards for all of them. You will spend hundreds in the pro shop for sweaters, hats, ball markers—proof you were here. Then you and your wife will meet back in the room and, assuming you aren't exhausted from the golf and she doesn't want to mess with her pampered vibe, you will have vacation sex and then go to one of the resort's five-star restaurants. If it rains, you cut a deal and go to a museum or some such nonsense. You might even do a couple's massage in the room, though you've seen that setup so often in porn you find it discomforting. The point is, you're a reasonable guy! Everyone wins! Until the credit card statement comes in.

Let's take your last excursion to Pebble. You stayed at The Lodge, because that's the only way to get preferred tee times on the course. That's $1,100 per night. You played twice, that's $1,200. Your wife's spa excursions ran $425 (not including tips). Between room service and eating out, you spent $815 on meals. And we still have to count the standard expenses of airfare ($1,300), rental car ($559, and the drive from San Fran to Big Sur totally lived up to the hype), and the new Club Glove you bought to protect your sticks ($289, but come on, you'll get so much use out of it that it almost isn't fair to count it). Finally, add $79 for the valet service at the airport you use to park your car.

The total for your Bucket List–Busting weekend to fabled Pebble Beach? Approximately $7,967!

Don't think about what else you could do with $7,967. Jack Nicklaus said that if he only had one round of golf left to play in his life, he'd play Pebble. And you, little old you, you know how Jack Nicklaus feels about something! Isn't that alone worth $7,967? Okay, yes, Jack never had to pay for a round at Pebble in his life, but that's beside the point.

So let's be rational for just a moment and review the cost of the Golf Bug in purely economic terms. Last year, in order to forge your garden variety, nothing-to-see-here, move-on-folks 11 handicap, you invested the following in what we would have to say is ironically, given your results, disposable income—

- Club Dues: $21,600

- Locker, restaurant and bag storage: $1,600

- Cart fees, guest fees, tips to ball kids and cart girl: $1,425

- Regripping clubs: $300

- Balls: $490
- New irons (every three years): $1,199
- New driver (every year): $599
- SkyCaddie: $399
- Shirts (1/5ᵗʰ of closet total): $963
- Pants/shorts (1/10ᵗʰ of your closet's total): $980
- Hats/Belts (1/5ᵗʰ of your total inventory): $270
- Shoes (1/5ᵗʰ of your 22 pairs): $516
- Trip to Myrtle with the guys (including air fare): $2,100
- Trip to Pebble with your wife: priceless of course, but let's call it $7,697 because that's what the credit card statement says

So last year, and pretty much every year since the Golf Bug latched on to you like a tick on a long-haired dog, your grand total in golf-related spending is $40,138. That's the average income in Louisiana and Mississippi. And if you sprang for the $65K golf simulator . . . well, you're now spending more than the average income in any state, and you're kinda my hero.

Clearly, from a purely economic perspective, you should quit golf and find cheaper ways to aggravate yourself. Your golf spending is going to forestall your retirement—a time in which, let's remember, you are planning to play more golf. The Golf Bug, like all communicable diseases, exists to devour its host body. It has no conscience.

"Okay, wait. I'm not being defensive, because I never realized I was spending $40K a year on golf (how did I know not that?), but isn't that what money is for? I work hard, and you can't take it with you, right?"

I should have known better than to run the numbers for you. Most people who get the Golf Bug have the means to indulge the Golf Bug, and the where-withal to live in denial. I could tell you that you spend $75K a year on golf and you'd say, "Hey, it's not like I'm making withdrawals from my 401(k) to play Augusta!" But we both know that's only because you can't get on Augusta.

For you, money is mostly perception. It's how adults keep score. And you want to be perceived as a golfer. Your eyes have always glazed over when the conversation turns to money. You've always made enough; you take care of your own; you have investment vehicles in low-risk funds, but the disposable part? Well, you "dispose" of it by playing golf!

So let's leave practical behind and get all up-in-your-face existential. "You can't take it with you," you say? Correct! You will, in fact, die.

So, in an average lifespan, we get about 27,375 days. If we take your age, currently 46, and multiply it by 365, we can figure that you have already lived 16,790 days (and have broken 80 exactly never times). Then subtract 16,790 from 27,375, and that gives you 10,585 days left before you die. You have already lived approximately 62 percent of your life. Sure, you may be that guy who lives to be 100, but you won't be playing golf at that age (and if you are, please God, don't be in the group ahead of mine). Then again, you could also have an aneurism before you finish reading this sentence. Still with me? Cool. So here is the question the Golf Bug coursing through your bloodstream doesn't want you to think about: Is playing golf the best use of whatever is left of your 27, 375 days?

Before you answer, think about how long it takes to play one round of golf. Oh, I know it's not like the old days when you were still learning and played five-and-a-half-hour rounds at the public course near the Target. Your club prides itself on four-hour rounds, and if you take a cart out late on a Saturday or Sunday afternoon, you've been known to play in less than three hours. But that's not the norm, and certainly not the whole story, is it?

Let's be honest about how long it really takes to play a round of golf. It begins during the week, with the group text about who is playing in what group and at what time, followed by confirmations, trash talking, and lowering expectations by letting everyone know your back hurts or you've been making swing changes. This process doesn't take much actual time out of your day, but it does start you thinking about the round, which gets you obsessively checking the weather, which, when sketchy, gets you praying to the golf gods for four hours of forbearance.

- Then, the day of, you wake up early and stretch. It hurts like hell. Your doctor says to do it after playing, but that is ridiculous and won't help you on the first tee. You have breakfast early because while you'll urinate in the woods, you won't defecate, mostly because the club is built among condos and you'd be seen, but also because you wouldn't want to hold up the pace of play. You have to drive to the club, and you get there an hour before because they don't take tee times and someone has to get your group on the list at the pro shop. Your kids are older, so you're elected, plus you're a Type A and you don't trust the others not to screw it up.

- Once your name's on the list, you warm up your short game—pitches, chips, bunker shots. One shank and you're in a panic. Then the putting green. You practice short putts even though you mostly have long putts. There are others on the green with you, so you chat. You complain that the greens are too slow or too fast, and you convince yourself they're not going in now but that means you'll make them all on the course.

- Next, you hit the range. Your pro says this should be strictly for purposes of rhythm, to not worry about where the ball goes. But that is impossible. Every off-line shot makes you evaluate what you're doing wrong. You make adjustments, which makes things worse. Now you can't get the ball off the ground. Panic sets in just as your group is called to the first tee. When this happens, you often hit a solid first tee shot. When the range session goes well, you usually top your first tee shot, and two of your partners are as silent as ascetic monks, which is horrible enough, but the third guy tells you that you "came off it." You remark ruefully that you didn't hit a single driver that badly on the range. This is not only untrue but completely beside the point. You wait for someone to offer you a breakfast ball, but the silence is deafening.

- From there, the four-hour round your club prides itself on becomes almost five hours because the group ahead of you is atrocious and they look for lost balls at nearly every hole. Also because your group is atrocious and you look for lost balls nearly every hole. At the four-hour mark, like clockwork, your wife passively aggressively texts, "How'd you play?" and you have to respond that you are on the 15th tee. This is why she says you lie to her, to which you respond that you are offended by the lack of trust.

- After you all remove your caps, revealing disgusting, matted-down, sweaty hair, and shake hands on the 18th green, it's time to settle up. Between the holes where there was candy, allowing for handicaps, and the side bets on birdies and sandies, it is ten minutes before you are asked to pay someone ten dollars. On the rare days you win ten dollars, you're not sure why.

- Before you can go, there's the obligatory chat with the ball boy who cleans your clubs and asks you, "How'd it go out there?" On a bad day, you say you had some good holes. On a good day, you tell him about your putts on 11 and 16, and he nods furiously since there is a direct relationship between the fury of his nods and the size of his tips. The ball boys who are willing to go far can actually convince you that they care. Then there are the post-round drinks in the grill room, which often turn into lunch, and then, well hell, DJ and Rory are tied with three holes to go, and it's so much more fun to watch it on the big screen with guys who understand the nuances. You hope there's not a playoff or there will be hell to pay when you get home.

And you do get home . . . right around three p.m. You left the house at seven a.m. And you need to shower because you are disgusting. And when you do, you feel better momentarily, but then you realize how tired you are. It must be the sun; I mean you rode in a cart, after all. You can't be physically spent. You're seriously considering lying down on the bed and resting your eyes, recharging the batteries, when your wife calls out that the kids are ready and you are leaving in ten minutes, and you yell out, "Gotcha!" even though you don't have a clue where you are going or what the purpose of the trip is. Weekend days for you are golf, followed by whatever else you can fit in before going to sleep.

You get off the bed to dress and realize you're not sure what you should wear since you don't know where you are going, but then opt for golf clothes. It's too late to be going to the beach, and golf clothes are suitable for all other occasions. You hope wherever you are going has caffeine.

So, if we don't credit the emotional and mental investment you make up front before even playing as actual time (which it is and you know it), it takes you eight hours to play a round of golf. Sleep also takes eight hours. That leaves eight hours for everything and everyone else in your life. One third of your day. And, your wife likes to point out, the best third of your day. The best part of you. Golf gets you; they get the leftovers.

You have 38 percent of a normal life span left. That's 10,385 days and counting. Today, you spent one on the golf course.

As your wife rescues you by asking if you know where you're going or if she should plug it into Waze, you have a brief moment of clarity. Is this how you want to spend your remaining time? In a meaningless chase for a little white ball? You're suddenly energized. You have seen the errors of your ways. You will be completely present in tonight's family activity, as soon as you arrive and figure out what the hell it is, and you will stay that way. Golf is about to get put in its proportional place.

Then your cell phone vibrates. A message from Stan, who played way over his head today. Had himself a damn day and shot 76!

"Today was a blast, dude. Good time, good friends. And I finally birdied #4! Can't wait for next week. You good for 8:27 at Cedar Ridge?"

You smile at your wife. After all, you're at a stop light. You're not texting and driving. Who does she think you are? Before the light turns green, you manage a response: *"Count me in!"*

CHAPTER THREE

Who Were You before Golf?

D o you remember you? The original you. Before golf.

Do you remember what you used to say at your first job interviews? God you were so earnest! "The purpose of life is a life of purpose," you would submit, without giving Robert Byrne his due attribution. And you believed it so much, you felt you would have eventually said it anyway had Byrne not beaten you to it. And do you remember how, when you said this, your interviewer would look away and fight hard not to smirk? Your friends weren't as kind; they would burst out laughing. You were so annoyingly sincere, so cluelessly sure of yourself! But you couldn't help it. You meant it!

And unlike your friends, who just wanted good jobs, their own homes, and healthy families without too much stress or selling out, you wanted stress. You were on the lookout for a buyer so you could sell out. You were acutely aware that you got one shot at life, that it would pass in a blink of an eye, and that while you might fail, you would do so without mailing in a moment of it. Your friends' biggest fear, even before they had taken on the world, was the fear of being consumed by it. They maybe didn't know what they wanted, but they were resolute about what they didn't want—they didn't want to burn out.

Putting aside the fact that they often said this while lighting up the evening's THC blend, you would look away and feel sorry for them. You were going to seek burnout, because if you burned out, that meant you had lived your life on fire.

Do you remember The Plan? At twenty-five, you had segmented your life span (that's what you actually called it) into three distinct areas of focus that you were convinced would come together and coalesce into what would someday be judged by others as time on the planet well spent. How this melding would happen, you weren't sure, and how other people would fit into this sublime scheme was not something you worried about—it would be such an amazing life that of course they would want to be a part of it!

It wasn't that you doubted that loving others was worthy and important, you just deemed it insufficient. Those without dreams and goals were often in love and loved by the people they frustrated and disappointed. You saw it all the time. Hell, that was your parents before they split up. But what you felt marrow-deep was that if you lived with purpose and prioritized achievement, well, that would attract love—love that would not be let down. You knew that you could love people you didn't respect, but that seemed lame to you. You wanted to prove that love that came from respect was better, deeper, and lasting.

It is embarrassing how much you believed in The Plan.

You remember one evening back then, as you sat in Yankee Stadium while the rain punished the tarpaulin and the players were nowhere to be found, noticing a vocationally disgruntled middle-aged guy next to you waving a rain-diluted beer and musing out loud, "Hey, it beats working, am I right?" You felt profoundly sorry for him. And yet now, when you lay the sod over a wedge and it lands in the water and you are staring a quad dead in the eyes, and your buddy says, "Hey, pards, bad golf beats working, am I right?" you sincerely reply, "Amen, brother!"

So what exactly was The Plan? It was simple. You were not only not going to consider your twenties your throwaway decade (you were not aware of golf yet, but you knew life offered no mulligans), you were going to see it as the decade of infrastructure. You were going to build a life based on a holistic three-part platform: Mind, Body, and Spirit.

First, let's tackle the mind. You knew knowledge was power, and it was time to stop taking a perverse pleasure in teachers telling your parents you could succeed if only you would apply yourself. It was time to stop pretending you understood cultural references made by your boss, the current president, or your girlfriend's parents. You needed to read! You made a pact with yourself to read the classics.

It was the era before Amazon, so you went to your local library and rather than browse, you made the librarian's day by asking for her go-to list of literary classics. You set out to read them all within twenty-four months. You then informed your friends and family of your quest, and this turned out to be a mistake. Knowing your timeline, they began to ask questions. Between having to log your eight hours at work and the fact that the days were so short and the books were so damn long, you began to skim. Descriptive passages had to be skipped over, as did all minor characters, flashbacks, and interior monologues. We get it, we get it, Atticus is totally opposed to racism, and Holden is depressed (though you didn't really grasp why, given he's hilarious and smart and able to wander around NYC at all hours of the day and night unsupervised), and while it was sexy as hell, you started to think no one in *Tropic of Cancer* actually has cancer, and it was hard for you to see what was so great about Jay Gatsby, given that he goes to the trouble of throwing decadent parties he doesn't even attend, and Jesus, what the hell was going on in Joyce's *Ulysses*? You just couldn't follow, and you were convinced Moby Dick would be so much better if it were shorter and just stuck to the action scenes with the damn fish.

Two years later, you called yourself on your bullshit. You had read some of all the books but all of none of them. This was not The Plan for your mind. You committed to reading one book all the way through and with total comprehension before you would start another. You chose Orwell's *1984* because it seemed relevant in a high-technology, privacy-shrinking world, and it was so much shorter than Tolstoy's *War and Peace*. It was crazy!

But then you realized, in the kind of self-serving epiphany that would rescue you when you really wanted to avoid something your entire adult life, that the classics, by definition, would always be there, and that the Mind part of your plan could be placed on pause. You could move on to the Body, and since the plan was holistic, your mind would still be improving as you prioritized your body! No one loses here!

You saw your body, which you began to refer to as your "unit" until someone let you know that was a penis reference, as the place where your mind and spirit resided. In order to make them feel at home, all facets of the body had to function at a high level. Your central nervous system was the air in the home, always set at an unflappable 70 degrees regardless of the season; your bloodstream was the unfailingly reliable well water; and your muscles and skin were the furniture, clearly created by an interior designer but not in such a heavy-handed way that the place felt like a museum. Your body would be lived in but well kept. In The Plan, company could stop by your body at any time, and you'd never be ashamed of the conditions they would find.

Full-body fitness started with cardio. Not having learned your lesson from overreaching with the classic books list, you first felt the ultimate goal for your body should be an Ironman Triathlon. Sure, a 2.4-mile swim, a 112-mile bike ride, and a 26.2-mile run was ambitious, but it seemed doable. Go big or go home! But then you found out that the biking, swimming, and running occur on the same day. Suddenly an Ironman went from ambitious to insane, and since you had never learned to swim anyway, you eliminated the goal and downgraded to running a full marathon. You ran for several months and worked up to five-mile runs, but you not only didn't experience the vaunted "runner's high," the idea of having to run actually brought you down. So you eliminated running and bought a bike. A very expensive one that weighed hardly anything and had clips for pedals and racing tires so thin you got a flat nearly every time you rode. Friends recommended a mountain bike with its thicker tires, but you found not riding to be a simpler solution. You did buy a rack to display the bike in your apartment entrance and it never failed to get a compliment, since it was the same bike Lance Armstrong rode. Later you sold it but continued to wear a Livestrong bracelet.

You then decided that flexibility would be your new focus in body design. "You're only as young as your spine is flexible" was something you heard a demonstrably insane person yell out on the subway, but you had also heard it in an infomercial and in some black-and-white footage from The Beatles' Maharishi period—you're pretty sure it was John, and he was the smart one. So it was clear The Plan would have to include being supple and lithe.

You would become one of those people who could sit on the floor at a party and seem truly comfortable, one of those graceful beings who seemed to float rather than walk. You bought a mat and signed up for yoga.

No one told you how *long* yoga classes are. You don't strike poses, you hold poses. You are encouraged endlessly to breathe, and then the pose—or the salutation to the sun—is repeated over and over. Rene, your ridiculously pliant instructor, looks out at everybody as she says it is perfectly fine if you can't reach your shin, but she means you. And you haven't been handed this many blocks since you were an infant. "Stronger students may want to lower their head to the floor" is said simply, but you hear "may want to defy the laws of physics and fly." At the end of the hour-long torture, you are encouraged to lie still and (wait for it) breathe, and "let the world fall away." You have no idea what this means; you are thinking about dinner.

When you tell your double-jointed friend who takes six yoga classes a week and is thinking about getting certified and teaching that it's not for you, she recommends hot yoga and begs you to give it a try. But if you are going to be in a room with a bunch of sweaty, nearly naked bodies, it's going to be an orgy, not a yoga class. You leave halfway through, nauseated from the 105-degree temps and convinced that a simple stretching routine every morning, targeting the big muscles and holding each stretch for thirty seconds, is all a person needs. Yoga, in your mind, is overkill. And you may be right, but since you never do the routine and have no data, it is hard to quantify.

Okay, hard pass on cardio and flexibility. Weightlifting is the way to go! There's a reason why Michelangelo's statue of David is ripped, with striations across his chest and the kind of intercostal definition not seen again until Brad Pitt and *Fight Club*. And it's not by coincidence that Rodin's *Thinker* has bulging lats—is he thinking, or flexing after a set of curls? Who is to say? But it is clear that strength has always been associated with accomplishment and success, that those who are "mighty," whether it's members of the armed forces or the league MVP or Mother Nature's latest hurricane, are admired not just when they use their strength, but even more so when they show restraint. They could crush you, but they choose not to, like a bouncer who calls you on your fake ID and merely points to the parking lot. The gentle giant is a beloved trope seen in works from Steinbeck to *Shrek*, and while those without muscles say, "The bigger they are the harder they fall," that has not been your experience. "The bigger they are, the more women fall for them" seems closer to the truth. (You picked up early on the fact that women will say they're not into muscles just to make the underdeveloped guys feel better. The next time you see an all-male revue in Vegas with guys with no muscle will be the first time.)

But to be clear, The Plan is not shallow! Vanity is merely a value-add. You want strength for Darwinian reasons, to maximize your survival and success. You join the local Gold's Gym for holistic reasons, and because you hear there are a lot of hot women who work out there.

You soon become the poster boy for the health club business model. In the beginning, you go every day. It is immediately apparent that the most muscular guys are doing free weights—bench presses, deadlifts, and squats. They put 45 lb. plates on the barbells. You struggle to do reps with 10 lb. plates, and you are embarrassed, so you switch to machines, which only require a pin to add and subtract weight. (And unlike the bench, you don't get trapped with the bar on your chest and have to squeal, "Little help?") After a month, you can do slightly more weight, but you see no change in the mirror, and you befriend a guy who is clearly a dedicated bodybuilder for pointers. He tells you to do an upper body–lower body split in order to let the muscles recover. You nod. You knew that. He also tells you to rotate heavy days with light days. But since they are all heavy days for you, this doesn't seem to pertain. Third piece of advice: Eat, eat, eat. Muscle growth comes from calories. Eat six meals a day. And drink 100 ounces of water a day. Muscles are mostly water. Never ever skip a workout or a meal. And finally, train to failure. On leg day, vomiting is a good sign. Wipe your mouth and continue squatting. "The best bodies endure the most suffering" is the musclehead credo.

A few months later, you are ten pounds heavier but it is all fat. You are sore all the time, and you find it hard to sleep. You got tired of prepping meals, so now you are eating less, and the workouts seem like a job, minus the paycheck. You're doubting you have the genetics to get muscular, and even if you do—however long it takes to get a great body—there is no tenure track! You have to keep doing it, or it disappears. How do people do this for their entire lives?

So the insidious business model kicks in. You stop going but the club keeps hitting your credit card, and you don't cancel because they require a thousand days' notice and an act of God, but also because you think you might go; you think you should go, and as long as you have the membership, you could go! This is why you saw the same twenty-five people in the gym regardless of the time of day and wondered how the gym stayed in business. You have now joined the three thousand members who pay every month and don't show.

You're no longer eating six meals a day, but you still push yourself to eat with intention. In The Plan, food is fuel. Its purpose is to sustain your body so that your mind and spirit are free to think about what matters most. The problem is food is often what seems to matter most and it seems to be on everyone's mind constantly. At work, people begin discussing where to go for lunch at ten a.m. At lunch, they discuss either what they had for dinner the night before, what they are having that very night, or what restaurant they are going to that weekend with their friends. They put down their sandwich to show you the restaurant's menu on their phones. You salivate at the photos even though you are eating while doing so.

But The Plan knows living well means being a member of the Underground Resistance. What others do when it comes to dieting is, by definition, the wrong path. You have decided that no food can taste better than being fit will feel. But which food?

- Initially, you try a high-carb diet because carbs are supposed to give you energy and burn glucose and as an active person, you need carbs. And this works! Until you become less active but don't cut the carbs. So you go low-carb. This works! But your friend at the gym says it's all water weight because carbs are water. ("Wait, I thought you said muscles were mostly water." "I did. Carbs are mostly water too." "So everything is water?" "No, and yes.") Two months later, you have raging headaches and feel exhausted all the time. And you crave carbs so much you dream of donuts and pasta.

- So you try fasting because you were told this will reset your metabolism and renew your body at the cellular level. Renewal sounds very holistic to you, but what really convinces you is the person who recommends it, a shredded coworker who claims that if you fast two days a week, you can eat whatever you want the other five days. ("Including carbs?" "Yep, go crazy, but you have to fast completely for two days. The only thing you can have is . . . " "Let me guess, water?" "Exactly.")

- But fasting doesn't work for you for two reasons: 1) You lack purpose. Gandhi fasted for twenty-one days at the age of seventy-four, but he was trying to end British rule. Margret Wallace Dunlop fasted to bring attention to the Suffragette movement. Cesar Chavez was trying to bring national focus to the plight of the migrant worker. You just want your clothes to fit well. 2) Fasting is hard to do when your access to food is so close. It's not a willpower issue for you, it's primarily a proximity problem. Plus, when you are not eating for two days, you have so much extra time. While this might sound like a positive, your lack of caloric intake leaves you with no energy to do anything except obsess over how much longer you have before you get to eat something. You become so cranky and annoying to others, people beg you to eat something, but not in a Gandhi, "save yourself" way, but in a "no one likes you like this" way. So you quit before you can experience the clarity fasting aficionados rave about. You were only clear about how much you wanted to eat. Crystal clear.

The Plan's final piece has to do with the spirit. In The Plan, you would be known to all as someone who "has spirit." You realized long ago that no one has ever said the words, "You're in high spirits today!" without a smile on their face. Spirit seemed to be the only attainable human trait not tied to time or circumstance. You could be young and be told that what you lacked in experience you made up for in spirit. You could be old and faced with late-stage cancer and be lauded for your fighting spirit. You could even die and people would gather and say, "He's with us in spirit." No one cares about the letter of the law, but they will argue passionately about the spirit of the law. Spirit is an animating principle of a high-impact life. To be a spirited person means you are joyful, generous, kind, and forgiving. We even tie it to a holiday season—it's getting cold, time to rev up the Christmas spirit. And when you can't get what you want with what you currently have, you can still have spirit. It doesn't cost anything or take any time, and everyone values it! In The Plan, you would be called, despite your youth, an "old soul" due to your obvious and indefatigable spirit.

But how to get there?

The majority of Americans—90 percent—believe in the soul. An awareness outside of the body that goes on after you are gone. Spirited people have no doubts; you have plenty.

It makes you crazy when a football player crosses the end zone, looks up, and makes the sign of the cross. You don't know if that's because you don't want to believe in a God that would care about such trivial things, or if you'd feel better about it if the defensive player who missed the tackle would look up and give the same God the middle finger. It seems hard to separate spirit from religion, and your innate logic and sense of fairness causes you to struggle with religion. The major religions, Christianity, Judaism, Islam, all have different creation stories; they all call their version of the chosen one by a different name—they can't all be right! And what if you grew up with one religion and it turned out it was the wrong one? Would you be consigned to hell even though you lived scrupulously according to the tenets of your assigned religion? And you never got a good answer from your folks or your pastor or your religious studies professor to the question: How does the nine-year-old who dies from famine or disease deserve to be judged by the Ten Commandments or the belief in a God they don't understand? And if God created the world, why did He have to wait thousands of years to send a Messiah to clean up all the bad behavior and forgive our sins? Why couldn't He just forgive them? Why the gamesmanship; why the drama? Why does He need to be adored and praised all the time?

Atheists are never considered spirited people. (You can be almost anything and run for president, except an atheist.) And yet something in you—is it spirit?—stirs when you listen to atheists say that we outgrew Zeus and in time we'll outgrow our present gods, that if you only behave morally and ethically because you are bargaining for eternal salvation, then you are not as good a person as an atheist, who does so simply because it is the right way to live and expects no reward. Life seems to have a sense of urgency for atheists (since it is over when it is over) that would serve The Plan well.

And so you attempt to develop your spirit while accepting that faith is a cop-out, a sign of intellectual bankruptcy. You know that one day science will sequence and compute and ultimately explain our inner life, and quantum biology will decode the soul. All you need to be a person of "high spirits" is to follow The Plan, live with purpose, and maybe download the Headspace app.

But it doesn't work. You do believe in God even though you can't explain it. And you do have spirit, but like everything else, it comes and goes. You don't seem to be able to summon high spirits nor banish low spirits. And your level of spirit doesn't seem to be tied to the current events in your life. You can feel an emptiness on days that are objectively positive and a deep sense of peace on days that are objectively horrible.

Maybe The Plan was always just a recipe for loneliness. Maybe you need to revisit it when you are older and wiser. Or maybe The Plan's real intention was to distract you from your own inevitable end. If that's the case, then maybe it has worked. Maybe it has served you.

Maybe golf is nothing more than a downsizing of The Plan. Maybe its intention is also to distract you. Maybe this is why non-golfers (and professional golfers who just choked) are fond of saying, "It's just a game, it doesn't really matter." How do you make them understand that the real allure of golf is that, in a world where nothing really matters, for four hours or so, *something* matters?

To the non-golfer, you are just chasing a white ball around a parkland. But you? You are really running from The Plan. The Plan, you have to come to realize, is gone. Golf is here. Play on!

CHAPTER FOUR

What You Tell Yourself When You Need to Quit Golf

I t is the presidential primary season. You are at a friend's house party to participate in the democratic process, become informed as a citizen, and get away from the kids. There are twelve candidates crammed on the debate stage. You have only heard of three of them. Your mind wanders quickly.

A candidate's carefully crafted one-liner causes your host to raise an eyebrow and say, "It's all about zingers. Sound bites. You know who started that? Kennedy."

And you nod and say, "You know, Kennedy was a pretty good golfer. He didn't like to talk about it because he already had this whole patrician thing to overcome, but he could play. I'd put him at a solid third place among the best presidential golfers in US history. It's really not a long list because most presidents who played were awful. Ford was flat out dangerous. Eisenhower played eight hundred rounds while President, ended most days by practicing his putting, was just obsessed, but not very good, so he's fifth. Clinton cheated like crazy on the course—that's called foreshadowing, huh?—but he could hit it.

He beats out Obama for fourth, but Obama started playing in his forties so he's probably much better by now. Then you have JFK, with a bad back by the way, at third, and then George Bush the Elder, played super-fast and pretty well. He was a legit 11 handicap. But the best presidential golfer of all time—and I know I'm about to piss off a lot of you, but I'm not talking about his moral compass or his handling of COVID-19 or the election nonsense, I'm talking about his quick hips and his 2.8 handicap on some tough courses. I mean, YouTube it, the guy could move it! Trump is the best presidential golfer of all time, no question. What? Why is everyone so quiet?"

Some people say you judge a man by how he treats his mother. Others say the better measure is how they treat their pets. But you have always held that you learn a lot about a man by how he treats people in service jobs. You can't abide people who yell at retail clerks over a missing price tag or snap their fingers to get a wait-ress's attention. But there you were at Sky Harbor Airport's baggage claim area, and all the bags had gone round a half dozen times. No new ones were being added. The red flashing light went out and the carousel stopped. And still, no golf clubs.

When you got in the American Airlines baggage claim office, you were ready to take no prisoners.

"You want to tell me how I can have a goddamn ninety-minute layover in Charlotte and you guys can't get my golf clubs on the flight? And how the hell did my bag of clothes make it but not the golf clubs? No, I don't have my claim ticket, can't you search by my name or address? I tipped the guy who checked in my bags twenty bucks this morning! Do you know how badly I will play with rental clubs, if they even have rental clubs? And I have to buy balls and tees and play in sneakers, and—What? Yes, golf clubs! In a golf bag! For the love of Christ, have you never heard of golf clubs? That might be a tiny part of the whole problem. Well, let me tell you, I have a badass lawyer with an ulcer and you don't want any piece of . . . What? Wait, what? There's an entirely separate carousel for oversized items like clubs? Oh. And where would that be? Number nine on the North side. Oh, okay. They're probably there then. So, anyway. Have a great day!"

There was a time when you saw no point in going for a yearly physical because you felt great and it took a lot of time. Then you entered a period where you didn't want to see your PCP because he would bug you about your weight, your cholesterol, and your genetic blood pressure issue. (You blame stress. He nods. You pretend you'll make behavioral changes. One more nod, and you're out of there.) Now you don't want to go because you're afraid he'll find something horrible in your labs, but today is different. You made the appointment today without any cajoling. In fact, your wife doesn't even know you're here. The purpose of your visit today? You want meds!

You begin your pitch by pointing out the reality that at any given time, 9–13 million adults suffer from ADHD, including 25 percent of all incarcerated males. It's a neurodevelopmental disorder causing untold amounts of pain. Your doctor politely says he's aware and asks if you have had difficulty staying on task at work. Are you not listening to others or finding it hard to remember chores or duties? Are you losing things?

Yes, you are losing just about every match you play, and you are losing $10 nearly every Saturday in side wagers. Plus you just lost 3Up to Raymond, who has this awful over-the-top move so ugly everyone looks away when he swings. You lost to Raymond! And you know why? Swing thoughts! You have so many of them going on every time you address the ball. A patchwork of lessons, suggestions from good players, and YouTube golf instruction have created a memory overload, a chaotic cacophony in your head. When you started you kept it simple. Swing easy was all you thought. But now, in no particular order, the following self-talk begins as you pull your club to hit every shot:

- Take it back low to keep from lifting.

- But don't snatch it back, you have more time than you think. Slow back, fast through.

- Keep as much width between your hands and your head as possible— don't collapse!

- Use the ground! Start your swing with your left knee, or if that doesn't work, the right knee, or try a bump feel. Slide the hips, but don't spin them! Slide good, spin bad!

- Release the club hard with your right hand, but not too early. That's casting. Casting bad, releasing good!

- Post on your left leg and clear. (What are you clearing? That's never been clear!)

- Cover the ball with your chest. (You don't know what that means, but everyone says it, so, I dunno, think about your chest too while you're at it.)

- Head still "through" the shot, but don't be afraid to move your head "during" the shot.

- Stay in the shot. Don't sway. But don't be rigid. Let it flow!

- And most of all, just look at your target and swing. Don't have *any* swing thoughts once you leave the range.

"So, as you can see, Doc, I need help. Vyvanse? Ritalin? Concerta? I don't mean to tell you your biz, but I heard the side effects are weight loss (which would be a bonus) and crankiness, but frankly, if they work and my handicap goes down, I promise I won't be cranky. Unless you think we should go the benzo or beta blocker route and treat this as an anxiety issue, because this is getting out of hand. I don't know if the intense terror I feel when I have a two-way miss going is a panic attack but it's something.

"What? A *therapist*? Why would I need a therapist? No, I don't want a referral, I want a scrip! Okay, okay, I get it, but I may be needing you to transfer my medical records soon—I had no idea you didn't play golf!"

You have been staring at the CGSA golf app for a while now, but there are still people logging on to the webinar, so you have a few moments to make this momentous decision. You shot 93 yesterday. It came out of nowhere. You've been playing pretty well lately, damn near scored 80 two weeks ago. (Okay, you were given three putts you could totally have missed and the OB call only went in your favor because they didn't want you to beg, but still, you had it going!) So now the big decision: Do you enter the score?

You debate with yourself as the idiots in the Denver office ask for the invite to be re-sent. You should post the score because it's the right thing to do. You did shoot 93, and this is an unassailable fact. By posting all your scores, your handicap is legit. It also makes sense for when you play tournaments. This 93 might give you a stroke (or a piece of "candy," as it is called by patronizing low handicappers), and it might be the difference between winning or losing a key hole. Some members of your club are accused of padding their handicaps in the leadup to the club championship by adding high scores they didn't shoot in order to get the aforementioned candy. This is as shrewd as it is dishonest. So you should definitely post the score.

You enter your password and pull up your account, and there it is. The last twenty scores you have shot. Available for the world to see. To keep a handicap on a database is to be exposed. In other walks of life, your flaws are also on display, but they fade with time. The details are forgotten, and you tell your own version of the story that differs dramatically from reality in outcome and intent. But a golf database is unsparing. It will not give in to your pandering. It cares nothing about your precious feelings.

The host of the webinar is thanking everyone for joining and apologizing in advance for his interloping cocker spaniel who will bark throughout his presentation. You have to make the call now. You realize that no one will really care if you enter a 93. You know that they too have shot 93. You understand that most people who play golf can't break 100, and you're being silly. A 93, while a terrible score, is not a reflection of your character. But then again, no one else will enter this score. You have the power. Unlike the multitude of times you have been humbled by life, this humbling can be avoided.

The host asks if you want to give a status update on your project, and so you are saved. You close the app. It's not like you're ever going to shoot a score like 93 again.

You sort of knew. If you only had a moment to wake up and gather your thoughts, it would all make sense. Why else would Barney's ex-wife be calling you close to midnight? You've always adored Clair, and when Barney told you two years ago they were getting divorced, you knew your role was to reassure him that he would find someone far better for him, and to totally agree when he listed the various grievances that made Clair a horrible human. And you did just that. You showed up for him! You told him the way to look at it was he got Clair's best years, and he laughed. But he also looked scared, and profoundly lost.

Clair apologized for the late hour and said simply, "Barney's gone. I knew he wasn't well lately, when he came to pick up Phoebe he looked bloated and disheveled. He wasn't taking care of himself. They found pills, but who knows? He was so overweight, maybe his heart gave out. Who knows? I guess it doesn't matter. Anyway, nothing made him happier than playing golf with you."

You sort of knew, too, that Barney worked very hard at being misjudged. If he was older, he would have been a hippie. He had long hair and took his bandana off in the parking lot of the golf course and replaced it with a golf cap. Because he was heavy and wore a thick beard, because he was able laugh out loud after a bad shot and say, "That's why I do something else for a living," everyone thought he was jolly. And it did seem like nothing bothered him. Not his failed career as a car salesman, not continued rejection from other sales jobs because he never went to college, not his inability to provide for his family at the level all the guys he played golf with seemed to do so easily. He was the guy you invited to your club because he was a good player and wonderful company, but he never seemed to fit. At your club, the head pro had sheepishly asked him to tuck in his shirt on the first tee, to which he shrugged and said, "I can try, but as soon as I swing, it's coming back out." You warned the head pro that you would resign your membership if he ever embarrassed your guest again.

Barney smoked pot on the course and off, and he was the rare golfer who played better the more beer he drank during the round. But he told wonderful, self-deprecating stories and was the first to ignore ticks and burrs and poison ivy and help find your ball. When he left the 19th hole to "get back to the old ball and chain," one of your friends would say, "You know, in a way I admire Barney," which of course meant they felt sorry for him and were grateful they didn't live like him.

None of them were at his funeral. Of course it was some sort of New Age church. When you walked in, there was a band behind the altar that looked no different than a rock band at a club. A guy who wore no robes or collar said he would be leading the service, and while he did mention Jesus, there were no recognizable prayers or readings. Classic Barney. His ex-wife gave an incredibly generous eulogy extolling Barney's virtues and recounting camping trips and how well Barney played Santa at the school where she worked. And when she spoke about how Barney sang their daughter, Phoebe, a lullaby every night when she was young, and even sang a verse of Phoebe's favorite, her voice breaking partway through . . . well, if you were there and your eyes were dry, you were hopeless.

And then it happened. And everything changed.

Clair gestured to the casket and invited everyone up to walk by and say their final goodbyes. She pointed out to us that since Barney had two passions, the Boston Red Sox and golf, that she was having him buried with the Red Sox flag that he hung at his house all summer draped over the casket and with his beloved putter.

Only it wasn't his beloved putter—it was yours! Barney had used a cen-ter-shafted piece of crap for years and flat out had gotten the yips. If he had a 2-footer to win a hole, nobody would give it to him anymore. He was that shaky. So a month ago, when you decided to go all in and buy the Prada of putters, a Scotty Cameron Special Select Newport 2, for $400, you gave Barney your almost new Ping Anser Platinum with the PP61 grip. And you know for a fact that he never got to hit it because you asked him two weeks ago how he liked it and he said he hadn't been able to get out, and then—ugh—the first snow had come early and the courses closed the first week of November.

His beloved putter? And she's having it buried with him? For eternity? Plus, you haven't really gotten the hang of the Scotty Cameron and you were starting to think you should switch it out with Barney and go back to your trusty Ping Anser.

You get in line to pay your last respects. You know Clair well. You have had Barney as a guest to your club a hundred times. Surely once you explain the con-fusion, she'll tell you to take the putter home with you. Or is that inappropriate?

You're at the end of the line, and she just exclaimed, "Uncle Dave!" and started crying and hugging this long lost relative. She is totally distracted. You have an overcoat. The exit is no more than twenty paces from the casket. You could wrap the putter in the overcoat, feign an overwrought reaction, and have this baby back in your garage in no time. And nobody would understand this move more than Barney. Irreverent, fun-loving, live-in-the-moment Barney!

You pick up the putter and look to see who is watching. You grip it and recall Barney's crosshanded grip, the way he would caress the club before wrapping his hands around it. You knew his routine well, could see it in your head. A big, exaggerated breath before he would take it back, the way he would tap the ground with his feet before settling in for the stroke, how wide his green eyes would get as the ball would approach the hole. He was so into it! Every putt, make or miss, was for him an experience to be completely savored. Each putt was its own miniature life span. It held promise, rolled an unknowing distance, and came to definitive conclusion. And best of all, there would be another lifetime to live the very next hole!

Clair is patting you on the back. She wipes away something on your face. She says she loved him too. You put the putter down.

It is customary to be quiet while someone is hitting a golf shot. This seems ridiculous considering how many demon voices are shouting at you inside your head. Once the shot is complete, it is okay and even encouraged to talk, but the following comments taunt you so much you are grateful they can't see your eyes roll behind your aviator sunglasses:

- "That won't hurt you." This means your shot was atrocious, but it went forward and not out of bounds, so you are technically still in the hole. Still, everyone knows your score will suck.

- "You can make four from there." That's the equivalent of saying you could win the lottery any given week. Yes, it is possible to make four from there, but not for you, and everyone knows it.

- "Get lucky!" Once a goal of your Friday evenings, now it is your partner trying to will the ball you just sprayed off the planet to hit a tree or rock and carom toward the fairway. It is intended as goodwill, but you hear it as condescending charity.

- "Better lucky than good." This is what you say if the ball does in fact hit a tree or rock and caroms back onto your fairway.

- "I got you, pards." Your better ball partner says this when you've just hit a horrendous tee shot and left him on his own for the hole. This is annoying, but you have found that if you do it on three consecutive holes, he says nothing at all, which is deafening, because you know he's thinking he never had a chance when he saw he was paired with you.

- "How does that not break left?" This is the absurd thing you say when, well, the putt did not break left because it was a straight putt. The more appropriate question, "How do you not know that read when you've been a member here for twelve years?" goes unsaid.

- "Is it still me?" This is not only an existential question, because sadly you are still you and you always will be, but it is also rhetorical in the extreme, as you and everyone else in your group knows damn well you are still away.

- "Pick it up, pards." This is golf euthanasia. Your whole group has lost count of your strokes. It's definitely not a double, probably not a triple, could be a quad. They tell you to just pick it up while there is still an actual name for your score.

- "How'd you play today, honey?" This is the most painful of all. Not just because it is disingenuous and your spouse doesn't care, or because it is the golf equivalent of "how are you?" (where to begin to answer would take you both on a complex and painful journey neither of you could bear), and not even because you are now indoors and your sunglasses are off so you can't roll your eyes without being busted, but because the question is beside the point. You'd prefer it if you could change the ground rules so that instead of your wife asking, "How'd you play today?" she would simply ask, "Did you play today?" Because that you can answer, that you can affirm, and that you can let go of.

Golf was first recommended to you as a way to deal with your genetic Type-A tendencies. A commune with nature. Breathe the fresh air and appreciate the trees and really, really notice your surroundings. (Look at that hawk! Is it a hawk or an eagle?) It's like an anger management class proctored by God!

And while you hated admitting you were a Type A, since they are generally considered assholes who don't live very long and then everyone is glad they're gone, you couldn't argue with the list of traits. Are you polyphasic? Do you do two things at once? You have never not begun shaving while still rinsing with mouthwash, and you brush your hair with your right hand while spraying deodorant with your left. Do you hate to wait? You will not think twice before going on the shoulder of the road to pass someone who is in the passing lane, and the look you give them as you are going by is inappropriately disgusted and threatening. Do you grind your teeth when you have things to do? Oh hell, you grind other people's teeth!

You do generally find golf has a calming effect on your control freakishness. That is, until you are waiting on the tee for a slow foursome to hit their approach shots. Then what starts as your inner voice decides to come out and introduce itself.

"What in the name of Christ are they doing!?"

"Do not tell me they are waiting for the green to clear so they can go for it in two. They are easily 320 yards from the green! If they could reach it from there, they wouldn't be there!"

"Where is the ranger? Why do we have a ranger if he's not out there policing these idiots?"

"One, two . . . three, that's three practice swings. Dude, I promise you that you could hit that crappy shot without any practice swings!"

"Can you believe this? Look where he left his pull cart. Now he has to put the flag in and walk backwards to get out of our way!"

"Hey fella, this isn't the Ryder Cup, stop reading the damn putt and hit it! Better yet, that's good! Pick it up!"

"I'm calling the pro shop, this is insane . . . Should I call the pro shop? What do you guys think?"

"He's not only taken way more than the allotted three minutes to look for his ball, but he's like 40 yards from where it went into the trees! Just drop a ball, I'll give you a goddamn sleeve of Pro Vs if you'll just drop a damn ball! You know what, I'm hitting. Screw it, I'm hitting into them. Maybe that will get their asses in gear!"

"No, you're not. Nothing they are doing would be half as wrong as that! If you hit into them, I'm calling the pro shop, but it will be on you!" That would be Scott. The guy with the James Earl Jones voice and the sweet, unrushed downswing. The best player in your group and as chill as they come. You would find out after that round that he told your playing partners that he didn't want to play with you anymore. He plays golf to relax, and you make that impossible.

On the way home, he is in the car in front of you, and you ignore the solid yellow lines and pass him only to catch the next red light. He is parked behind you, and you see in the rearview he is shaking his head and wondering what possible difference it makes to you that you got to that light a few seconds before him. If you had his cell phone number, you would text him the answer: "Because you were ahead of me and now you're not!"

According to the American Heart Association, golf courses rank fifth among public places where people have heart attacks. Even more cheery, 95 percent of heart attacks on golf courses are fatal. Some say this is because you are often so far from the clubhouse, where the defibrillators are kept, and you need help within five minutes to survive a heart attack. Others say it is because the sport is populated by older men, and so cardiac incidents are more likely. And of course a case can be made that more clubs should offer CPR classes and more members should take them. You suspect that even if they did, some members would simply step over the body and play through.

You are well aware of these statistics, but you don't worry about them because you always take a riding cart. To you this should be an easy call. You play faster with a riding cart. And a cart means there's a place to keep your stuff! Your layering of clothing in fall and early spring, your water bottles and snacks, plus you've been striking it poorly lately so you have your extra box of balls and several training aids you used on the driving range. Not to mention, there is GPS on the cart, so you don't need to shoot any distances. And a port to charge your phone! But most of all, you don't get as tired. There are more hills on the back nine and when you walk your legs are gone by the 14th, but the 15th and 18th are the longest holes on the course. You need energy! You don't do this for exercise, you do it to play golf, damn it. You do something else for exercise. (Well, you could, if you were so inclined.)

But then the kid taking your bag asks, "You're playing in the 8:47 group with Mr. Moulton and Dr. Guyler, right? You walking or riding?" You say you'll find out who the fourth is and then decide. If the fourth member is riding, you can keep him company. It doesn't screw up the pace of play. No judgment.

Moulton is on the practice tee. You ask him who you are playing with, and he points to a guy much younger than both of you who is ignoring the "PLEASE DO NOT HIT BALLS OVER THE FENCE" sign. He is wearing shorts to show off his bulging calves; he has 460cc calves to match his driver clubhead. There's no pushcart near him, but that's because he's carrying.

When do we outgrow peer pressure? These guys don't really care if you walk, ride, or take an Uber to your ball. Just play the game and keep up. Your means of transportation should be a decision left to you and you alone. It is your doctor who told you he was concerned about your blood pressure. Your wife who you told that on occasion when you walk you get a little lightheaded. Your college-age daughter who gave you the aforementioned data on how dangerous it was to walk a golf course due to the risk of cardiac incidents. You long ago learned that you didn't need to drink a shot just because they brought a tray of them to your table and everyone else was doing it. You're mature enough to say, "No, thanks," and go home when the downtown biz dinner was over and the "guys" were going out to "see what's going on," which was usually code for going to the strip clubs. You finally understood, albeit a little late for a grown-ass man, that people don't think of you as often as you think they are, and you shouldn't do things to please them if it's not in your best interests. You have learned the invaluable life skill of saying no.

"Hey, it's a beautiful day, we're all walking, but you do you."

"What, no! Hell, I always walk, I just ride if everyone is riding so I don't slow anyone up. Walking is what golf is about, right?"

You always hope to play "lights out," and with this decision, today could literally be that day.

The logic is impeccable: If someone is in a cart playing by themselves and you are a foursome ahead of them, you should let them play through. It is both a pace of play issue and one of the inherent, unselfish niceties of golf. "We don't want to hold you up, you go right ahead," is what every respectful foursome should say to the single player behind them. There is a mathematical beauty to it. A lower number of players should not have to wait for a higher number of players, especially if 1) there is a hole open ahead and 2) they are riding and you are walking. And ironically enough, you actually enjoy "hosting." If a twosome is sitting in their cart on the tee of a par 3 and you are in a foursome, you are the first to wave them up to the green. You whistle and wave your arm to get their attention, and they wave back and give you a beaming smile. This confirms you are a wonderful human being, attentive to the needs of others and always willing to sacrifice. Never fails to lift your heart. As is customary, once they arrive on the green, they act sheepish and grateful and promise you they will "get out of your way" as soon as possible. But ever the gracious host, you not only assure them that they should take their time, you repair their ball marks for them and offer to pull or tend the flagstick. You yell "get in" when they putt, as if you are watching the Masters and you have put money on them. And you always, always, tell them to enjoy their day. You love when you get to host someone playing through your group.

This is ironic because you live in fear of having to play through a host group. When you are alone and you come to a tee with a foursome that asks you if you want to play through, you're not above reassuring them that the pace of play is fine, and you're just enjoying the day, and no, no, you guys go ahead. Sometimes you are let off the hook when they say, "Dude, we'd let you through but there's nowhere to go—the course is packed!" And you nod and sigh like it's so true and so sad, but you feel your pulse rate starting to return to normal. And sometimes you escape because the group in front of you is either ignorant of the custom or oblivious to your presence. In either case, they never offer to let you play through, and in those instances, you get to be offended without having to actually perform.

But sometimes there is no escape. You walk to the tee and look out at the group in the fairway, and they are waving you through. They are too far away to tell them that you're playing two balls or not in a hurry and they pull their carts over to a shaded area under a tree to not only let you through but to judge your skillset. And now your mind races:

"If I don't hit a good shot, they'll think I suck and rue the moment they decided to let me play through."

"Maybe I should drive up in my cart and just tell them I'm going to skip the hole so I don't hold them up."

"I should put my driver away and hit hybrid. I could totally block driver and hit their cart."

"If I hit hybrid, I'll have a super long second shot and take too long to play the hole."

"Get a grip. When you're hosting, you don't care where they hit it. You don't judge them. Why should it be any different now? (Answer: Because it's you and you suck.)"

"They're waiting. Just hit the freaking ball. Okay, stick to your pre-shot routine. Take a breath. Ignore them, the ball doesn't know you're playing through, the ball only knows how solidly it's been hit. Just have one swing thought and pull the trigger." (Your swing thought is, "Please don't let me hit such a horrendous shot that I'm humiliated." Not optimal.)

When you get to the green to play your fourth shot from the rough on this par 4, you apologize and promise to get out of their way ASAP even though three of them are on their phones and not even paying attention to your situation. The fourth member has repaired your ball mark for you, tells you to take your time, and offers to pull or tend the flagstick for you. As your putt rolls egregiously off-line, nowhere near the hole, he yells, "Get in!" Then he sweeps the four-footer up and tells you to enjoy your day. Who does he think he's kidding?

Your mother has been conclusively proven wrong about so many things she told you with utter certainty and confidence in your youth. It turns out that when she struck you, it didn't hurt her as much as it did you. It is absolutely possible to love material possessions as much as people; college debt is not even close to being worth the ROI of a bachelor's degree, and as Jack the Starter proves every time you see him, you *don't* have to keep busy, keep learning, keep contributing, or keep improving.

Jack has no clients that cancel meetings and don't have the common decency to give you more than an hour's notice even though you were up to until one a.m.

making the PowerPoints. Jack doesn't deal with refunds or irate customers claiming the product was misrepresented. (Oh sure, people get mad on the golf course about the snack shack's menu, or the restroom's cleanliness, or the temp green on 12 no one told them about when they booked the round and paid full price, but they complain after the round. When they encounter Jack, they are by definition "starting"—nothing has soured them yet. They are innocent and as such, happy.) Jack doesn't have to learn a new computer system every few months; no one offers Jack free upgrades or requires him to power down in the middle of his report and restart.

Jack never has to jump—not on a call, not on a hot stock, not on a sales lead. Jack's feet are flat on the ground until he raises them up to go to sleep. Jack isn't asked to join team building events where he has to give his assigned partner "objections" and roleplay their "rebuttals." No one asks Jack why he didn't come to the virtual happy hour, or what car he drives, who he voted for, or what town he lives in. No one complains to Jack's boss about his attitude, hygiene, or lack (or worse, his excess) of ambition. Jack doesn't make anyone feel threatened or overlooked. When you try to put Jack in one of life's two buckets, Giver or Taker, he is neutral. You can let your guard down around Jack. There'll be no price to pay, no tracks to cover. Jack the Starter, unlike everyone else in your life, has no angle.

Jack has become a homeostatic structure in your life. When every day seems so fragile, Jack is solid. He is there every Saturday and Sunday. He stands by the starter lectern with his clipboard. When you are about to pull onto the course, you go right by the first tee, and it is oddly pleasing to see him in place and to wave at him. It is an extended part of your first tee pre-shot routine. Jack is there, Jack is smiling, and everything is as it should be. This day is intact!

And Jack's first-tee homily has become sacred to you. And while it occasionally does contain info you need ("Guys, we had some rain last night, so we're cart paths only on 7 and 9"), it is the needless repetition of his script that is the most affirming. You know what he's going to say, and yet you don't turn away because you somehow need to hear it.

"Morning! Beautiful day to go low! Anyone need me to find out what the course record is so you know where you stand? No? Okay, well gentlemen, we are playing hole location #3 today; it's at the top of the scorecard. Greens were rolled so try to keep the swearing down to a dull roar. Carts at ninety degrees, Sharon will be out there with beverages, we expect you to keep up with the group ahead, and you should be shaking hands in four and a half hours! Balls in the air, please! Have a great round!"

In the grill room after a Sunday round, with Monday's chaos looming for everyone in your group, especially if the sun goes behind the clouds and the temps drop and the light changes, the mood can shift from relentless reminders of choking on putts and sarcastic commentary on the day's news to a suddenly serious discussion about what you will all do when you reach "that" day. Americans as a whole work until they no longer have to, financially. And then the exodus begins. To a warmer place. With lower property taxes. There have to be golf courses, for sure. Myrtle Beach? Hilton Head? Scottsdale?

But once in a while, the conversation gets past the deflection of place. What would you do with all that time? You can't just play golf. And some have laudable plans. Jeff and his wife are going to start a foundation for cerebral palsy to honor his brother who suffered so terribly. Mark plans on a second career developing property and flipping houses. There is lots of talk of giving back, of staying active. There is palpable fear. Everyone also knows someone who died shortly after retirement. They had stopped doing, they had no plans. While no one can prove the theory with any sort of clinical data, it is agreed, with a toast of the glasses, that if you stop waking up with a plan every day, you won't get many more days.

Somewhere, your mother is nodding. Damn straight.

But Jack seems happier to you than everyone at the table. Jack seems more centered and peaceful than anyone you play with. Everyone assumes that at his age, Jack is working as a starter because he needs money. Poor guy is here at six in the morning to greet the first groups. But does he? You can't ask, plus you don't really want to know anything real about Jack. You don't want to look behind the curtain. Besides, you truly believe there's nothing more to know. Jack is deeply content. You can feel it.

It's your turn to pick up the check, and everyone starts to gather themselves to leave. Knees crack, and dealing gingerly joints make the process of pushing back the chairs and standing up longer than it used to be. Maybe it's as simple as this: You have all finished your round and are starting to realize you are also getting closer to finishing far more. Finishing is coming. Everything you do after your work life is mostly intended to distract you from this fact.

But Jack is the Starter! Jack's whole reason for being is to help you start something that could be potentially wonderful on any given day. And he is only on the first hole at his lectern. He is never by the 18th green when you finish and your hopes have been diminished or dashed, or even, rarely, fulfilled. He knows better.

When you finish, you tell yourself, you want Jack's job.

CHAPTER FIVE

A Homework Assignment

'm just going to say it: I'm starting to worry about you. By now, most peo-ple in your situation have started to tire of golf. They realize there is more to life. Even the hardcore have at least taken a sabbatical if they're not ready to quit altogether. But not you. You're getting golf alerts from Google and scrolling through Facebook Marketplace for a deal on a new Integra Ultralite 45-gram graphite shaft to replace the one on a new club you haven't even hit yet—**while reading this!**

Can you at least make an effort?

Maybe you're not able to see the forest for the proverbial trees, which is sur-prising considering that's where you most often play from. Maybe you need more incentive. Tell you what, before we go any further, I have a little homework assignment for you. Put the book down and make a list of **things you can do in four hours besides play golf**. Just free associate. No judgment—there are no right or wrong answers!

Okay, what'd you come up with? If you don't mind sharing . . .

"I could fly to Las Vegas, if I were willing to endure the cattle call of Southwest, otherwise it's two connections. I could play two rounds in the amount of time it would take to get there if even one connection was delayed."

Okay, true, but let's stay focused here. The point is that, yes, in the amount of time you take to play a standard, been-there-done-that round of golf, you could be in a completely different time zone, in a totally new culture, experiencing new things!

"Right, right, and desert golf has no trees or water hazards. There's a lot to be said for that. No rain delays or mosquitoes, and if I stayed at the Wynn, they have a course right at the casino, right on the Strip. It's crazy!"

Sigh . . . Let's move on, shall we? What else?

"I could watch two movies. Unless I was playing a public course, then I could watch seasons one and two of *Fleabag*."

Precisely! Surrounded by your family, bonding with the people you love, sharing an emotional experience.

"Right, right, but full disclosure, my wife falls asleep twenty minutes into any movie. Doesn't matter the genre. Scariest horror premise, most intriguing whodunit, or funniest comedy, she's out with her head across my lap. If I move to go to the bathroom, she wakes up all grumpy; if I don't move, she goes into deep REM and starts drooling on my leg. I've seen her get through forty-five minutes if Jason Momoa is the lead, but movies have become complete pretense for us—we're just too embarrassed to go to bed that early. So back-to-back movies? Four hours? That's hilarious. That's as likely as me shooting even par."

Okay, at some point you need to Google "caffeine" and maybe update your video streaming repertoire, but let's stay on point here.

"Right, next idea. I could go back to volunteering for Meals on Wheels."

Yes, now you're getting it! I love this, volunteering your time to help other people. You did this? When?

"Yeah, when I first got out of grad school, and it took about four hours. It's funny that back then I was all about giving to people less fortunate even though I didn't have any money either. I was pretty damn unfortunate myself, but, I don't know, I'd take my deathtrap of a Blazer with like 200,000 miles on it and I'd drive into the worst part of Bridgeport, pick up the meals from the community kitchen along with a list of addresses, and I'd go do my thing, like a foodie version of Robin Hood.

"There were no navigation apps then, so I'd get lost and end up in some sketchy areas where they'd either ask me if I wanted drugs or tell me to get the hell out of there if I knew what was good for me. But the elderly people I delivered to, they were amazing. They seemed happy all out of proportion to their circumstances. They'd chat me up, some insisted on tipping me a dollar or asked me to come in and share the meal. I never went home feeling like I had wasted my time. I never felt there was something else more important to do. Then I got my first job and stopped. No, no that's bullshit, that's an excuse. I could have done it on a Saturday or taken an evening shift. I just stopped."

Hey, that's fine, stuff happens, but the point is you could reconnect with that part of you. You could recapture those good feelings! You could stop playing just one round a week and do a Meals on Wheels shift instead!

"Yes, I should do that! I mean, there are some complications now. A beat-up Blazer nobody touched, but my Maserati GranTurismo? They'd have it up on blocks by the time I delivered the first meal. I mean, I could use my daughter's Camry, but my wife would go into cardiac arrest if she knew I was going into Bridgeport. And back then, I had nothing to offer these people but the meal I brought in. I was a kid. Now I could help more, but how much more? And where would that end? Now I'd feel . . . I don't know if it would feel good anymore. I think it would make me sad. I mean, I want to quit golf and add more meaning to my life, but . . ."

But not if it inconveniences you or makes you face the privileges you take for granted?

"Well, don't put it like that. I've earned every damn thing I've got. I just don't want to quit golf to go feel sad instead. Is that wrong? "

Well, I promised not to judge, but yes!

Okay let's pivot. Something you can do in four hours that would make you feel good. Something simple. Go!

"I could have sex I'm not having now!"

Okay, but what would you do with the remaining three hours and forty minutes?

"No listen, it's kind of perfect. On Saturday morning both kids are out of the house by eight a.m.—please don't ask me where they go, I don't know—and my wife and I have the whole house to ourselves. And tell me if this is too much information, but we've gotten to the point where when we say we can't wait to go to bed together, we normally mean we have clean sheets. We're both exhausted by 9:30. Our lovemaking frequency has really dropped off."

Well, according to a study published in the *Archives of Sexual Behavior* (a periodical I have time to read because I quit golf), the average married couple has sex fifty-one times a year, which comes out to about once a week. That's down from eighty times a year for a married couple in their twenties, so you're not the only ones.

"Okay, well . . . we'd still have to rally in the last few months of this year to be average."

Oh. Well, remember that the study defines sex broadly, so any sexual act counts, not just intercourse.

"Still not helping. But no, this is good, this would be a great substitute for golf! I would have more energy in the morning, and it being Saturday, no work in the back of my mind. Plus, it would be a set thing, like a tee time!"

Uh, whatever works, but aren't you worried about loss of spontaneity?

"We've been married twenty-two years and lived together for three before that. There is nothing spontaneous about our sex life. Now that I think about it, it's very much aligned with golf: We start off knowing our goal, we know each other's bodies enough to know the scoring zone, and she's made it very clear what's out of bounds and when I can go ahead and hit it."

I'm a little uncomfortable with the intersecting vernacular, but at least you're finding—

"Gotta say, first thing in the morning, after a night's rest, I'm not going to be able to use my standard excuses if I'm not, you know, up for it. What if I'm trading in golf performance anxiety for sexual performance anxiety?"

I really think you need to dial this back and stay in the present and—

"Never mind, won't work, I just texted my wife to discuss and she said she's taking a ceramics class on Saturdays. She also said she's told me this several times."

"Putting aside how easily ceramics could lead to celibacy, what could you do alone?"

"I could take a coding class!"

Really? You, coding? I don't mean to imply . . . I mean, that would be great! The golden trio of HTML, CSS, and JavaScript would be my recommendations. Learning computer skills is great for older people. There's a lot of research showing that it may have similar cognitive effects as doing Sudoku puzzles or learning a new language. It could help you avoid Alzheimer's or dementia.

"Okay, settle down, I'm not a hundred years old. I can navigate my company's CRM, I can attach and send photos, I'm on Insta and X (formerly known as Twitter), and I know how to pretend I've read your post and feed your ego with a like or a thumbs up. I'm not a Luddite."

Okay, but this would be programming. That's quite a step up, and it would take a lot more than four hours. Where is this coming from?

"You ever see the PNC Father/Son Challenge on TV? You have to be a PGA pro who has won a major or be in the Golf Hall of Fame to qualify, but if you are and have a son or daughter, you play in this 36-hole best ball event on a ridiculously easy resort course. And they have tees for the kids, and tees if you're over fifty-five, and tees if you're over eighty. Some of these guys you haven't seen in years and they're all fat and grey and their swings are just slower, shorter versions of what you remember."

God, it sounds sad, and awful!

"But see, it's not! It's kind of wonderful! Their kids, some of them are twelve years old, some as old as thirty-five, they don't just swing exactly like their dads. They move like them, they walk in step, they have the same pre-shot routines and waggles. They roll their left arm sleeve up like Dad did when he was on the 72nd tee at Oakmont, they hitch up their pants like Dad before moving in to address the ball. It's eerie to see the power and, I dunno, the charm of DNA. Tiger and his son dress the same, bust their opponents' chops the same; the smile is the same, and they all want to win so bad. The kids may not end up being as good as their dads at golf, but they have the same drive, the same intensity. And even though NBC lays on the sentimentality a bit too thick, even they can't ruin the love of the game and how happy these parents and kids are to be with each other for four hours, doing something they both want to do. It's not one side placating the other to have 'quality time.' When the kid makes a putt to win a hole or hits it close, you see the look on the dads' faces and you just know . . ."

You know what?

"That there's nowhere else they would rather be."

Okay, I get that it's an awesome made-for-TV golf event that sounds like it could be simulcast on Lifetime, but uh, you're not a PGA pro, let alone a major champion or Hall of Famer.

"It's not just the pros, I see it every week at my club. A dad taking his son or daughter out to play in the late afternoon when the course is empty. Sometimes they play until dark. I don't think they even know what time it is. It must be an awesome feeling."

I'm sure. You have a son, right? Does he like to play golf?

"He hates it. Hates it! Does he hate it because I love it? Does he hate it to send me a message? Did I push him too hard? Not enough? It doesn't matter, because now it's a thing. The word 'golf' is officially eyeroll-worthy to him. He talks about it with a lovely combination of disdain and disgust."

I'm sorry, that has to be tough for you.

"Nah, I've let it go. Really. You know what he does like though? Like, with a passion?"

I'm going to go with coding.

"Yeah. Coding. Whatever that is."

"Let's stay with what you know. You must have had some things you did before golf, a crew you hung out with. What about them?"

"Yeah, I used to cycle on weekends with a group of guys. That took at least four hours."

That sounds promising! You should reconnect with an old crew. Cycling still gets you outdoors, and it's great cardio. Do they still ride?

"Oh yeah, I get the Facebook updates. With the analytics. They post the route they rode, the calories they burned, their resting heart rates, their blood oxygen levels."

Well, like golf, each pursuit has its own metrics and markers.

"And oh my God, the way they go on about their damn bikes! The chromoly frames, the hydraulic brake calipers, the gearing, all the penis envy nonsense of

'Look how aero the drop clamp frame and carbon wheels make my new $12,000 Roubaix.' I mean, the way they go on and on about technology and performance and how they're faster now than when they were thirty—it's silly!"

Um, yeah, golfers aren't like that.

"I mean, my Cannondale is like ten years old. I'd have to get a new bike, and the clothes—you have to have the clothes. They've got shirts that don't hold on to sweat, they've got pants that have gel cushions that protect your testicles and keep you from becoming infertile, though that ship has sailed. I'd steer that Roubaix right into oncoming traffic before I'd take all that on again! And the helmets, I'd have to upgrade the helmet. With all the distracted drivers texting, it's a matter of when, not if, you crash."

Maybe you just take one weekend ride on your old bike before you even reach out to the crew—see if you still enjoy riding.

"You know what? I quit because I couldn't keep up enough to even draft with the stronger riders, and because my forearms ached after ten miles, and because from the moment we started all I thought about was stopping. With golf, when we're done, I always wish we could play more. When I cycled, I never felt that. Ever."

You need to stop overthinking this. Is there something, anything non-golf related that you told yourself you would get around to if you ever had the time? Come on, there must be something. Look, let me help—how about travel? You live in New England, so you are a four-hour drive from some epic tourist sites and a four-hour flight to some of the wonders of the planet!

"Like what?"

How about DC? The White House? The Smithsonian?

"You want me to give up golf for a kids' field trip?"

How about New York City? The Holocaust Museum?

"Too depressing. Humans are horrible. I concede the point, I don't need reminding."

Okay, how about zoos? You're not far from some phenomenal zoos!

"Right, but lines are long for the good stuff like the silverbacks and the elephants, and sidebar, zoos are like strip clubs."

Wait, in what way?

"You start off staring in amazement, then you get bored, and ultimately you feel sorry for those getting gawked at."

Wow, okay fine, get on a plane. The Alamo in San Antonio?

"Seen it, crazy let down. I can't believe how small it is. No wonder they got massacred."

The Grand Canyon?

"A really big hole. I don't get it."

Mount Rushmore?

"Only Lincoln looks like himself, and that's because no one else has ever looked like Lincoln. The rest need Photoshopping, plus it's in South Dakota! You see it and then what?"

You're not really approaching this as I'd hoped. How about Niagara Falls? Please do not tell me it is not awesome. You park your car, and you can hear it before you even get near it. A loud, low rumbling, like God clearing his throat. And then, as you get closer, it starts to rain, only it's not rain, it's the water bouncing off the damn bottom of the Falls! It is an ongoing testament to the power of nature! It will stagger your senses. They say there are no atheists in foxholes; I promise there are zero atheists at Niagara Falls!

"Whoa, okay, settle down, you convinced me! I will give up a Saturday of golf and make the drive. But I did hear that it is much better on the Canadian side than the American side, and I would have to update my passport. And the kids don't have passports, so I'd have to leave them home—who knows what we'd come back to? And I have also heard that customs these days is painfully slow. And I hate to admit it, but I am a bit of a hotel snob and I hear that area hasn't recovered from the last recession and the accommodations are subpar. But hey, the great thing is Niagara Falls isn't going anywhere, right? We can go anytime, like maybe after golf season some year!"

I get it. Intrepid you are not, so stay at home. But there must be something that you feel would be worthwhile to do with all the time you dedicate to golf. Maybe something entrepreneurial! Something that you think would add to the common good. Something you'd be remembered for. There are millions of golfers, but what could you do that *only you* could do?

"Entrepreneurial, well . . . No, you'd laugh. It's stupid . . ."

No, look, we're down to stupid! What have you got?

"Okay, now I haven't fleshed this out yet, but I think it would be both helpful and potentially a sick moneymaker. So, if you're a guy, once you get to a certain age, and from that point until you die, you have to pee all the time. During the night, during movies, during dinner, during everything, and always at the most inopportune time. The toast at the wedding, the moment the killer is revealed, when you're in an interview and they ask you why they should hire you. And it's not like when you're younger and you go, 'Oh, I have to go, but now is inconvenient, so I'll wait until the flight is over because the guy in the aisle is sleeping.' No, there's urgency now! You cannot wait, and beyond a certain point lurks humiliation. It's one of the things that you love about golf: You can go anytime. There's always a tree nearby, and if there's not, no one cares, as long as you don't do it when it's your turn to hit. A urologist can slow this process with drugs, but the prostate eventually becomes like a wedge with no grooves—it just won't hold."

Yet another example of the indecency of aging. So what's the stupid idea, you want to make bedpans that fit in laptop bags?

"No, but that might be better than my current idea! I'll have to sticky-note that for later. Anyhow, trust me that the worst part of this affliction is when you are in the car. A traffic jam causes panic attacks, a gas station you barely make it to only to find there are no restrooms is soul crushing, and to be on the highway, holding on, shaking your legs, which doesn't help, tapping the steering wheel while searching frantically for rest areas, is both painful and inevitable. You simply can no longer go an hour without access to a bathroom, ever . . . so I have my notes!

"I have compiled an exhaustive list of all the public places in New England that have bathrooms. Some are obvious, but some are sneaky, like certain grocery stores or retail stores that you wouldn't think of (every Target, for example, has super clean and reliable bathrooms). I also save you from stopping at the places you would think have bathrooms but don't. (CVS, no; Walgreens, yes!) I can tell you which exits to take, which construction sites leave their Porta Potties open, and, in a pinch, which dark roads in residential communities have plenty of bushes and no street lamps. I even have a bonus section of super nice people who will let you in to use their bathrooms when you have to take a dump.

"It's taken me years to collect this knowledge! I could self-publish, or create a website, and I could spend my weekends driving and expanding it. It would never be a finished project, it would just keep growing, and eventually I could hire other people to start adding info for their neighborhoods and states; I'd give them full access to the site. We could call it Wee-kipedia! And yes, we could eventually take on ad revenue, and maybe I'd make serious money and we'd go public or position ourselves for takeover, but honestly, the idea of guys like me being able to relax when they start to get the urge, knowing they can trust my app or book or site or whatever to bail them out, I mean, that would be so satisfying to me. To eliminate that fear for others, to keep their loved ones from feeling momentarily abandoned . . . Yes, I would do that. For that project, I would give up golf! Absolutely!"

That's a real breakthrough, the fact that you can see yourself doing something with purpose that has nothing to do with golf! So try to keep that in mind when I tell you that you can already find detailed data on "places near me with restroom facilities" on several popular apps. The info's all already out there. (Other than the construction sites, which is weird and probably illegal.)

"Oh. That's very disheartening."

I'm sure. I'm sorry.

"No it's okay, but look, I did your homework assignment, and all it did was make me realize how limited my life has become, how I really don't have anything better to do in four hours other than play golf. In fact, I could have played a round of golf rather than do this stupid exercise."

Okay, now you're pouting. You're such an absolutist! How about a golf-related activity that would satisfy your urge to be involved with the game and yet wean you off your harmful tendency to construct your life around playing golf?

"You quashed my dream, but whatever. So you're telling me I can keep playing golf while weaning off golf? How?"

How about, instead of four hours, you take one hour every weekend, go to the driving range, and instead of playing golf, you teach your wife how to play! Now you're doing something together with the person you love most, and over time . . . Wait, what's going on? Are you okay? I don't mean to alarm you, but I think you're having a stroke.

"Have you discussed this with her? Tell me exactly what you said to her!"

What? No! I don't even know her. You need to breathe. Is your left arm tingling?

"So she knows nothing about this very, very, very bad idea? You swear?"

I promise, I was purely spitballing! Just lie down. How many fingers do you see?

"For God's sake, man, church and state! Church and state!"

CHAPTER SIX

The Center
Will Not Hold

"Hi, where are you?"

"I'm at work. Why, what's up?"

"You're at work?"

"Uh . . . yeah."

"Because I'm at your office and you're not here."

"Well, I didn't mean I was physically at work, I meant I was working. You know our office has a hybrid model, and I don't take advantage of it enough. I decided to work from home."

"So you're home?"

"Not at the moment, I'm running some errands. But I'll be home soon . . . where I'll be working. Why are you at my office?"

"Today was the continuing education seminar. They had it downtown, so I thought I'd drop in and make your day."

"Well, you would have for sure!"

"What errands?"

"You know, the usual mundane stuff. I'm getting gas at the moment."

"You are? That's so weird, because I'm parked right next to your car in the club parking lot, and I don't see any pumps around, and I sure as hell don't see you."

"Okay, okay, scary enhanced interrogator lady, I'm playing golf! I was heading home to work and thought I'd get in a few holes. It was just a spur-of-the-moment decision; you don't have to freak out."

"'Spur of the moment' . . . You know, you should tell your boss to give Brendan a raise. That's one dedicated kid. The only guy at the office today after your boss told your whole team *yesterday* that you had hit your quarterly goal a week early so he was giving you all the day off today. Brendan said that after you all cheered, you hit the phones trying to get a foursome together. Brendan said he doesn't play golf, but he should probably take it up because you seemed so excited."

"Brendan skateboards. He can do that anywhere. By himself. Who is he going to call? I understand that's not relevant. "

"You told me you were going to work! You dressed for work! I saw you putting golf clothes in your backpack this morning! You flat out lied to me!"

"You are making this into something ridiculous. I thought you were working all day; I knew you thought I was working all day. The weather guy said today was going to be one of the top ten days of the year! He only says that like ten times all year! When we got the day off, I saw it as . . ."

"As what?" Her voice is dangerously low, like her next step was either to scream or burst into tears.

" . . . a victimless crime. I knew I'd be home the same time I always am. Nobody gets hurt."

"But somebody did. Me."

"Only because you found out."

"No! You don't even see it, do you? What hurts is I wasn't the first call! What hurts is that you got a bonus day off, one of the top ten days of the year, and you never even thought to ask me if I could get the day off. It never occurred to you that we could spend the day together. We could celebrate the office success, go somewhere special with friends, with the kids, by ourselves. You'd rather golf than be with me. That's what hurts."

"I'm with you every day of my life. I don't golf every day of my life."

"I think you would if you could. If you could switch those two things around, you would, wouldn't you?"

"I'm not going to answer something so ridiculous. You know my back wouldn't hold up to playing every day."

"I think you need to come home."

"Look, you're being crazy, and I can't stay on the phone. There are three guys on the tee, two of them guests I invited, waiting for me to finish out the hole. I'm sorry I didn't tell you. That was wrong, I get that."

"But that's not all that's wrong. I think we need to reevaluate at a pretty basic level what we're doing together."

"What? I have nothing to reevaluate!"

"But I do."

Two of the guys in your foursome were married. They gave you a look that said, "Been there dude," once you hung up and apologized for the holdup. The fourth, engaged to be married, gave you a look that said, "Is that where I'm headed?" You three putted from 4 feet when you got to the green, and your best ball partner said, "We'll chalk that up to your wife's call." When you somehow were able to hit the next tee shot out of bounds on the widest fairway on the course, your partner said, "That one's on you."

You couldn't have survived in a corporate environment as long as you have without learning to count to ten before reacting in anger. Oh, you learned that if you say, "Hey, I didn't mean that," people will nod and say they get it, we all do it, it's all good. But they don't forget. And it comes back to you. In a pending promotion that gets put on hold, in the table they assign you at the quarterly President's Club dinner, in how long it takes you to get a simple email response. You said it, it's out there, and you can't take it back.

So you knew better than to follow your wife's directive and rush home after the round. Instead you sat in the grill room and watched the PGA event on the big screen and felt even worse than you already did when the announcer informed you that Tony Finau had 187 yards to the flag and was hitting a stock nine iron. You had to figure this out before going home. Your wife would not be overtly angry. There would be no histrionics. No, she'd smile sadly, would be eerily calm and kind. She would tell you she just wants to understand. That she's coming at this from a place of love, that (and this is the part that kills, right out of your mom's playbook) she's not angry, she's disappointed in you. She thought you were better than this. She could give a masterclass.

"Go with your first read. Just like on the greens!"

Chad had pulled up the stool next to you at the bar. He was in your group and witnessed the call. He had actually patted you on the back when you got in the cart after you hung up.

"Chad?"

"You're obviously trying to decide how to handle things when you get home. And I'm telling you to go with your first read. Like a putt, it's always the right call. What do you really want to say to your wife?"

"That I didn't do anything wrong."

"There you go. Say it to her."

"But I did. I did do something wrong."

"Because you played golf?"

"Because I made her feel like I prefer golf to her."

"And you don't?"

"I think I do. And that's messed up. That's messed up, right?"

"I was always clear from the jump with my wife: when I'm playing golf, don't call me, don't text me, I don't exist. I'll be present with you if you let me be present without you. That was our deal."

"It *was* your deal? Not now?"

"I'm talking about my first wife."

"Right. And your current wife?"

"Oh, she'd never go for that."

"Did you ever lie about where you were when you were playing golf?"

"With the first, or second, or current?"

"We're up to three now?"

"Doesn't matter. The answer is yes across the board. It never bothered me. Also I never got caught."

"Well, it bothers me. I should have just told her. She probably would have said 'fine, go ahead.'"

"Sure, but she wouldn't have meant it. And you would know that she didn't mean it, and she would know that you know that she didn't mean it. And then you know what happens?"

"Apparently multiple divorces."

"You play badly. Like today, you were playing pretty well today until she called."

"I did shoot 38 on the front, and I couldn't believe I parred 11. I never par 11."

"Swing looked smooth. Just saying."

"She got me worked up and then my tempo was shot."

"Yeah, awful. Last five holes you couldn't find the planet. Not that it matters, you know, big picture, but she lost us the match. If my wife—my current wife—called me and took me out of rhythm and then I lost the match, I'd make her pay me back the twenty bucks we lost. Including the press on 18."

"You would? Sidebar, do you have, like, a boilerplate prenup you just update as needed?"

You picked up Chad's tab and thanked him, even though the only thing clear in your mind at the moment was that going forward, whenever you had a problem in life, if you asked Chad for a solution and did the complete opposite of whatever he advised, you'd probably make out pretty well.

You went out to the deck that overlooks the putting green and mindlessly checked your emails while watching members putt. You noticed, not for the first time, that Mark practices putting more than anyone in the club. And he's a horrible putter. By the time he's within 5 feet of the hole, everyone puts him out of his misery and concedes. Mark is proof the game is 100 percent mental.

You were so apprehensive about going home that you even checked your junk folder, where you find job offers by ZipRecruiter, vacation homes by VRBO, and requests for donations from politicians running for Senate seats in states where you don't live. Then the ringtone—"The Lady in Red," chosen by your ginger wife. You got it on the second ring and faux mouthed an apology to Mark, who would have missed his putt anyway.

"Hi, I'm heading home in a bit, I just wanted to give us both a little time to breathe, you know?"

"That was considerate, and I do need to breathe, because I've been laughing so hard. I got into your computer."

"What? How?"

"Seriously? Every password you have ever had in your life is a combination of your first dog, good ol' Roscoe, and something your baby brain can remember. Roscoe plus your birthday for your debit card, Roscoe plus the kids' birthdays for streaming services, Roscoe plus my birthday for Venmo . . . "

"Because family is what matters to me!"

"What matters to you is golf, so guess what? Roscoe plus your precious GHIN number opened your laptop. And by the way, hacker alert, your GHIN number is on every piece of mail the club sends us."

"So you went through my email?"

"Oh no, not just email. Recent documents, archived files, browser history— now that was illuminating."

"Can I just say, compared to most guys I hardly watch porn."

"Agreed, you seem to watch less than I do. But honestly, how disappointingly vanilla, you only search for 'busty MILFS.' Hell, I'm a busty MILF!"

"Right, I would think you'd find that reassuring."

"When exactly was I going to be notified that you are going to Bandon Dunes with twelve guys the last week of July?"

"That's, uh . . . not in stone. That's just being tossed around."

"Stop! I read the emails! You used your company credit card for the flights and hotel so I wouldn't see the charges. Do you want me to read you the confirmation numbers?"

"We're well within the cancellation period. That time of year that place fills up fast, just wanted to have options."

"Tuscany is the option! We are going to Tuscany! With the Krausses and the Pattersons! A trip a year in the making! You know this, we talk about it when they come over, we had a Tuscany-themed dinner party a goddamn week ago, you were there! We looked at the websites of tour guides, we watched a YouTube video on where to go in Florence!"

"Okay, calm down! Of course, it's not that I forgot about Tuscany, I honestly thought, for whatever reason, it was next year."

"Next year! Do you get how crazy and hostile that sounds to me? Every night in bed I have the Rosetta Stone app up on the iPad, I have earbuds in, and I'm talking in Italian! You make fun of me for it, then I tell you it won't be so funny when I'm the only one who knows what's what in Tuscany! Why would I do that a year in advance?"

"It did seem to me you were being over-the-top proactive."

"I can't. You're not present anymore. Ever. We get remnants of you. Jesus, honey, it's a game. Just a game. You're not supposed to live for it."

"I don't! I live for you guys. Seriously, you know that."

"Nope, I don't know that anymore. And you know what makes it harder to understand? You're not even that good. I think it would be easier for me to understand if you found this thing late in life that you were crazy gifted at. I probably shouldn't say that."

"Because it's cruel?"

"No, because you'll probably see this whole conversation as motivation to improve."

"Look, I'm coming home."

"Don't. Or do, it doesn't matter. I won't be here. I'm going to stay at Melissa's for a few days. Maybe longer. I need time to think. You need time to come up with a new password."

"What about the kids? You're going to leave that all on me. That's my punishment for a round of golf?"

"Oh right, I forgot, you have become disassociated from time when not on the golf course. Our kids are now teenagers! Jordan actually drives a car, where he keeps condoms in the center console. You ought to introduce yourself while I'm gone, it'd be great to catch up. I'll be in touch."

"Can I just ask you one thing before you disappear? Are you at all sorry for invading my privacy?"

"At the moment, I'm sorry I didn't do it sooner."

"That's fair. Do me a favor, and I'll let you go. Search for 'Sharon Ducci.' Email, social media, Word docs, browser history, whatever you'd like. Can you do that please?"

"I already did."

"Find anything . . . Anything?"

"No . . . no, I didn't."

"Can you please try to keep that in mind?"

"I think I had more of you even then. You keep that in mind."

From (408) 734-4456: *Smokeshow goes low!*

That was the text Sharon had sent you three years ago. It had come in when you left the table to go to the restroom. Beyond the flirtatious subject line, there was a video attached and you could see Sharon, in shorts and sleeveless golf shirt, her body mostly covered by the play button, but your wife had seen enough to forego your longstanding agreement not to look at each other's phones. Sharon was participating in a scramble at a conference, which is exactly where and how you met her, and had buried a putt from 40 feet. Your wife played the video and Sharon's impromptu celebration showcased not only her hip-hop dance moves, but also her tendency to play golf drunk, leading your wife to believe all scrambles and corporate outings are not for networking but sanctioned debauchery.

By the time you got back to the table she had excused herself, and you didn't realize she had your phone until several minutes later, when she abruptly tossed it in your lap in front of your friends and, wait for it, went to Melissa's for a few weeks, taking the kids with her. Her first night away, you realized that, other than business trips, you had never spent a night apart. You roamed the empty house like a male version of Gloria Swanson in *Sunset Boulevard*.

The emails your wife uncovered that time were both incriminating and exculpatory. You had only seen Sharon twice at conferences. You had never kissed her or even been alone with her. You could even say you hadn't touched her except for high-fiving when a good shot was struck or hugging upon greeting or ending a round. All of this backed up by the emails from Sharon herself!

But that wasn't the whole story. You were allowed to be someone else with Sharon in the course of your long-distance email relationship. You were funnier, looser, and one would read the emails and think you could turn anything into sexual innuendo. You were clever and chill. And she reciprocated. She was verbally agile, and she matched you inference for inference. Seeing her number pop up in your phone was an oasis on an arid day. She was self-deprecating, sharing her disastrous stories from the dating apps. "You have no idea how many loser men are out there," she wrote. "Your wife is so lucky." And that led you to occasionally confide in Sharon that no, she was the lucky one. Marriage and kids were dull and enervating, that you longed to have one thing happen to you that was new and exciting, that you had started to feel stuck. You often included a sad face emoji or the GIF of a famous actor shaking his head.

You imagined your wife reading the stock driving-range-longsuffering-husband emails you exchanged with Sharon and realized it would have been less damaging if Sharon had sent you photos of her in a Victoria's Secret bombshell lace teddy. The lack of these photos was really your only defense. But it wasn't enough. Because your wife knows you, and when you told her that you were just taking your wits for a walk, that it was harmless banter, just another golf buddy who just happened to be beautiful and a little younger than your wife, when you told her it didn't mean anything and that she was being ridiculous, she saw through you. The truth was that the texts and emails you got from Sharon sustained you. You never intended to take the relationship to any next level, but the possibility that you could, that someone like Sharon might want to . . . well, it meant a great deal to you.

You had to agree to cut off all contact with her. You had to agree to allow your wife access to your phone at any and all times. Without eye rolling. You had to agree to allow your wife to verify this arrangement by calling Sharon herself. Mortifying. You had to agree to see a marriage counselor, a colorful guy who tested your willingness to do the work by opening with a joke: "Couple goes to a marriage counselor and it's not working, bickering and battling for six months, counselor says, 'Someone has to change,' and the husband says, 'Well I'm not changing and she's not changing, so I guess *you* have to change.' Are you guys willing to make changes?"

And you were. And you did. At least you thought you had. At first, the agreement was that anytime you went to a conference, you had to provide a list of attendees so your wife would know Sharon wasn't going to be there. But it wasn't long before your wife stopped requesting to search your phone, and you stopped even thinking about Sharon. It wasn't as much about rebuilt trust as it was exhaustion. You never contacted Sharon again, and to her credit, she apologized to your wife and blocked your number.

You thought reminding your wife that you kept your promise and erased Sharon would count for something. But it didn't and it shouldn't. It wasn't that hard to do. Partly because it was really, at its core, a distracting ego biscuit. But mostly because you're a golfer. You have to have a short-term memory if you're going to be a golfer. The shot that matters is the one in front of you.

You texted your kids and asked if they wanted to do something. Dinner? Bowling? (Did they still bowl? Did you just embarrass yourself?) But they both responded that they weren't home and not to expect them until late. Your wife had gotten to them first and they knew she was going to Melissa's. (Condoms in your son's center console? Was she trying to scare you? You would need to verify that.) There was still an hour of light left, and the idea of going home and being by yourself all night, an idea you often fantasized about, seemed incredibly depressing.

You had been sitting for almost two hours since coming off the course, and when you went to pick up your bag at the bag drop, your knees made a crunching sound and your back was so stiff you involuntarily made an old man sound, like you were clearing your throat before telling some kids to get off your lawn. You started for your car but you had to walk past the driving range to get to the parking lot, and you told yourself 1) maybe hitting some balls would give you some clarity, since obviously you needed a next move here; 2) in a few months, when the course would be closed and you wouldn't be able to hit balls, you'll wish you'd seized this moment; and 3) God, your hybrid was costing you strokes. Everything was low and left with that club. Gotta fix that.

You were going to warm back up with some wedges. But you just grabbed the hybrid, dumped a bucket on the mat, and swung at full speed. Some were still low and left, some you were able to pop up, but it didn't matter. Your mind was gone. You knew you had to go to Melissa's and confront your wife. That alone would get through to her, right? Send the message that you didn't just let this linger? I mean, if you really were so unhealthily obsessed with golf, then you could have just let her stay at Melissa's and played golf all day tomorrow, and the next day too. Hmm . . . maybe a cooling off period would be a good idea, and you saw on the tee sheet that Walt had an opening in a foursome at eleven tomorrow morning. . . No! Focus. You needed to go to Melissa's and agree not to play golf tomorrow and to offer to do something around the house or go somewhere instead. But no, that would not work. It was too soon and too little. You needed to go big in order to go home. You needed a Big Gesture! One that would surprise her. One that would shake her up. But what?

By now, every time you turned away from the ball your lower back stiffened a bit more. Your turn was restricted. Get your left shoulder under your chin to complete the backswing. You narrowed your stance to allow more turn. Okay, that helped, that last shot was pure!

Okay, Big Gesture . . .

Got it! You needed to write a resignation letter to the club president. You would reassure him that your decision to resign had nothing to do with the club's amenities or the quality of the golf course. You would go to great pains to thank the course superintendent and his wonderful staff. You would compliment the attitude and courtesy of the ball kids and say that you very much appreciated him stopping by on occasion to give you tips when he saw you struggling on the range. You would tell him that it was, in fact, a very emotional decision for you, since the members of the men's club had become like a second family and you would always cherish the relationships you had forged while you were a member and you hoped someday to be able to revisit this tragic and difficult decision, but that after much soul searching you had realized your real and actual family was at an inflection point. In a blink your kids had become teenagers, and you wanted to spend as much time with them as you could before they went on to make their mark in the world. And you wanted to take time, as well, with your beautiful and devoted wife, to strategize what your life as empty nesters should look like. It's an exciting albeit daunting stage of life, and you needed to put the clubs away and focus. In fact, you and your wife and some wonderful friends were going to Tuscany to plot out your course in a new and nourishing environ. You hoped that someday, if things worked out and golf once again fit into the plan, that the club would consider taking you back.

So you would draft the letter and send it to your wife to ask if she wanted to see any changes or if you should send it as it was. Then you would wait for her reply, which had better be that while she appreciated the Big Gesture, it wouldn't be necessary, and she's sure the two of you can find some middle ground. If she said, "Yes, that's great, please send and CC me on it" . . . Well, no, she wouldn't do that! Would she? Well if she did, then you were going to have to resign. And that would be that. You said you wanted to know how to quit golf, and this would be how.

They say that 70 percent of what we worry about never happens. You're such a chronic worrier that you worry if that number is real. Is it too low? Have you wasted that much energy? Or is it too high, and your default setting of expecting the worst all the time is the only way to survive? Hard to know definitively, and we will never know if you invested too much energy in worrying about whether your Big Gesture would get your wife to come home. Because the question of whether you were capable of quitting golf answered itself—in one disastrous swing!

It's tempting to blame Bryson Dechambeau and his speed training. The way he hovered the club over the ball and huffed and puffed and shuffled his feet like a bull at the exact moment they tie his testicles (the bull's, not Bryson's, although you don't really know that) and lift the gate. And then the huge turn, and he exhaled and swung as hard as a human can swing from the ground up, the club recoiling off his back and the tee flying further than many of your tee shots. Maybe this is unfair to Bryson, since he gets blamed for ruining golf. Isn't it piling on to blame him for ruining your golf game and your physical well-being, too? Wouldn't this have happened even if you were visualizing the easy power and grace of Adam Scott or In Gee Chun? Isn't it just that you were tired of your hybrid going twenty yards shorter than the target? Or that you had not properly warmed up? Or that you had just played eighteen holes and let yourself get stiff while moping in the grill room and then, with the sun going down and the temperature dropping, you took it upon yourself to swing your hybrid as hard as you could? Isn't it just that you are getting old? In the end the cause doesn't matter—the effect does.

You would tell the doctor a few hours later that it felt like you'd been shot in the back. Before you went down, since you didn't hear a shot and a silencer was unlikely at such a posh club, you actually turned to find out who the idiot was who had shot you.

You had told yourself to stop swinging like a wimp, to make a full turn and fire your left knee at the target and then to release your whole body as hard as you could. It didn't even matter if you missed the ball entirely, you were going to get some damn speed in your swing. You were just past the ball when the spasm started. You were not even onto your left side when your back locked. By the time you were on the ground, the pain was radiating down your lower back through your glute, and any attempt to move only made it worse. You lay there for a moment thinking you had "tweaked" something, and since you were alone on the range, no one would even know. You would get back up, stretch a bit, and maybe break out the sand wedge for those last dozen balls in the bucket.

Instead, the assistant pro started running at you with the defibrillator unit they keep on the wall of the pro shop. You were somehow offended that he could mistake you, a paragon of fitness, for someone who could have a cardiac event, even though you were lying flat on the ground and moaning. Soon half of the grill room was watching as an ambulance pulled up incongruously among the golf carts. (Seriously, sirens? Jesus, now you might as well resign. There would be no living this down.)

You told them this was all a bit dramatic, you simply pulled something in your back and just needed some help getting up and maybe a muscle relaxer or two. But when they tried to roll you over, wicked spasms ran through your entire posterior chain and only lying completely still would stop the radiating pain. So you had no choice. They strapped you to a stretcher like they would an NFL player who had been hit above the neck and wasn't moving. (Unlike in the NFL, none of the members huddled up and locked hands and said a prayer, and no one cheered when you showed you could move your toes.)

It's amazing what runs through your head in such moments. You were overly concerned about your clubs. You didn't usually store them at the club because you liked to play at other courses with friends who weren't members of the same club, and you often hit a driving range near your office, so you needed reassurance from the head pro that you could leave your clubs and that someone would mark them with your name. You insisted the ambulance driver reach into your pullover pocket and take out a twenty to give to the kid who had brought your balls to the range and cleaned your clubs. So many members were notorious for being crappy tippers, and you would not be remembered that way. And suddenly you remembered an interview late in his life with Arnold Palmer. They asked him if he would have done anything differently in his playing career. He was notorious for hitting the ball low. He never tried to change his shot shape to land the ball softer, and even though his putting got suspect as he aged (he never won another major after thirty-five), he never tried a cross-handed or claw grip. But all he said was, "I wish I had stretched more. I lost my legs because I wasn't very flexible." And that's all you thought this was, a reminder to be more flexible. It never occurred to you that this was one of those life-trajectory-changing moments. Golfers have bad backs. You'll deal.

The ambulance driver closed the back hatch, told you to relax, and asked you a simple question. "Sir, is there anyone you want us to call for you?"

And you realized that this question could solve a lot of short-term problems for you. You didn't have to quit golf right now. You didn't have to worry about your wife realizing she preferred her life without you, never coming home, and toppling your entire life's infrastructure. All of these decisions were now put on hold. Your physical pain, searing as it was, was going to allow you to kick that can right down the proverbial road. Your wife would be home tonight! She just has to make one stop first. As bad as you hit it, that hybrid range session turned out to be an intuitive act of survival. Genius.

"Yes, my wife. I'm sure she'll want to meet us at the hospital."

CHAPTER SEVEN

The Liar in Winter

As far as your wife was concerned, you were through playing golf. But you saw it not as hanging up your clubs for good, more as the kind of medical extension the PGA tour allows its members. Of course, you wouldn't be getting the $10,000 a month they pay their injured members, and you weren't guaranteed a certain number of starts when you recovered. And unlike the PGA, which has no limit on how long a medical extension can last or how many times you can apply for one, your club has a medical "freeze" policy that allows you to retain membership and pause payments for up to one year.

The real bonus was your wife was willing to come home and care for you and not add to your stress by relitigating the serious golf-fostered grievances that sent her packing for all of four hours, but she did make it clear that this had better be a time of self-reflection and reevaluation. Because after the three months your team of doctors predicted it would take for you to be close to fully functional again, she wanted you to come back to who you once were and have been pretending to be . . . or not. Your call. She said this while standing over you with her arms crossed over her chest in her quintessential, "Do I look like I'm messing around?" pose, but her lips were also trembling, and her eyes were filling up. She felt she had to say it, but she was such a good person the guilt was getting to her. You were in so much pain, and here she was issuing an ultimatum.

"So choose wisely, my friend." ("My friend" was her signal that this was a line in the sand. No one in the family had ever come out unscathed when she started a sentence with, "Let me tell you something, my friend . . .") "But for right now, try to rest. What can I get you, baby?"

It is supposed to be one of the laws of golf, an immutable truth, like the fact that all putts left short do not go in the hole, that if you play golf long enough, you will have back pain. But it is a myth! Sure, the constant repetition of a movement as contrary to proper kinetics as the golf swing is bound to cause problems in your back. You are creating torque by disassociating your upper body from your lower body, and the more pressure you can withstand when you turn your back to the target, fire your hips, and violently uncoil your body in a forward motion as fast as you can while still striking the ball with the center of the club face, the better player you are likely to be. And it takes its toll! Tiger Woods was a lithe twenty-one-year-old when he first won the Masters and made the course look like a pitch and putt with his prodigious length, forcing the Augusta National powers that be to attempt to "Tiger Proof" the course, but that was also the year Lee Trevino watched him swing and predicted serious back trouble. That was four back operations ago.

But that's not acute back pain, that's chronic back soreness brought on by repetition. You have now learned the profound difference. People mistake the chronic for the acute all the time. When you are chronically late for social events or professional appointments, it's considered rude, but if you are late for boarding a flight, the result is acute because they're closing that door with or without you and you have now lost an entire day of your life.

Until that day at the range, until you hit the ground and couldn't move, you would have told everyone you knew that you had back pain. But you didn't, you had chronic back soreness. Here's how you know the difference in life: When you have chronic pain, you don't stop doing the thing that causes you pain. Oh, you complain; you talk about it way too much to people who are tired of hearing it; you even plan on someday taking some steps to rectify whatever is causing your pain, but you never get around to it. For most golfers, that means standing on the first tee and faux stretching their back, asking if anyone has Advil, and wondering if anyone would recommend Pilates. But they continue to play.

Acute pain is different. You stop doing what's causing the pain. Your choice is gone. It's your body's emergency broadcast system. If you pull a muscle, you suck it up and continue skiing down the mountain, but if you break a leg, you will lie there until the ski patrol arrives. If you are in a job that pays well but is no fun or has no long-term potential, you sigh and go to work every day. That's chronic pain. If you are in a job where the boss demotes you or the workplace is unsafe or you get your salary cut in half, that's acute pain. Chronic pain can be ignored for a time; acute pain is urgent! You must deal with it now!

Now that you have officially graduated to acute back pain, you long for the halcyon days of chronic back soreness.

But it isn't all bad. You got to play the martyr at work. Your boss felt horrible and had the HR manager call you immediately and run through a dizzying array of options: use accumulated PTO, access the short-term disability plan, or even take the ninety-day sabbatical that is available to employees once every three years as a measure conceived to reduce burnout but is generally exploited— either people went on sabbatical but took another job immediately and collected two salaries until someone at the new company insisted on adding their bio to the website and someone from the old company saw it and blew them up, or people spent the time writing their memoirs.

But you are one of the roughly 25 percent of Americans who can work remotely. Ever since the early days of COVID-19, you were allowed to work from home as long as you had the proper computer connectivity. Your company now has a hybrid model where you should be going in three days a week, but nobody ever figured out how to police it, and it soon became the Wild, Wild West. No one knew who was supposed to be coming in on any given day, and it just became who was bored at home or wanted to get away from their kids or got sick of seeing the same four walls every day. It was all about results. Your boss only cared if the work got done. If it did, where it was done from was not his problem. If it didn't, very much his problem and soon to be yours!

You said to him, "I got this. Give me a few days to get off the painkillers and I'll work remotely and get after it. No problem." Your boss was duly impressed and even picked up the phone to tell you all about his miracle worker naturopath who changed his life.

And that's how it started. Nothing makes people happier in the social media epoch than making a medical referral. Despite knowing next to nothing about your actual diagnosis, they insisted their referral was the one and true way to a quick recovery. The referrals fell into the following distinct camps when it came to back injuries.

Naturopathic Medicine

Along with your boss, many people offered neuropathic medicine as the cure to not just your back pain but all of life's worries. Natural-based "alternatives" to conventional medicine, they said. Friends started texting you links to plant resins from the Incas, as if that meant anything to you—as if ancient and traditional necessarily meant effective. As if the Incas were paragons of health. Coworkers sent you "studies" on vitamin C, or D, or folic acid, or echinacea. You noticed the studies were often funded by the same company that sold the product. Everyone had an anecdote of how someone they knew, frustrated by the results they were getting from their doctors, recovered immediately after trying acupuncture or yoga or tai chi. When you pointed out that maybe in the time it took for them to find their pseudoscience of choice, they had simply healed up, they got angry. "Don't be so closed-minded," they would chide, "why would so many people go to retreats with crystal therapy or aromatherapy or Reiki or moxibustion if they didn't see a difference?"

But you couldn't find any clinical data to support any of these modalities. And none of them were paid for by your insurance. And nearly all of them played unbearable music, like whale songs, during the treatments. Besides, they were all considered "holistic" approaches, which to your cynical mind was just cover for "everything but the kitchen sink." It just seemed to you that alternative medicine was one more way for us to show we are special and unique.

You went to Sedona once for a conference (and to play golf in the desert where there are no trees and hardly any water hazards and the ball flies forever at altitude), and every evening before dinner the hotel offered a free drink and a chance to stand in a circle, hold hands, and "feel" the electromagnetic energy of the Sedona Spiritual Vortex, which supposedly encompasses twenty-two miles. You were supposed to feel the intensity, the euphoria, the surge of learning. Your hands were supposed to tingle; your senses were supposed to switch on to high alert. A buzz should have permeated your body, but you felt nothing. And you didn't believe the people who you were with did either. But after a seven-hour flight, a two-hour ride, and $799 a night for the room, nobody wanted to admit they were being conned, and one woman, tipsy going in, said she was unable to lower her arm because it was "caught up in the Vortex." It took everything in you not to slap her arm down to her side.

Even the most ardent admirers of alternative medicine would concede it's not optimal for acute conditions. You don't break your leg and rub elderberry on it and expect to walk; you don't get diagnosed with cancer and drink chamomile tea and meditate. That's all you needed to hear. Your back hurts! And the golf season is coming! No alternative medicine for you.

Orthopedic Surgeons

They wanted to cut you. They told you that all other options were half measures. They told you chiropractors are charlatans, and physical therapy is useless with its "if you just listen to your body, it will tell you what you can do and through trial and error you can regain range of motion all by yourself" pablum. They told you fusing your back—permanently connecting two or more vertebrae and eliminating motion—was the only surefire way to eliminate your pain and lead a normal life. A short hospital stay, a few weeks of recovery, and you would go back to living your life pain free! That sounded awesome, but then they told you that they couldn't guarantee you could resume activities you had previously enjoyed. Some people could play golf, but with limitations. Well, you already had limitations, namely your golf skill set and your fragile golf mind. Blaming bad shots on your fused back would get old quickly. Surgery wasn't happening.

Chiropractors

They told you to avoid surgery at all costs. Surgeons are paid fortunes to perform operations, they said, so they're trigger happy. Surgeons don't understand the musculoskeletal system, and they hate that chiropractic care is relatively inexpensive and produces instant results. A big part of you, always looking for the easy way out, wanted to buy in. Insurance covered chiro care, and a member of your club had a practice near your home.

But just a few years ago, when your back would get so sore by the end of a round that you found yourself shopping online for one of those suction cups you stick on the end of your putter grip so you could retrieve the ball out of each hole without bending over, you went to this guy. It bothered you that it took longer for you to fill out the release forms saying it wasn't his fault if you had a stroke than it did for the actual adjustment, and as you sat on the cushioned table with the hydraulics waiting for him to come in, you weren't pleased that instead of a medical school diploma, the "degree" on the wall was an accreditation from a chiropractic college in a small town in Wisconsin. You made a mental note to Google whether it took longer to get certified as a personal trainer or a doctor of chiropractic medicine.

You got precious solace from the rubber vertebrae hanging from a hook that he breezily pointed to as he explained how lucky you were that you had a soft tissue injury and not bulging discs, and that chiro was your best bet. He said you'd have to come three times a week initially, but then it would be twice a week, and eventually you'd hit maintenance stage where you'd still have to come in regularly "to keep things tracking." You couldn't help but admire at some level a biz model based on dependency. And it did seem something good had to be happening when you turned on your side and pulled your legs up to your chest, he pushed your shoulders in the opposite direction, and a loud cracking sound filled the room. It seemed to make him very proud of himself, and when he turned you over and created a diversion by asking you about the family while he jerked your head sideways and an even louder crack ensued, he smiled and in a very smug voice said, "Exactly!" But an hour later at home, you were listing to the side, favoring your back, and reaching for the NSAIDs in your medicine cabinet. So this time around, with your back in far worse condition, you couldn't get excited about revisiting the turf wars between orthopedics and chiros.

Pharmaceutical Solutions

No one over the age of twenty-five plays golf without the help of an anti-inflammatory. Yes, you knew at some level they weren't good for your stomach and could raise your blood pressure, but if they raised your blood pressure as much as the triple bogeys you carded once your back got sore and you started lifting off the ball, you would have been diagnosed with chronic hypertension long ago. But this was different. NSAIDs weren't touching your acute pain. When they released you from the hospital, the doctor gave you a script for a dozen Vicodin®, a lightweight Schedule II opiate. He said you wouldn't need any more than that and not to take them unless you were in distress. You told him to relax. You had seen enough documentaries on Purdue Pharma and the Sackler family to know the drill. First you use Oxycontin® for some legitimate injury and then you build up a tolerance so you need two to take away the pain and then three, and pretty soon you realize you haven't left the couch all weekend and you want the oxy even though the injury has healed and no doctor will give it to you because now you're in a database. So you turn to street drugs like heroin and . . . well, in the movies someone saves you, but in real life no one can save you, and things get dark, sometimes irretrievably so.

You knew all this, and yet you adapted quickly from the Vicodin® making you so groggy you couldn't function to being able to function on it and feeling awake. At first your stomach couldn't handle it, but damn, it took your back pain away completely, so what's a little digestive trouble? But when you woke up in the middle of the day—in the house you'd designed and built seventeen years ago—and momentarily had no idea where you were or what day it was, you gathered yourself, decided you wouldn't become this cliché, wouldn't put yourself or your family through the nightmare that would inevitably follow, and you flushed the remaining tablets down the toilet. Instead, you would complain, feel sorry for yourself, and lament your lost youth to anyone who would listen—like a real man.

Massage Therapy

In the seventies, Mimi's "home office" was literally a hot dog stand. It was right off a main drag, and you practically had to park in the road. And if you went in thinking your car wasn't safe, Mimi didn't exactly give you the sense your back was in any less danger of being totaled. You knew she wouldn't be in scrubs (you didn't even know if there was such a thing as a massage therapist uniform) but Mimi dressed like a senior citizen in Palm Springs playing paddle ball: a pink velour track suit, a bandana, and tiny-framed eyeglasses hung from a lanyard around her neck. She croaked when she spoke—either a Harvey Fierstein homage or a lifetime of cigarettes. She asked you some questions about how you hurt yourself, what the doctors had said, and sat back patiently as you tried to impress her by telling her that you understood that contemporary medical science advocated for massage therapy, that it had been proven to improve range of motion and raise both serotonin and dopamine levels. You also said that you had read a lot about the difference between conventional deep tissue massage and neuromuscular "trigger point" therapy, and that while both were effective, it seemed like the NMT got better results because it improved blood flow, which in turn increased the oxygen levels, which reduced the lactic acid buildup that caused the pain. But what did she think?

"I don't know what NMT is, and I never heard that massage raised dopamine levels, but I do know mine has been dropping since you started talking. I'll step out, you get naked, and we'll start on your stomach. Use the face cradle."

"But what's your overall approach? Is it purely pressure point? Do you use tapotement or vibration modalities? I'm not trying to give you a hard time, I'm just trying to figure out how I'll know if this is right for me."

"You're in pain, right?"

"A lot of pain."

"Can you touch your toes right now?"

"Only if you cut them off and hand them to me."

"So if you stop talking and cooperate, lie down, breathe through the pain, and generally stop acting like a little bitch, in one hour you will not be in pain and you'll be able to bend over and put the entire palms of your hands on the floor. That's what I do. Talking to you about how I do it seems like a waste of time, and I've got an appointment after yours. I'll have you playing golf again before the snow melts, but only if you let me step out, you get undressed, and start on your stomach. Use the face cradle."

You saw Mimi twice a week for the entire winter. Neither of you spoke during the sessions. She never asked you which scented oil you preferred or what type of music you wanted to listen to. She was on a search for knotted muscle, and when she found one, she showed it no mercy. She would tell you to breathe and she would dig her elbow into the middle of the knot and hold it there for longer than it takes Bernhard Langer to hit a shot. It made you glad your face was buried in that cushioned cradle, because you were pretty sure you were crying a little, but then you could feel the muscle release, and the knot and the pain were gone. You could tell this was immensely satisfying for Mimi.

It wasn't a conventional massage. There was no effleurage before, no pulling your feet and separating your toes after. There was no eye mask for her to lift off you while she massaged your temples and in a quiet voice said, "Take your time getting up. I left some water on the table." She had identified key areas specific to your body and your injury. Your neck was a rigid nightmare. Your glutes were weak and tight. And your hips were fossils. She actually spent very little time on your back itself. "Aren't you old enough now to realize that a pain's source and its location are two very different things? My mom is a huge pain in my ass, but she lives in Florida."

Mimi was torn about golf. She thought it was silly at its core, a waste of beautiful land and resources so you can try to find a ball you intentionally tried to lose, but it also was a big part of her business. Golf long enough and you're going to need Mimi. She was also grateful for CrossFit. Take middle-aged people who haven't worked out in forever and have them do Olympic weightlifting moves as fast as they can—what could go wrong? Mimi planned to retire on golf and CrossFit (but not to Florida).

Mimi told you the same thing your golf pro tells you after every lesson. The same thing you've been told your entire life whenever something worthwhile is at stake. "It's a process. This will take time."

In the meantime, you were home. At first your wife told you to simply rest, but she couldn't hide her pleasure when she noticed, as you improved, you started to do some of the little projects around the house you had neglected. You did some online research for your daughter's science contest entry, and you made pharmacy and grocery runs and even had dinner waiting for all of them a couple of times a week. "Who are you and what have you done with my husband?" And you had to admit, you really enjoyed rehabilitating your image.

But what they didn't know was that while you were home all day, able to work remotely and simply stay logged on to the office CRM, what you mostly did was watch golf.

CHAPTER EIGHT

All Access Programming

I f it's true that we make choices and in the end our choices make us, then it's not a fair fight. You were truly trying to quit golf, and you thought being injured in the dead of winter would allow you a much-needed bridge, a way station where you could rest, reset your values, and redefine a way forward as a non-golfer. But we all end up genuflecting at the altar of technology, and between your ability to work from home and your bundled Xfinity internet package that ties in your TV, phone, and iPad, well, your willpower and good intentions were no match for your self-imposed weapons of mass distraction.

Golf programming on TV slows for the holidays, so at first you thought this would be easy. There are no tournaments between early December and the January Tournament of Champions in Hawaii, the kick-off to the season and a boondoggle for the winners of tour events the previous season. It is played on the goofy Plantation Resort course, and it is the official green light for golfers in the colder climates across the US to start swinging weighted clubs in their finished basements, putting on rugs into water glasses. Two days into watching the tournament, you typically begin shopping online for new clubs and gadgets. And you would usually reach out to your club pro to schedule lessons in the feckless hope that this could be your year. But this year, you had almost a full month of no tournament play to wean yourself off the game. Every competent nutritionist charged with helping a client lose weight will recommend emptying pantries and refrigerators of unhealthy foods—you can't eat what's not there. (They also recommend eating your meals naked so you can see your slovenly self as you chew the chocolate cake dooming your A1C levels, and you wonder, do these people all live alone or are they in dieting communes?)

But you trusted yourself to simply make a good choice. Besides, it's the holidays—what's on that's worth watching anyway? Turns out when you are as golf-starved and obsessed as you are, even the filler programming Golf Channel replays over and over so they can stay on the air with minimal staff and effort is must-see viewing for you!

Golf Movies

You have Netflix, Apple TV, Hulu, HBO Max, and Amazon Prime, but you watch golf movies over and over. You, who refused to watch *Titanic* with your wife because, "I know how it ends, the ship sinks, everyone dies." The following list contains a few of your most played.

TIN CUP

Once truly amusing and even moving, as we'd all like to believe in long-shot second chances and romance, it now makes you toggle back and forth from *Yellowstone* just to see how much hair Kevin Costner has lost. The low production values make it hard for you to take the golf sequences seriously, and the dated golf apparel is laughable. But you have now watched it eight times, and it's not even New Year's. Even Rene Russo in her sexy prime makes this excessive.

SEVE

The only movie with subtitles you have ever been able to watch. The big takeaway is Seve was a great player and a really disagreeable kid. You watch it now because there are lot of shots of a thin and dynamic Johnny Miller, whom you only know as an overly critical commentator, and because you find it fun to count how many times they tell you Seve was handsome.

THE LEGEND OF BAGGER VANCE

You first found this film engaging because you could relate to Matt Damon's crisis of confidence on the golf course, and the heft of the cast (Damon, Charlize Theron, Will Smith) seem outsized for a cable golf movie. You've watched it six times, but post-2022 Oscars, you wonder if you will ever be able to watch it again without imagining Will Smith slapping Damon for hitting his tee shots into the hazard.

HAPPY GILMORE

You're up to twenty-one viewings, and it takes everything in you not to go out in your yard and attempt a "get a running start and swing out of your shoes" drive into the woods behind your property, but that would mean a trip back to the ER and the waste of a lot of rehabilitation.

CADDYSHACK

Thirty-seven viewings. Let's face it, there is *Gone with the Wind*, *Citizen Kane*, *The Godfather*, and *Caddyshack*. To date, Bill Murray has still not gotten the Irving Thalberg Award for the film and that seems as cruel and unjust as a 360-degree lip out.

Replays of Famous Golf Tournaments

This is another category of watching where you already know how it ends. Even though there are approximately fifty PGA-sanctioned events each year, plus four majors, and they have been filmed since Arnold Palmer grabbed the public's imagination and made golf on TV weekend must-see viewing—so let's say approximately 3,500 televised events—during golf TV's holiday hiatus, your choices narrow considerably to a few choice tournaments.

THE 1986 MASTERS

Jack's last hurrah was stirring stuff, and you wish you had seen it live, but you were a teenager and spending a few hours watching golf would have been deemed cruel and unusual punishment. But by now, the events of the 1986 Masters have been so seared into the minds of all golfers that when they have Jack himself commenting on his amazing back nine, even he seems bored. Before Jim Nantz and Verne Lundquist say, "The bear has come out of hibernation" and "Maybe . . . Yes, sir!" you are mouthing the lines yourself. You've now watched it enough times to have a critic's eye. No doubt Jack caught lightning in a bottle and was absolutely on fire and never wavered, but now you can see through the magic of editing, because in the replay they move on quickly from what must have been obvious in real time: Seve and Norman choked like dogs. You know Jack had help winning that sixth jacket, and yet every time it's on you watch it. And every time the putt on 17 goes in and the crowd goes insane, the hair on the back of your neck stands up. And when Jack hugs his son after putting out on 18, your eyes get wet and you want to go hug your own son, who would be mortified.

THE 1997 MASTERS

Tiger's coming out party and total domination. When you saw it years ago, it was a testament to his budding genius (he shot 40 on his opening 9 on Thursday and still ran away with it). The friendly smile belied the assassin's heart. He would crush everyone and do it with a joy that was contagious. But now, having seen it dozens of times, you are reminded that we somehow thought baggy pants, modeled after the zoot suits of a bygone era, were perfect for an athletic pursuit like golf. It also reminds you that Tiger had yet to break up with Butch, after which he would never again regain the perfect swing they'd built together; had yet to lose the father he embraces on 18, or the wife he would sacrifice on the altar of entitlement; had yet to embrace the Canadian doctor well known for giving HGH to athletes or trade in the wiry, lithe frame he was blessed with for the look of an NFL cornerback, ushering in back and knee issues, which then ushered in an addiction to painkillers, which ushered in an obvious need to either always use Uber or come to the realization that, along with a caddy, Tiger needs a chauffeur.

These two iconic tournaments seem to be on as much as *Law and Order*, but if you're an Augusta devotee, you can certainly watch Phil Mickelson's first win in 2004, and his well-inside-the-leather vertical leap when the putt drops. Or you can easily find the 1996 Masters with Faldo's win over Greg Norman—two egomaniacs so universally loathed that even now you watch it hoping someone else will win in the end. Or you can watch Bubba's hooked wedge from the pine straw, or Jordan's meltdown on 12, or Rory's drive on 10 when he had the Sunday lead that went so far left, Faldo, by now a commentator who had been coming to Augusta for thirty years, said, "What is over there?"

If you prefer links-style TV golf and never got to watch the Open live because it was on at the exact same time you were playing, the holiday hiatus will be happy to show you Jack and Watson's epic battles; Tiger's dismantling of St Andrew's; Jordan's twenty-five-minute drop from the driving range and the subsequent superhuman putting display; or Tom Watson again, this time age fifty-nine and on the brink, failing to get up and down on 18 and making us wonder why we were foolish enough to think Father Time wasn't toying with us. And of course, at almost any time, the Golf Channel is happy to rerun Jean van de Velde's tragicomedy. You still yell at him to not hit driver, you still tell him to not even think about taking his shoes off, and when he drains the putt for triple bogey, you can't help but say to the screen, "Stop pumping your fist like you did something great! You're an idiot!" You never watch the playoff. No one has ever watched the playoff. Paul Lawrie's mother has never seen that playoff.

If you wear your patriotism on your sleeve, you can go into your channel guide or tell your remote to find the US Open and you will find no shortage of time slots for Tiger's fifteen shot lapping of the field at Pebble Beach, prompting

Roger Maltbie to improvise: "It's not a fair fight." Jack's 1980 win at age forty gets a fair amount of play, and you can even go black and white and see ol' Arnie humble Ben Hogan and hold off a buzzed-head amateur named Nicklaus at Cherry Hills. For those looking for a bit of schadenfreude, it's hard to beat the ever-present 2006 Open, where Phil finds yet another creative way to throw away the only major he's never won.

For the jingoists and the Saturday morning game purists, the holiday hiatus gives you the Ryder Cup reruns. Eat your heart out, Theresa Caputo, no one has shown more psychic powers than Ben Crenshaw the night before the 1999 comeback at Brookline. (The first few times you watched it to see the miraculous putt on 18 by Justin Leonard, but now you watch for the amusement of the vulgarity; the spectacle of players and their wives, some in dress shoes, storming the 18th green and stomping on Olazabál's line; the inexplicable chicken dance David Duval performs as he closes out his match; and to wonder anew how anyone could have selected the hideous shirts the Americans wore.) The Golf Channel loves to show the 2008 "pod" cast, where Paul Azinger's pod approach is treated as a momentous feat of neuroplasticity, when in fact what happened is the USA made a few putts.

But even when they are showing one of the many Euro blowouts (with the cheeky Seve always getting into everyone's head), you watch the Ryder Cup because it mirrors what you do every week. You play with a partner, in better ball or alternate shot, and your actual score doesn't matter, it just has to be one better than the other team. You read each other's putts. (You say, "I got it just outside the right edge, but it depends on speed," as a way of having a disclaimer in case he misses.) You pick each other up when one hits a bad shot, you bump fists when you win a hole, and when you're down two, you pat your partner on the back and say, "Lots of golf left, pards." And when you're down two at the turn you say, "We got them just where we want them, pards." And when you lose 5 and 4, you shake hands and say it wasn't your day (and then wish you could ask Paul to get out of this loser pod). You feel the Ryder Cup in a way you can't feel majors.

Your wife calls you on your hypocrisy and says, "How can you make fun of me for watching a movie more than once when you watch these tournaments over and over? It's the same thing, isn't it? In my world, Channing Tatum gets the girl; in yours, Tiger wins. How can you watch it over and over?"

Because it's not the same thing, you insist. "If I were to watch Channing Tatum over and over, it would do nothing but remind me that I don't look like Channing Tatum and am out of the 'get the girl' market permanently. But if I watch golf, while I know what happens, I might glean something from how it happened that I didn't notice before. I might get better at golf by watching golf. Now, I have never, in fact, gleaned anything that worked, but it could!" And if watching tournaments doesn't help, well, no worries, the holiday hiatus still has you covered. Welcome to 24/7 golf lessons!

Golf Instruction

You thought the only thing you'd learned from your high school phys ed teacher was that becoming a high school phys ed teacher would be a very bad life choice. Coach "G" had checked out long before you were in his class. He was completely disinterested in teaching you the intricacies of soccer, or flag football, or proper calisthenics or stretching techniques. The athletes who were on varsity or intra-mural teams were given a hard pass on PE, so the only people in his class either actively didn't want to be there or had deep insecurity issues about how their bodies looked or their lack of hand/eye coordination. Once it was determined who would be shirts and skins in the pickup games, no one cared about the score or developing skill sets. It was a mandatory hour, and everyone was putting in their time—no one more so than Coach G.

How utterly weird then, now that you are trying to quit golf while simulta-neously trying to improve by viewing it, that it is not Butch Harmon, or Bob Rotella, or Sean Foley, the gurus of the game, whose voices resonate with you. Instead it is an offhand comment made by Coach G, not to you but to a student who was trying to help another student learn to serve a tennis ball by telling him he had to get his right hand in "back scratching" position while simultaneously reaching up to strike the back side of the ball to create slice spin. When the ball caromed sideways less than halfway to the net, Coach G shook his head and said something you now know to be profoundly true: "You can't do something well while thinking about how to do it well."

And yet as a Type A with some level of accomplishment in life, you can't accept it. Everything you have ever achieved, everything you have ever been recognized for, has come from working harder than the other person. More is better. More hours, more phone calls, more preparation has always resulted in more money, more status, more options. How could golf be any different? You just haven't found the right swing thought or training aid, haven't heard the right tip that speaks to you from the right pro. When the student is ready, the teacher appears, and you are more than ready for your aha moment, damn it! You just have to keep looking, and the holiday hiatus machine is happy to oblige with any number of instructional options.

Playing Lessons with the Pros

You can hear the pitch made in a production meeting at the Golf Channel: "They'll love this. We get a pro and an analyst together (they all live within a few blocks of each other in either Orlando or Scottsdale anyway) and have them walk nine holes. The pro will do it for nothing so his sponsor's logos and equipment get free air time, the analyst we're paying anyway, the resort course gets showcased—everybody wins. The touring pro tells you what he or she is actually thinking as they execute the shot, and the analyst shoots every shot on a laser so we get money from Bushnell. We sell it as a no-fluff, no-theory, no-stuffiness lesson from a guy who was *Golf Digest*'s Teacher of the Year twenty years ago. It's the best kind of reality TV!"

Except, if it's true that "those who can't do, teach" then these shows prove that those who can do, also cannot teach. These elite pros are so good and have been for so long—most have been playing since they were little kids—they have become unconsciously competent. When the unfortunate analyst hosting the gig asks them how they produce a draw, the featured pro waggles, hits a draw, and says, "Kind of like that." The analyst, masking a little exasperation, tries to lead them: "Uh, yep, great shot, but how do you do it? Do you strengthen your grip or move your ball position further forward to give it time to release?" And the pro gives him a quizzical look and says, "You know, I try not to think too much. I just tell myself I need to hit a draw and just trust it, you know?"

Uh, no, we do not know. That is why you are on the show. To explain it to us. Watch enough of these segments and the only thing you'll learn is that these pros have hit thousands and thousands of shots. And in the countless hours it took them to do so, they figured out how it feels when the ball goes high or low, left or right, and their bodies and brains can now replicate the feeling and produce the shot on demand. It's amazing to you and makes you wildly envious, but is not helpful. The show's premise, that you would get inside of the head of the best players in the world, is not disingenuous. It's just that the show reveals the simple truth that when they swing, they think about nothing.

School of Golf

If you prefer academics, then check out this Martin Hall and Blair O'Neal act. Hall is British, so by law he sounds really smart, and there is no question he gets how the golf swing works. And he tells you, over and over again, about path, and shallow versus steep angles of attack, about the basics of ball position and grip and posture. Realizing that he has covered this threadbare territory ad nauseam, he falls back on three constructs:

1) He is a shameless name dropper and feels if he starts his story with "the great Sam Snead showed me this . . . " you'll be more impressed than you were when he said the same thing the week before.

2) He does show-and-tell with homemade training aids that you will never bother to emulate, much less try. You're not going to paint golf balls half blue so you can aim at the inside, you're not going to take clothes hangers and twist them into a device that will create width in your swing, and you're not going to a construction site at midnight so you can steal orange cones or two-by-fours to keep you from coming over the top.

3) When all this fails, and it fails weekly, his go-to is right out of the Fox News playbook: keep the audience watching by having the winsome Blair showcase his

"lesson" by taking a swing. In theory, she is replicating his lesson of the day, but every week she takes the exact same swing—as well she should since she is an excellent golfer. But we all know at some level that the majority of the audience is watching her form and not her, well, form.

YouTube

The internet gives everyone a TV channel—this is its great promise and its greater horror. The holiday hiatus machine has credible instruction, but YouTube is a jungle. Every famous PGA pro's swing, past and present, is available for dissection and analysis on YouTube. Some of the "instructors" are perfectly legit, and credibly draw their shoulder planes and swing planes and point out the key moves that make these swings great. But others have low production values, with grainy, snuff-film-like video, and they never mention anything about their credentials. They don't even ask you to subscribe or hit a Like button, they just say, "It's Rick on golf here, and today we're going to look at the swing of Ernie Els." You get the distinct impression that Rick is living in his parents' basement and hiding from the insurance investigators trying to deny him his worker's comp complaint.

Mobile App-Based Subscription Services

Digital optimization from places like GolfPass or Revolution Golf allow you to continue to get instruction even when you are away from home. Gone are the days when you spent your car rides listening to the news and staying current with world events. These days, you watch Rory tell you how he reads putts. At first you did this only when you were stuck at a red light or when your wife was on speaker telling you about her day, but now you find yourself driving at 80 mph on the highway while simultaneously watching a lesson on hitting a high lob off a tight lie. You know you shouldn't do this, but you also know how many shanks you've hit off of tight lies. You're trying to maximize value! You've even been known to pull over into gas station parking lots and highway rest areas so you could step out of your car and immediately try the tip you risked your life to watch. The tip about turning your shirt buttons through the shot before letting your arms fall seems exactly right, and you have to get a club out of your trunk and try it right now!

There is so much instruction out there that it quickly becomes a blur to you. You either forget to try it at all when you get to the range, or you do try it and it's a massive letdown. As sure as you were that it would add 20 yards when you saw it demonstrated by Devan Bonebrake, as well as it worked in your living room using a broomstick, and on the range with actual balls, it not only doesn't work but you're making horrendous contact, so you give it up within a few swings. The following day you get another tip, rinse, and repeat. You do this despite knowing in the marrow of your soul that any golf tip of value for your swing, body type, and age works within a few swings or it doesn't work at all. You do this despite your anecdotal survey of the best players at your club proving conclusively to you that they own their swing, practice what they own, and don't make changes. They watch golf tournaments, but they never watch golf instruction. Even during the holiday hiatus.

But they are good and you are not. And you prefer to hope. "Hope," wrote Jean Kerr, "is the feeling you have that the feeling you have isn't permanent."

The Golf Announcer Subculture

You have argued with your son for a long time about smoking weed. You tell him it's addictive, and he sends you articles from medical journals proving that is not clinically true. He tells you it's better than drinking and driving, and you tell him that's a false choice and unknowable. He tells you it relaxes him and is better than antidepressants and antianxiety meds, and you ask him what the hell he has to be anxious about. The only thing that has ever given him pause is when you told him it kills brain cells, and brain cells are finite. He is making himself "less than" before his time. To his credit, rather than push back, he nodded his head and drew in a deep breath. Then again, he could have been high.

Whatever his brain cell count, it has to be higher than yours, since you waste yours on detailed and completely useless information about golf announcers.

You do this year round, but the holiday hiatus gives you even more time to spend contemplating futile questions:

- Why didn't Dottie Pepper get the coveted anchor analyst gig when CBS booted Lanny Wadkins or when Johnny Miller retired? She's a major champ, super articulate and smart, and knows the game's finer points. She's not even afraid to call a choker a choker. To you this is obvious and terrible sexism. You have no idea if Dottie wanted the job; for all you know she turned it down, but you seethe for her. Just in case.

- Why doesn't David Feherty quit? You can tell he doesn't want to commentate anymore. He's mailing it in. He really wants to do stand-up comedy. You've been in corporate America long enough to know burnout when you see it. You also know that Feherty at 50 percent effort and wattage is more interesting than everyone else on the telecast.

- Are Arron Oberholser and Colt Knost sad? They sure make you sad. They're both insightful and energetic, and they bring a player's insight to each shot and situation. Knost especially is super relatable and hilarious. But they are both younger than many of the players they are covering. You know Arron had injuries and Colt got sick of losing his card. But having to give up the game and then walk alongside the players they used to compete against and give them score updates and ask for a few minutes of their time for an on-course interview seems piteous to you.

- Who does Brandel Chamblee think he is? Mark Twain with a less feral but no less luxuriant head of hair? Who appointed him the poet laureate of golf?

- Now that there are no longer toll booth operators or dispatchers or customer service humans, network TV rules officials must have the loneliest and most boring job on Earth. They are on "stand by" in case there is a rules question. Despite golf being a game of integrity where players police themselves, there are times when the convoluted rules are in question and the network has an ex-official ready to explain. And it happens! Like once a week! They guy watches 72 holes and 156 players so he can explain a single ruling for 30 seconds. Worse, the players call in rules officials even though they know the rules but are paranoid they could be disqualified or lose a stroke (fair enough, with the money at stake), and because the networks have sophisticated microphones, we can plainly hear the on-course rules official explain the rule to the player. But the drop is taken, and the network cuts to our lonely appointed rules official anyway, and he says, "Yep, what Jeff did there was exactly right." You would feel even more sorry for this guy than you do, but he's being paid to watch golf.

Your next Zoom call for work—a training on the scintillating new HRIS dashboard—doesn't require you to be on video, so you wander out on your deck to log on. It feels pretty warm for March, or maybe that's just because you are bathed in sunlight. As you wait for the host presenter to let you into the meeting, you wonder why you expend so much mental energy on your second family of golf analysts, instructors, and fledgling players and caddies-turned-announcers. Why do you care if they are okay, if they are being left out, if (God forbid) they are forced to do infomercials for golf clubs so awful even Amazon won't rep them? Because even though they all reached some level of excellence and credibility in the game of golf (which you never will), they are just like you—they talk about golf because they can't play it well. They want to stay connected to the game in whatever diminished capacity, because it beats the alternative: letting go of the game.

You step away from the screen, take in the sunlight and the green patches showing through your snow-covered yard. It won't be long now. A few weeks, maybe less if we get some dry days and the course superintendent had covered the greens in time for the first storm in December. You take your golf posture and gingerly make a half swing. No pain in your back. Another swing, this one harder, and you hold the pose. No pain. You would run to the garage and get a club and try one for real, but the host is laying out the goals of the call. So you will wait. You've waited this long. But you now know that the holiday hiatus is over.

You really were done with golf. But is it your fault if it's not done with you?

CHAPTER NINE

Golf's Fifth Major

Your frequent urination issue is problematic when you travel alone. With your family in tow, it is flat out humiliating. This time, you are standing in front of a urinal at a rest area in New Jersey, the fourth such stop this trip, and you just know a portable urinary catheter, maybe with an analgesic gel pack attached to help ease insertion and removal, would make long trips in the car for middle-aged men so much shorter. Why haven't they invented that yet? When you put the signal light on for this stop, your son wailed, "Jesus, really? We're on a schedule!"

You are unmoved. You have seen four colleges in three days and not one of the schools' reps have been on time. Your son is in the spring of his junior year, but you're pretty sure not peeing your pants takes precedence over this multi-state fact-finding mission. You also don't know why, besides the obvious genetic factor, he's so stressed about getting to a state university on time. He is only looking at the school because your wife insisted he at least use it as a point of comparison. She loves the idea of him being around twenty thousand kids in a big campus setting. The diversity. The community spirit. The state tuition.

But your son is set on Colorado. Of course he is. He says he wants to explore nature while it still exists on our dying planet. He wants the fresh air, the hiking trails, the sublime experience of seeing the Rocky Mountains outside his window every day. He also feels his studies will be aided by the serenity of the wide-open spaces. There'll be fewer distractions. His therapist says it will help him with his anxiety and his PTSD. His therapist also says getting away from home might allow him to cut the dosage of his antidepressant and antianxiety meds. His therapist makes no mention of the fact that your son, without you and your wife to monitor his swollen eyes and giggle-laden walks to the fridge, will ingest so much weed he will never attend a class. Colorado? Give me a break. You saw him ask the bot on the school's website if there were any work-study jobs at marijuana dispensaries.

The private school outside of Boulder costs $72K a year. They have offered a $2,500 scholarship, and your son brags about it like he is being given a MacArthur Fellowship. Your son has no clue what he wants to major in or pursue as a career. Which is fine—why should he at sixteen? But you argue that while he is figuring that out, why not take the same prerequisite courses they make everyone take in their first two years at a community college, and then transfer someplace that makes sense once he knows his direction? He could work part time, live at home, and build up some savings. Generally this is the point when he starts asking his mom how she is going to feel when she finds him hanging from the crossbeams in the basement. Somehow, when you were out of the room, they decided that he would consider a private school on the beach but no less than three hours from home, and he would even deign to fake his way through a tour of this crummy, $50K-a-year state university, with its student unions and intramural club teams and booster nights before he spent the next year begging and plotting to get to Colorado.

So here you are, at the urinal. You wander into the adjacent convenience store to buy a KIND bar and the Gatorade that will cause the next stop in approximately forty minutes, when your phone pings with an incoming text:

Golf's Fifth Major!

Hey, what's up, pards! The Major Member-Member is in 6 weeks! It's so on! I figure this is our year because after your sabbatical, you must be fresh and hungry. Seriously dude, I heard about the injury, and I've even heard you were quitting the club and taking up macramé or something. You know I love you and we have the best time every year, but I totally get it if you're not up for it or can't do it. I can you let me know ASAP though? Because Joey Lamontagne asked me to play, and while it wouldn't be anywhere near as fun as partnering with you . . . Joey IS a stick, and I don't want to miss out on the tournament if you had to pull out last minute because you're injured. (Let's be real, you are kind of a pussy about these things. JK!) But can you let me know?! LFG!!!

As you approached your car and your family that was irritated out of proportion to the offense of having to pee, it killed you not to reply to your partner's text. You fought your puerile desire to at least write back, "Joey Lamontagne is a stick and a dick." You were self-aware enough to know that at some level, if you were being serious about giving up golf, then by default, you were giving up Golf's Fifth Major. Your club's Major Member-Member (MMM) Tournament. Three sacred days of complete golf immersion. And knowing that, it would be incredibly unfair to your wife and son to not stay present with them as you toured an institution that could both shape his future and save you from needing to take out a second mortgage.

Besides, your partner was a solid friend for even texting you. He could just as easily have assumed you were out and committed to playing with Joey. Or is that what he did? Maybe he is just covering his ass and he banking on you texting him back that you can't play. Joey is an excellent choice, and maybe now he'll have a shot at winning. Maybe he's watching his phone this very second hoping to God you're going to be gracious about this, because if you text back that you're recovered and totally all in, then he has to figure out what to tell Joey—or what to tell you! What if he then—knowing you killed yourself rehabbing and practicing and that the only thing that kept you going through this physical and emotional hardship was the goal of being ready for the Major

Member-Member (cause that's how thick you'll lay it on)—what if knowing all that, he still chooses Joey? How could he do that to you? What kind of friend is he? You know what, he and Joey are both dicks and belong together riding around for fifty-four holes in their double-dick cart.

Your wife says you missed the turn. Your son is apoplectic. He wants to know why you didn't listen to the GPS lady who clearly said, "Turn left in one-quarter mile." But it is hard to hear her, and them, with all the other voices clamoring in your head. You gather yourself when you see the apprehension on your son's face in the rearview mirror, and pull into campus.

So you know you filter all life experience through the prism of golf, but even your wife smiled when you were welcomed by Lisa, the university tour guide assigned to you and your son. The university took its cue from the cart girl theory of sales. Cart girls know their audience, and the happier they are, the more drinks they sell, and the more drinks they sell, the more tips they make. It's primitive really, and we all should be able to see through this by now, but we don't. Or we do and it works anyway. All you knew was your painfully shy son, mortified to be on the campus of a state university, was chatting up a storm with the winsome Lisa. Lisa was young, beautiful, and over-the-top happy. She was a public health major, and when she asked your son what he wanted to study, guess what? He had always had interest in public health too, and the program here was one of the chief reasons he was here. As Lisa led you out of the library and began the tour, your son walked side by side with her and hung on her every word.

Lisa had been well trained. She asked open-ended questions so she could figure out what to emphasize and what to leave out in her description of campus. "There are a lot of spontaneous touch football games in the courtyard. Are you into sports?" Once she realized she had a geekish stoner on her hands, she never mentioned sports again. And she had talking points!

"We've got a kind of small-school feel but with all the resources of a world-class university."

"*Princeton Review* ranked us one of the Top Fifty Best Value schools in the country!" Your son shamelessly said he had read that.

"There's an 18:1 student to faculty member ratio. That's an amazing ratio, by the way!"

"We have 110 undergrad majors and 1,400 faculty members."

"We have a dining commons, but there are fifty-two dining halls around campus. Try the gluten free chocolate chip cookies, they're insane."

"We have 3-D movie theaters, and lounges in every quad."

When she asked what other schools your son was looking at and he mentioned Colorado, she smirked in a way that said "amateur hour," but then replied, "Oh, well, sure, I looked at those schools too, but I don't know, I wanted more! You know?" And your son couldn't have agreed faster or with more vigor. He nodded like a bobblehead doll on a dashboard going over a speed bump.

Then she started in on the work she does for the Racial Justice Coalition and how there was a rally for women's rights that very night, if he wanted to come. Your wife saved him, telling Lisa that while we would love to because women's rights is all he talks about at home, we have to beat the NYC traffic and get home to tend to our dog. Your son shrugged and gave her his best "see what I put up with?" face.

When the tour was over and we were headed to the dean of admission's lecture, Lisa told us what a pleasure it was to "hang with us" and then gave your son a full-on hug. She left him with, "Remember the best reason to come here—I'm here!" Signed, sealed, and delivered. Shameless. Like all good cart girls.

Considering your creativity as an undergrad in coming up with reasons why you couldn't go to the library after dinner to study with the rest of the guys on your floor (the one unimpeachable excuse you found was that you were still in mourning over Kurt Cobain, even though you loathed Nirvana), it's ironic how annoyed you were that your son didn't want to check out the university library. But it had a modern, mysterious allure to you. What in the world went on in a college library in a world of cloud-based storage? There couldn't be books in there, right? They couldn't sign them out, could they? Surely artificial intelligence had replaced indurate librarians and the Dewey Decimal System, so what reason could there have been to walk across campus to plug in a laptop and do what you could have done from your dorm? What went on in this rococo palace that looked like it could have been an Airbnb for the X-Men? Why did university libraries still exist?

But your wife and son were already taking a brochure from the nurse outside the 24/7 infirmary, and truth be told, the best practices and services offered at the infirmary were far more important than whether the library was still a sanctuary of learning, given your son's proven lack of knowing when enough was enough. Then a kid with a bullhorn announced that the university dance team was about to do an impromptu version of the hip-hop routine that qualified them for Nationals in the courtyard. You turned to your son to snarkily point out that it seemed anything but "impromptu," but he had already joined the throng running to get the best view.

Your wife said, "Let's give him some time, we can text him later." She took your hand and the two of you began to walk. Where? Neither of you knew. The campus was sprawling, and over time anything sprawling had become scary and bad. But, somehow, this wasn't. For a few moments there was no conversation. You just wandered. The day was a classic tease weather-wise. Winter wasn't quite done; it would return, but today was a glorious respite. Warm, with the slightest of breezes. Your wife tapped your shoulder and gestured to two girls sitting on a blanket, their faces turned up to the sun and their eyes closed. They didn't yet need sunscreen; there was no fear of damage or disease, just the rich satisfaction of the sun's rays. You nodded. Some guys—worked up over some minor transgression, their testosterone levels at a peak they would one day seek gel packs to restore—were yelling profanely. When they saw your wife, they calmed down instantly and waited for you to pass. Your wife giggled. Neither of you said a word, but you were both thinking the same nostalgic thoughts. You met on a campus not so different from this one. And while you didn't have the earbuds you now saw everywhere, while she didn't wear leggings, and neither of you defaulted to looking at your phones every few steps, you did take walks together, and you did hold hands. You did cut deals with roommates to give you a few hours of privacy in your dorm. And somehow, here you were, still walking a campus, still holding hands, still looking forward to the occasional date night.

You sat on a bench across from the Life Sciences building. The seat was rustic-looking, made of wood, and yet on each arm was a USB port, simultaneously ruining the period effect and impressing you for their attention to real-life needs. And then, was it the breeze, the music from the courtyard? The proximity to young bodies? You put your arm around your wife, leaned over to kiss her, and squeezed her boob.

"Really?" she exclaimed, more amused than surprised.

"This isn't real life, this is college! We can do anything here."

"Is that what we're paying for? For him to take a four-year break from life? Or will he learn something?"

"It's not either/or. But yeah, for a short time, he gets to be with only people his age, only caring about the things they care about."

"Dead certain that they know everything and that we have left them with a broken system and a dying planet."

"Which they will fix the moment they graduate."

"After they get a car, an apartment, and a gig at a socially conscious company with unlimited mental health days."

"You're very sexy when you're cynical. I'm going to sit on the other side of you now so I can squeeze the other boob."

"Do you ever miss it? College?"

"Hmm . . . not generally. I remember it as this chaotic, stressful period where I didn't think I was smart enough, didn't know what I wanted to major in or do. I just knew I had to get a degree so I could get a job, because if I didn't get a job your dad would tell you I wasn't good enough for you."

"Oh stop, you got a perfectly fine job and my dad still thought you weren't good enough for me."

"He wasn't wrong. Do you miss it?"

She thought for a moment before answering. "I miss the immersion. College isn't real, but in some ways, it's *so* real! For a short time you experience everything so intensely, and everyone around you is doing the same thing, in their own way. You eat together, study together, sleep together . . . though we only slept with each other, and I know we both regret that. You're part of something bigger than you for the first time, and it all happens when you're at your physical peak. Even a family isn't the same sort of immersion, because college is immersion without consequence."

You would later take great pride in the emotional growth that allowed you to show some restraint. Before your decision to quit golf, you would have been unable to suppress what you were thinking, even though what you were thinking is true: Golf is immersion. A scaled down, four-hour version of college. A group of guys trying to navigate four white balls around a landscaped labyrinth is objectively not real life. Nor is it important. But while you're immersed, it feels like everything depends on it. And while you have traded in your GPA for a GHIN, while the stories you tell once "class is over" are different, you are still recounting the day's events over drinks and/or drugs with the people who lived it with you.

But you would never have pointed out that your wife had put her finger on golf's central appeal: short-term immersion. She would have thought you weren't listening to her. But then she surprised you. And while it is true that surprising moments come less often in a long marriage, when they do come, they have more impact, and you get reminded how much more there is to learn about each other.

"It's probably what you love about golf, right? I can see that."

"But you have your versions, right? Your yoga peeps, the book club, the fund-raisers. I mean, it's awesome what you do."

"It's not the same."

"You don't feel immersed?"

"No, it's more a feeling of being engulfed."

"I'm sorry. Really."

"It's okay. I think you should play in the Major Member-Member. I know who's blowing up your phone. I know you want to play. So play."

"Nope, I quit golf."

"I never asked you to quit, I asked you get some perspective. And you did. This winter has been amazing for me, for the kids. So play. Just keep it under control."

You knew better. She was testing you. You needed to prove that you had perspective. You needed to stick to the plan—give up golf. It is for the greater good, and she's right. You do feel closer to her, to your kids. You do feel better. She brought this up to see if you have really changed. Now is the time to let it go. It will make her so happy to have offered you this generous way back and to have it turned down because you prioritize her and your life together more. Maybe it's not too late to once again be as immersed with each other as you were when you first strolled around campus together. Who's to say it can't be better now? But you have to start. You have to commit. You have to pass this test.

"Thanks, baby, I really appreciate that. I'll text him right now before he reaches out to Joey Lamontagne. That's guy's such a dick. We are totally winning this year!"

CHAPTER TEN

The Comeback (Let's Not Call It a Relapse)

Your first boss would whisper, in a conspiratorial but creepy tone, that "if you don't have a plan, you're part of someone else's." Then he would nod solemnly, giving the Orwellian impression that the office was bugged, and walk off. It occurred to you that it was probably never his plan to be a mid-level manager in an insurance company at fifty, and so you ignored him and have been improvising your life ever since. But really, how has that worked out for you? Benjamin Franklin said, "By failing to prepare, you are preparing to fail" and he lived to be eighty when the average life span was thirty, so maybe if you really want to win the Major Member-Member in your epic return to golf, having a plan might help!

You set about making a fitness plan to chart your return and give yourself the best chance at success. You have now seen your swing on video enough times (an experience akin to watching a horror movie slasher scene, where you look away in disgust and wonder why the first fifty passes with the ax are not sufficient to prove the point) to know it doesn't change all that much. Your swing change, which feels radically different to you and is sure to produce a high, soft draw, looks exactly the same as your old swing, and the accompanying analytic readout shows no difference in trajectory, swing path, or distance. You have come to realize that your swing will change when your body is more flexible and supple. To produce better results, you have to be able to put the club in better positions. No more triage and bandages, no more adjusting your ball position and alignment and grip to allow for your body's limitations. You have six weeks until the Major Member-Member and a whole golf season ahead of you. Fix your body, the swing will fix itself!

In prehistoric times, let's call it twenty years ago or so, you would have to go about finding a fitness trainer by word of mouth. Ask some friends you see as fitness-conscious; maybe ask the guy at the club who is married to a chiropractor; work your inner circle, and hope someone knows someone and then actually remembers to have them call you. When this process inevitably fails or takes too long, you cast a wider net, moving from friends to allies and acquaintances, or more likely, you give up.

But not anymore. In the golf equivalent of the Kevin Bacon game, you found Felicia within two degrees of separation. You asked your head pro if he could recommend any golf-specific fitness programs, and he mentioned that there is such a thing as a TPI certified therapist, a physical therapist or sports medicine professional who went to the Titleist Performance Institute and got certified. They would test you according to TPI standards and create a program custom-designed to improve your swing. Awesome. You hung up and entered "TPI certified therapist near me" into your mobile browser, and Felicia's smiling face appeared on your phone. A few minutes later, you had booked your first appointment for the next day. You know it's not cool to say; you know you would release a torrent of resentment and accusations of privilege if you said it; you know that you would be practically inviting karma to kick your ass, but seriously, sometimes life these days is crazy easy!

Felicia cleverly called her physical therapy practice The Body Shop, and it turns out you've driven by her signage before without ever questioning how an auto body shop could be in a strip mall of bougie stores. The build-out was ultramodern. Black massage tables, power racks, and dumbbells contrasted against stark white walls. You instantly noticed the area dedicated to golf, a driving range mat and a bin of clubs, with a balance board and a few TRX bands on the floor. She was super fit, adorned in the requisite Lululemon uniform, and had the natural warmth therapists and healers so effortlessly exude. You could tell she really wanted to help her clients. When you gave her the elevator pitch of your golf journey, injury, and nascent comeback, she nodded gravely and took notes.

She was not a golfer, but she was an entrepreneur. When she was looking for ways to scale her business, she did an analysis of the types of problems her current clientele came to her with, and high on the list was the ailing golfer. The bulging discs limiting something called "the backswing," the arthritic hip keeping them from "clearing on the way down," and everyone whispered to her ruefully that they wanted more "turn"—the Holy Grail of shooting close to par. She knew shooting "par" was a good thing, but her husband was a hunter and her kids never cared about golf. But she knew there were no less than four country clubs within ten miles of her office. That's a lot of potential business.

Fearless, she called the general managers of each club and offered a strategic alliance. They would promote The Body Shop to members, and she would give the clubs a cut of the revenue. Everyone wins! But the walls went up right away. There are tons of sports medicine clinics and orthopedic practices with golf-centric programming in the area. (Some of these medical specialists are members and would not take kindly to competition.) And as one GM said to her, a little too archly for Felicia's taste, "You don't get it because you're not a golfer." To Felicia's credit, rather than launch a diatribe about how her expertise was in body form and function and she could make anyone better at *any* physical endeavor, she said, "Thanks very much," and started to do her research.

She didn't know much about golf but she knew good branding. The Titleist Performance Institute's methodology has been used by eighteen of the last twenty major championship winners. Twenty-five of the top thirty players in the world have been advised by a TPI certified pro, and forty-seven of *Golf Digest*'s fifty top PGA pros are either TPI certified or TPI advisory board members. If Felicia got certified, their credibility would be hers! She Googled and found zero TPI physical therapists or ortho practices in the area. She went on social media and still couldn't find anyone. She didn't trust it—she wasn't going to go through the expense and time to get certified if it was already being done—so she called the head pros at all the area courses—even the public courses—to ask if they knew any certified therapists. Nope! The only TPI folks were the teaching pros. Her lane was still open!

That was a year before you walked in her door. Now she smoothly rolled out the TPI value proposition like a seasoned Realtor who could show a house in this neighborhood with her eyes closed.

She said that most golfers never improve in any real way. She cited a stat that sounded true based on the laments of several retired snowbirds in your club: most people who retire and can play every day actually get worse at golf! But that's because their bodies are older and they don't pay attention to diet, sleep, recovery, or—and here is where she comes in—their flexibility, joint mobility, and balance. This matched up with what you'd observed at the club. Even some of the best golfers, once they hit their mid-forties, would no longer be able to get out of the car, walk to the first tee, and stripe a drive. They all needed to attempt feebly to touch their toes, take two clubs and swing them together like they were in an on-deck circle, and then top or skull a half dozen balls on the range before they could start to make decent contact.

You told her you understood, that with your recent injury you had already bought in to physical therapy and off-course training, you just needed to know you could make significant improvements in time for the Major Member-Member.

She smiled, but it was strained. Her eyes said, "All you jokers want miracles without putting in the effort." But she bit it back and deftly changed the topic. "First, we have to establish your handicap!"

You told her you were a 10.8 and offered your GHIN number if she wanted to verify, hoping you could now skip a step and get on with it.

"No, not your golf handicap, we need to test you using the TPI guidelines and establish your mobility handicap. I'll take you through a series of movements and golf positions, take a picture of each, and the TPI software program will automatically measure you compared to a touring pro's range of motion and position. It will take a half-hour and ideally, your TPI handicap will equal your golf handicap. In your case, if you score a TPI 10 or 11, we don't have much work to do. If not, well, let's not worry about that right now. You ready?"

Felicia took you over to the scale to get your weight. She asked if you felt dizzy or had any blood pressure issues, and then she made you wonder just how bad your current level of physical presentation was by asking you if you had any metal plates or medical devices like a pacemaker? When she snapped her first picture to establish your profile in the program, you felt yourself suck in your belly. You really are ridiculous.

For the next thirty minutes, as she tested your range through various movements and positions, that feeling of ridiculousness only grew. The take-home report she gave you at the end of it didn't make things any better. Here are some choice excerpts:

> **Shoulder Rotation:** *Reduced external rotation in the right shoulder of a right-handed golfer creates a flying right elbow and often results in getting trapped and coming over the top and changing your swing plane in the down swing. Reduced external rotation in the left shoulder for a right-handed golfer results in an inability to rotate the left arm through impact, resulting in the dreaded "chicken wing" position at impact and causing poor contact and low ball flight.*
>
> **Tour average:** *Over 90 degrees.*
>
> **Player tested:** *Less than half of that.*
>
> **Leg Balance:** *As measured by the ability to stand on one leg with eyes closed. Balance is critical to a repeatable swing and allows the better player to adjust for the never-ending array of lies a golfer faces in the course of a competitive round.*
>
> **Tour Average:** *20 seconds.*
>
> **Player tested:** *2 seconds. Highly unlikely this player could post on their right side or stay stable during the backswing.*
>
> **Lat Test:** *This test measures the flexibility of the shoulder girdle, which will allow or limit a player's ability to make a full shoulder turn.*
>
> **Tour average:** *170*

Player tested: *114. Incapable of getting completely behind the ball.*

For the following areas, your scores were so far off the tour average that they didn't register in the software program:

Lower Quarter Rotation: *(hips, knees, ankles): All areas so restricted that player is unlikely to be able to stay in a golf posture and will often sway in the backswing, resulting in poor outcomes.*

Wrist Hinge: *(radial and ulnar deviation): Player's wrist mobility is so poor as to make it difficult to hinge the club freely, often resulting in setting the club too late and altering the proper release, resulting in poor outcomes.*

Pelvic Tilt: *(lumbar spine): Player has little to no control of the pelvis, making generating ground forces and disassociation (moving the lower body before the upper body in proper swing sequencing) nearly impossible.*

Overhead Squat: *Player was unable to achieve any depth and pitched forward.*

Players with such overall immobility will generally "bring a different golf swing" to the course every day, depending on factors like firmness of mattress, length of time in a car in transit, and the amount of anti-inflammatory drugs ingested pre-round.

TPI Mobility Handicap for player tested: *34*

You're a 34 handicap. In golf terms, that is a beginner. In golf terms, that is someone you don't want to play with, someone you don't want to play behind, and someone you don't even want to know. A 34 handicap hits Pinnacle golf balls and plays out of his grandfather's bag twice a year. A 34 handicap wears a tank top to the golf course, and his chief goal is to sneak his cooler of alcohol onto the golf cart. He takes huge divots with his driver, laughs, and yells, "Get in the hole!" A 34 handicap drives his cart on the fringe of the green and when the ranger chastises him, he thinks he should be able to go wherever he wants because he paid the greens fees. These 34 handicappers know they suck and don't care; golf is a respite from their life, a time out. There is no difference in their minds between badminton, horseshoes, and golf. They are merely ways to drink, get a tan, and be outside without working up a sweat. Once a day, they hit a drive straight and long, or a double breaking 50-foot putt goes in, and that is all they remember—the few things that went right. For a real golfer, a golfer with an index they want desperately to lower, all they remember are the bad shots, the ones that kept them once again from shooting the score they could have "if only" those shots didn't happen.

"So, just so I'm clear, my actual index should match my TPI. So my 10 handicap means I should be a 10 on the TPI?"

"Right."

"And I'm a 34 . . . "

"Exactly"

"So this test says, basically, I'm physically incapable of improvement. A lost cause."

"No! No! You're looking at it the wrong way! This says you must have amazing hand/eye coordination, and tremendous drive and grit. You're a 10 handicap with the physical limitations of a 34 handicap. Isn't that better than having a TPI mobility handicap of 10 but shooting the scores of a 34 handicap? Imagine how frustrating that would be."

"I mean . . . I guess."

"A golfer with a 10 mobility index that shoots in the low 100s is wasting their gifts. You have fought your way to a very respectable handicap level with *no* help from your body. You found a way! That's very inspiring!"

"You think? I mean, I feel like I do have grit."

"Right? And here's the great news. Think of yourself as trying to play golf while wrapped in plastic wrap. That's basically what you've been doing with the stiffness in your joints and the tightness in your muscles and connective tissue. I can unlock you. We can tear off that plastic wrap. In time, you'll make huge improvements that no number of golf lessons or buckets of balls on the range can match!"

"Yeah? And I would imagine, and tell me if I'm being crazy here, but if I've gotten to a 10 handicap in real golf terms with a 34 mobility handicap, I don't have to become super supple and all rubbery. If I got to a TPI 15 handicap, I might be a 3 or 4 handicap in real life, right?"

"Well, maybe. That would be a good goal. We should start with some near term, reachable goals, like touching your toes with your fingers."

"Okay, but bottom-line this for me. Have you ever seen a 34 TPI handicap become a 15?"

"No, but that's only because I've never seen a 34 TPI handicap."

"Oh."

"But listen, I have absolutely seen people become more flexible and mobile if they're willing to put in the work. I can put you on a program that I know will not only make you a better golfer but will have you feeling better—"

"Right, and the feeling better part can wait, but would I see a big improvement golf-wise in, say, and I'm just making stuff up now . . . six weeks?"

"Absolutely not."

"Ah, I see! I see what you're doing. Managing expectations! You want me pleasantly surprised rather than let down. Very savvy, well played. Okay, let's do this!"

Within an hour, you had paid for twelve hours of mobility sessions, three TRX bands, a foam roller, and a Theragun. A $1,600 investment.

But you had learned your lesson. The new you wouldn't let your wife see the credit card bill and ask you what the hell this Body Shop charge was. You walked in the house, showed her your purchases, and assured her it was more for your back than for golf. You just wanted to be healthy. You were not going to let this age thing take you down without a fight. To keep her from asking too many questions, you turned on the Theragun and ran it down her upper back. She was experiencing too much pleasure to interrogate you any further.

CHAPTER ELEVEN

What Men Talk about When Playing Golf

S ix weeks out. You scheduled yourself a club fitting.

"So let's take all the tension out of the room. We are brand agnostic."

That was Lane's way of telling you they didn't care whose clubs you played. They represent all of the major brands, so from a clinical, detached, business point of view, they don't care which clubs you buy, and since they charge $500 for the fitting, they don't even care if you buy any clubs at all. Today was about enjoying your experience and learning about yourself and your golf game in a nurturing, positive environment.

He asked you if that made you more comfortable, and you nodded but didn't bother to explain that it might be because agnostic was sort of your spiritual default setting.

Then he asked if you wanted an unsweetened vanilla shot in the coffee he was brewing just for you.

Lane was not going to be fitting you. Lane was your personal fitting "ambassador," and his job was to introduce you to Spec-Fun's passion for golf, show you their cavernous space (in a previous century a turbine blades factory), tour the sixty-five hitting bays (each with food and beverage service), walk you through the men's locker room (where he recommended a steam sauna after your fitting), and finally, introduce you to your fitting "artisan," Stewart!

Stewart was absolutely beaming. He didn't seem capable of being agnostic about anything. Stewart seemed to be a true, zealous believer. He was going to change your life today. With a golf swing fitting.

The whole setup seemed so overwrought that you felt you had made a mistake. Your clubs were just a year old, the grooves on your irons were deep, and your driver clubface immaculate. But when you sheepishly told Stewart about your farfetched hope that a fitting and maybe new clubs or adjustments on your current clubs might help you in the Major Member-Member coming up in just six weeks, his eyes got Charlie Manson wide.

"Six weeks? That's an eternity in golf! Let's get you spec'd up and get that W!"

So, here's a thought: Maybe when you've spent the winter rehabbing from a serious back injury, the best thing to do is not commit to a professional golf fitting where you will hit more balls in ninety minutes than you have hit in your life. The bottle of Advil on the table where Stewart entered data into the computer might have been a tip-off. Or maybe they were for Stewart, who once upon a time was a solid D1 college player hoping to become a tour pro, but instead is watching hacks like you make the same bad swing over and over.

After a short warm-up, Stewart asked you to hit some stock 8 irons, and when you cut across one so badly it hit the support bar of the overhead screen and nearly caromed off Stewart's head, you said, "So what am I doing wrong, pro?"

Stewart's face grew deadly serious, and he slowly, solemnly shook his head. What you just did was clearly forbidden.

"I'm not here to fix your golf swing, I'm here to fit you for the golf swing you have. We do offer lessons, and you can see Lane about that when we're finished. Okay?"

Stewart put tape on your clubface, and you hit some balls. Then he handed you the next club and you did it again. Then he moved to spraying your club with a substance that would wipe right off, but not before showing how far off the toe or heel you were hitting it. Once in a while, Stewart would look at the screen, a bewildering cacophony of data showing loft, lie angle, path, and degree of clubface squareness at impact.

After twenty minutes you were given a break, a hand towel softer than anything you have in your entire house, and your choice of ice or tap or sparkling water. You thought you'd hit a few drivers and be out of there just before the back spasms started.

"We good with the irons?" you asked, hoping to get an idea of how much more was in store for you.

"Absolutely. Well, I mean as far as the Titleist irons, I don't like them for you. Let's move on to Callaway."

It may have been the repeating dismal data Stewart got from your twenty minutes with Callaway, and your next twenty minutes with Ping, or maybe it was the fact your swing speed was dropping like December temperatures once the sun goes down, but Stewart decided to skip Taylor and PXG.

Now it was time for the Big Stick. As tired as you were, you got excited. Even before the back issues, you'd needed more distance. You were carrying the ball 211 yards. If you turned one over or it was a dry day, you might get another 10–20 yards of help from the ground, but you were a popcorn hitter, often hitting hybrids and even fairway woods into the long par 4s while your opponents were hitting short irons. It just wasn't a fair fight.

After you'd hit your own driver, last year's Callaway model, you'd expected Stewart to hand you an assortment of new weapons. Instead, he looked at the screen and nodded sagely, a scientist having to hand it to his graduate assistant for catching something he'd missed.

"That's the right driver for you. The issue is the shaft. It's too light for you."

"You don't want me to buy the new driver?"

"Dude, it's a paint job. You need a heavier shaft. Let's try 60 grams."

You knew it the moment you hit it. Then you hit another one. It sounded different. But when you looked at the overhead readout, the carry distance was only 3.5 yards longer, giving you 214.5.

Stewart could see your frustration. He paused for a moment. He took pity on you and made a decision to break the rules. Proof positive that even the agnostic go to sleep at night wondering if there really is something greater than all of us guiding our lives. Stewart came over and told you to take your golf posture, then he yanked the club way inside. So far inside it felt like it was behind you.

"What does that feel like?"

"Like I'm trapped way too far inside."

"That's because you have never been inside the golf ball in your life. You take the club way outside and then drop it in, but you're so far outside you can't do anything but chop down. That's why you hit that pussy fade. I want you to feel like it's so far inside that it's insane. Listen to me—*you* can't get too far inside, get it? Now try it with the 7 iron first."

It took ten swings. On the eleventh, where you felt the club was so far inside you were forcing yourself to come way over the top, the ball compressed perfectly and the top tracer showed it carrying 160 yards in a tight, high draw. Stewart told you to do it again. And again. Then he told you to take the driver and, for the love of God, don't change anything. Every shot was pure. Suddenly your back didn't hurt a bit.

Stewart pointed to the screen. You carried the ball 234 yards and with the draw induced roll out, the overall distance was 251 yards. You thought you were too old and cynical for this. You thought you could only experience this emotion now through kids and grandkids. But you felt a sense of awe and wonder, and you never wanted to kiss anyone in your life as much as you wanted to kiss Stewart right then.

Stewart then showed you your swing on video. An experience that for you has always been akin to the moment when the dentist asks you if your mouth is numb from the novocaine and turns on the drill. Sheer terror. But Stewart split the screen between the swing you came in with and the swing he had just forced on you. The "insanely inside" version was exactly on plane. The club intersecting your right shoulder, the butt of the club aimed directly at the ball, and on the down swing, the club dropped slightly to the inside. The path was inside-to-out-to-inside. The ball *had* to go right to left and draw back toward the target. You asked him if you could see it again, and he laughed and said he'd send it to your phone so you could watch it as often as you liked.

Now, if humans were logical creatures, you would have reasoned that you really weren't hitting any of the new clubs with their new, amazing technology any better than you were hitting your current clubs, which were chock full of last year's new, amazing technology. You only started hitting it great when Stewart broke the rules and gave you a lesson. So clearly, there was no reason to buy any new clubs. Except to maybe put the heavier 60 gram shaft in your old driver.

But, new clubs come individually wrapped. It's like fourteen years of Christmas presents every time you buy a set. And the virgin iron heads are so shiny and pristine. The grips have never had an ounce of sweat on them, they've never been choked and dented by your hold-on-for-dear-life pass at the ball. Emily Dickinson got it almost right: "Hope is the thing with feathers." It has to be airborne, and new clubs perch in the soul the feeling that this time, with these clubs, you will fill the air with just the right shots, at just the right time . . . "and never stop at all."

And you owed Stewart big time. He could have mailed in the session, sold you some sticks, and forgotten about you ten minutes later. Maybe he still will. And you don't really know if he gets paid a commission or not. You hope he does. Because you bought all new irons, a driver and three wood and two hybrids, all with new shafts. And hell, why not, even though you never even tested any putters, you bought a brand new Scotty Cameron limited edition blade. Throw in the cost of the fitting and you walked out of there $4,200 lighter.

Stewart walked you over to Lane to conduct an exit interview rating your customer experience. But before you got within earshot of your trust brand ambassador, Stewart leaned in. "Look, the next time you go to hit balls, the new inside move might not work as well as it did today. Do *not* abandon it or try something else. You have six weeks before that tournament. Your goal is to make that swing and only that swing for the rest of your life."

"I get it. It's just . . . it's so hard to trust it. It feels so wrong."

"That's because you've been doing it wrong for so long."

"Yeah. Listen, dude. I know you're not paid to give lessons and you didn't have to do that. So thanks. Seriously."

"Truth is, pards, it was so ugly I couldn't take it any longer. You broke me."

Four weeks out. You decided to play nine holes, strictly by the rules.

The courses were open. Well, not your course. The greens were still covered at the club, but the public courses, eager for revenue, were open at reduced greens fees. There were still frost delays, the ground was still muddy, and the shaded areas of the fairway still had snow piles obstinately making their last stand. The driving ranges weren't open—there was no way to get the machinery out to collect the balls without it getting stuck—but that didn't matter.

Felicia had given you a fifteen-minute pre-round stretching routine. First the big muscles: the back, the glutes, the quads. Then the shoulders, hands, and fingers. Once you could do fifteen strict overhead body squats without pitching forward, you were ready to swing. No balls necessary.

It was time to test your new swing and your new (sort of) supple body in the elements. Oh, you had put your time in indoors, at those virtual golf lounges with their bowling alley vibe, the simulations of famous courses, the freedom to play matches while drinking with your buddies and eating pizza, but you weren't there for the fun! So you'd reserved a bay in the corner, chose the club you were hitting from the main menu, and pounded balls.

Take the club so far inside it feels insane, you reminded yourself. You would check your distance and ball flight and clubhead speed, and then grab another club. Rinse, repeat. Inevitably someone you knew would come over, beer in hand, watch you hit a couple of balls and say, "Dude, you're yanking it inside. You're going to get stuck back there." If you were in a good mood, you'd thank them and tell them you were working on something a *professional* had recommended. And if you weren't in a good mood, or if you had just hit one poorly, you'd look through them with laser beam eyes and say, archly, "I can't tell you how much I value your opinion."

But the Major Member-Member wouldn't be played on a simulator. Your misfires wouldn't hit a net and roll back to your feet. Your shots wouldn't be played on even lies on a rubber mat. It was time to test the new swing outside. In real life.

Even though you could have asked some buddies to go slumming on a public course, or just asked the starter to hook you up with a group, you decided your new swing was still in beta—you needed to test it in the elements without facing the judgment of others or investing any energy in the back-and-forth decorum of playing with others. You needed to focus strictly on you. You knew between your debilitating ADHD and your back's lack of endurance you'd never be able to play a full round, so you paid for nine holes, rented a pushcart, and waited for the group ahead of you to not only clear the green but tee off on the next hole before you went to the first tee.

This was completely foreign to you. You never played alone. When you saw a "single" out on your course, often playing two balls, you just couldn't understand it. Why would someone want to play alone? The fun of golf was playing with other people. It was the only game where you could compete and yet still have interesting conversations. You had played pickup basketball for years, and sure, you could go out after for beers, but no one ran up and down the court, thrust their butt into someone's stomach to box them out, smacked them in the face when their attempt to block their shot was miscalculated, and then, in the ensuing twenty seconds before the ball was taken out at the top of the key, said, "Did you catch Joe Rogan's podcast yesterday? If he survives this there is no such thing as cancel culture." You needed that time to clutch your gym shorts and try to catch your breath!

When you saw singles out on the golf course, generally in the late afternoons or early evenings, you made judgments:

- Poor guy has no friends.
- Guy's golf game is so bad, he doesn't want to subject himself to the humiliation.
- He has schizophrenia and thinks he is playing with others.

Like most of your baseless judgments about people you don't know (and let's be fair, even the judgments you make on people you do know), they don't hold up under the most superficial of scrutiny. The guys you saw playing as singles were among the most popular guys in the club. Boisterous, extroverted people. And some of the singles you saw were excellent players. Maybe their golf games were *so* good, they didn't want to subject themselves to others holding them back. When you let one of these "singles" play through your group, you often saw amazing drives and stiff tee shots on par 3s. And when you came off the 5th green, you could look across at the 9th and see them walking off, heading to the parking lot. So maybe it was time management?

But they never got to hear anyone say, "Nice shot!" They never got to mention how great the conditions of the course were or bitch about how fast the greens were rolling or help someone else find their ball. They never got to thank anyone for the small acts of grace—fixing someone's mark for them, asking them if you were in their line, pulling the flag for them. They never got to hear the genuine empathy when their putt lips out and their partner says sadly, "Aww pards, you got hosed!" And they never got to take their hat off on the final green and thank their partners for the gift of their time.

And what if it happened? At long last! What if you got your first hole in one, and no one saw it? Who would believe you? (Maybe this is why great players go out alone? To avoid buying everyone a drink? Can anyone be simultaneously that cheap and that self-assured?)

You would rather not play at all than play alone.

But you were now on a mission, and if you wanted different results, you would have to prepare differently. And since you were now in tournament prep mode, you were going to do this right! You were going to walk nine holes and play strictly by the rules. None of the Saturday morning, best-ball-pace-of-play rationalizing. You would putt everything out. You would play the ball down. (Wait, the course just opened, there'll be hideous mud balls, surely you should . . . NO! Play the ball down!) If you hit it OB, back to the tee. And three inches OB is, guess what, still OB! Walk of shame back to the tee! You would take a proper drop from all hazards. Not back to the fairway, one club length. And there would be no mulligans. Every year in the Major Member-Member, you see guys choking on short putts and hitting horrendous shots out of divots. That's because the rest of the year, they're told to "pick it up" or "hit a breakfast ball." Today is the start of playing every round between now and the tournament strictly by the rules.

You've seen singles playing two balls, and it made sense. If they were behind a group who was not letting them through because there was no place to go, it would keep them occupied while also allowing them to play a full round of golf in nine holes. So that was your plan. Until, off the first tee, you hit ball one dead right and ball two dead left. Without a cart, you were going to be exhausted by the third hole. Playing two balls is only a good strategy if you are a straight hitter or a jogger in your spare time.

Speaking of jogging, you never realized playing alone and walking the course gave you time to notice your surroundings. To a competitive group, the golf course is a playing field, no different than a track or a court, just a place where the game happened. But golf is played in emerald fields.

As you stood in the second fairway, dying to level out your side hill lie, a jogger came down the cart path of the fourth fairway that ran the opposite direction. In a group you would have either ignored him or, more likely, you would have yelled for him to get off the course. You would have been infuriated that the jogger could have so little courtesy, could be so selfish as to trespass on these hallowed grounds. You'd sneer that if a golf ball hit him in the head, he'd be the first to get an injury lawyer and nowadays would probably get a big payday, too. You'd shake your head until he was out of sight and then blame him for ruining your concentration when you fatted your next shot.

But now, newly single, you could see it from the jogger's perspective. Of course the golf course is a great place to run! The surroundings are serene and beautiful, there are no cars commandeered by distracting drivers that could end your life at any minute. You knew walking a golf course was a five-mile journey; runners knew it too. You were suddenly sad that he was running in the other direction. You would have liked to give him a wave.

You were waiting for the fairway to clear on the next tee box, and so you tossed grass over your head to judge the wind. You did this for no discernible reason since you were going to hit driver regardless of the wind's direction or intensity, but you're trying to get better at this since most of the time when you do it you get a face full of grass. That's when you saw a hawk fly across the tee box and into the tree beside you. It was no more than 30 feet above your head, and it was massive, and it stared at you utterly unimpressed with your entire being. You couldn't help but remember all the times you had stood over a shot, trying to decide if you should hit a low cut around the tree that had snookered you or if you should try to go over, when your concentration would be broken by a playing partner saying, "Hey, check out that hawk! It's massive!" and you would roll your eyes. Who cares?

But now the hawk broke its contemptuous stare as it spotted something to the side. You followed its gaze and saw a squirrel running down the base of a tree and making its way through the rough toward the fairway. Your nemophilist enjoyment suddenly became a life and death situation. What should you do? Distract the hawk? How? Warn the squirrel? How? You grabbed your driver and started waving it at the hawk and yelling. The guys on the green thought you were demanding to play through even though they were 400 yards away, and they raised their hands in a WTF group gesture.

The hawk lifted its wings and made a beeline for the squirrel. You knew how this would end, had seen it before at your club: the hawk lands directly on the hapless squirrel's back, you hear the pitiful sounds as the talons dig in, and it flies away with its prey. But in the past, you were never really engaged. It happened; the group saw it; the requisite jokes were made about Darwin and how there are days when you play so badly you wish you were the squirrel. But moments later, you're reading the line of your putt and the hawk drama is out of your mind.

But this time the hawk didn't dive-bomb. It hovered, flying in small semicircles. Was it taunting? No, it had miscalibrated. It couldn't find the squirrel. You rushed your tee shot (no, no mulligan, even in cases of crisis; the tournament is still in a month) and hustled down the fairway. When you got to the general area where you last saw the squirrel, you stood your ground like a silly sentry. The hawk made one last pass, then lifted away, talons empty. You felt the tension leave your shoulders and your anxiety level drop. And you started to laugh. Whatever had just happened, it was unlike anything you've ever experienced on a golf course. And it happened because you were a single. Because you were alone with your thoughts.

You've always been afraid to be alone with your thoughts because without interruption, you tended to gravitate to the melancholic and then nosedive into the morbid. Was your mom's Life Alert® device working? You should see her more. You hadn't gotten a shingles shot yet because you were burned out on boosters and flu shots, and yet people say you could go blind from shingles, so you should suck it up and stop by a CVS. And money . . . always money. Did you have enough? Were you spending too much? Was your 401(k) too risk averse? What if you lived to ninety-five and ran out of money? Wait, who wanted to be ninety-five and in a home, muttering and drooling?

But today, on a nine-hole stroll, your thoughts have not been morbid; they're just reactive to the stimulus you encounter. Is this what your wife calls a "flow state"? Being so absorbed in an endeavor that you don't notice time and don't need to talk—you're just *there*? You'll tell her about this, but you doubt she'll believe you. Because for all the golf-related compromises you've come to terms with as a couple, there is one area in which she will cut you no slack. She will not concede an inch. It is anathema to the social core of her being to believe you when you come home from a round of golf and, when she asks, "So what did you guys talk about for four hours?" you say, "Just golf."

"I get it," your wife says, tired of the chase "There's a code. You're not supposed to tell me."

Nope. There is no code. Blood is not shared on the first tee. No solemn oaths are taken.

"So what do you talk about? And don't say, 'just golf.'"

Just golf.

"For nearly five hours?"

Yes.

"But you're on the same course every time, with the same people, playing the same game you played a few days earlier. Don't you run out of golf stuff to talk about?"

We do not.

Now your wife's head is about to explode. A head consumed every day with notifications on her phone from several news sources and innumerable activist celebrities she follows on Twitter.

"The world is on the precipice of collapse! You don't discuss the economy? The climate crisis? China's saber-rattling over Taiwan? The fact that democracy itself is in peril and America is a fading empire on a doomed planet, and that between gerrymandering and a bought-and-paid-for Supreme Court, we have given away our power to save ourselves?"

Now she's making you sound like bad people. But no, none of that.

"Jesus. How about your families? You walk around for eighteen holes and never discuss family?"

Well. Sure. How's everything? How's the family? How's life? But . . .

"It's rhetorical?"

Pretty much.

"You're lying. I get it. There's a code."

But there is no code! Your wife doesn't play golf but she comes back from her Thursday book club and can't wait to give you the community download. Rumors of infidelity are confirmed and/or denied, often by the same person. Horror stories of inept general contractors, the insanity of the city council's latest street signage recommendations, referrals to nail salons and personal trainers, warnings about the folly of CoolSculpting®, and after enough wine, debate over whether prosthetics are used when a penis is shown on HBO. When you ask if they found time to discuss the book, she raises her middle finger and makes a shoveling motion with her elbow. For women, a recurring social event is an alibi for talking about their lives. The activity is somewhat supplemental.

So it makes perfect sense that they feel they are getting played when you deny having touched on any conversation topic outside of golf. They are more than willing to share with you exactly what was said at their meeting or sport, why can't you reciprocate? Why do you have to insult their intelligence and try to get them to believe the absurd notion that all you talk about is golf? You guys must really talk about some disturbing stuff to come up with this code of honor!

How to explain this to your non-golfing wife without hurting her feelings and scaring the crap out of her? How do you say to your life partner that she is on a need-to-know basis? You share everything measurable—an address, bank accounts, credit cards—you are each other's emergency contacts and beneficiaries, the person who will one day make the "do not resuscitate" decision that will seal your fate. But there is so much she doesn't need to know: your inner thoughts, irrational fears, the scar tissue of a thousand slights, the adamantine hold of breached trust from a caregiver long since out of your life. Your ongoing terror that your wonderful life will be taken from you, while at some point on the same day hoping it will happen so you can finally do whatever it is you were meant to do.

A round of golf is the only place in your life where there is no conditional status. No one is on a need-to-know basis. All information is free. It is given without fear of reprisal. Even in the midst of intense competition, you give all the info you have wholeheartedly, and if someone beats you because of it, good for them! And there are no hidden meanings or loaded phrases that will come back to haunt you days later. "Did she mean that? Was she sending me a message? Am I overthinking it?"

The repetition of golf speak is soothing. Yes, everyone knows the false front on number two means you have to carry it all the way to a front flag, but someone says it anyway. Yes, everyone knows there is fescue on the left on number seven and it sure looks like your ball landed right in it, but someone will offer the blatant lie of saying they think you'll have a shot. Everyone can feel the wind howling and everyone knows number fourteen plays dead into it, but someone will mention that it is at least a two-club wind today, and everyone will nod grimly like they've been given the nuclear codes.

It's not that golfers aren't interested in juicy gossip, or that they're not interested in and appropriately distressed about current events. And sure, they'll brag about their kids or mention they just locked down a timeshare in Hawaii. But that is a small fraction of what they discuss during a round of golf. And before you judge them as being detached or callous, remember two central mindsets that justify the communication style of golfers.

Mindset number one: Golfers can't multitask! Well, in reality, no one can. Multitasking isn't even a human term. It's a computer science concept from the 1960s that emerged when they were trying to get two processors to talk to each other. When our attention spans started shrinking, we appropriated the term and started claiming that unlike older generations, we could multitask, but your brain's structure only allows for one conscious thought at a time. You think you're doing two things at once, but you're really just switching back and forth. Golfers know this intuitively. "I would love to discuss the rise of fascism with you, but where is my ball?" "I am concerned about the effects of artificial intelligence on late-stage capitalism, but is that stake yellow or red? Where do I drop?" You can't expect a golfer to carry on meaningful conversations when they're playing for money, they're down two with five to play, and their opponent is stiff for birdie and they're 30 feet above the hole putting for par! Until there comes a time when golf balls always go where they are intended, golfers will not be engaging in discussions of any depth while golfing.

1. Mindset number two: Golf is how guys get to be kind. In the real world, especially for men, there is a tension between being told to "man up" and being told to be vulnerable. You're taught from the jump that the world is fraught and hypercompetitive, and a degree of toughness is not only in order, it is imperative. From getting promoted to being found attractive by potential mates, projecting strength is a requirement. And yet a certain level of softness is in order too. Acts of random kindness are noticed, lauded, and appreciated. But no one tells you where the line is drawn. And if you guess wrong, you can pay a price. What is worse: being cold and bottom line–oriented, or being perceived as weak, overly sentimental, or ineffectual? Everyone wants to be kind, but no one wants to guess wrong.

2. So where is it okay, no questions asked, to be kind? Yep, the golf course. A foursome playing in tough conditions would make an anger management therapist weep with joy. Terry likes to bust balls, but there he is, helping his opponent look for his ball, ignoring the three minute rule, and finally offering, "Dude, just drop it somewhere in here, don't take the stroke." And in return, Jon, who launched said ball into the junk, reminds everyone that there is poison ivy in there and not to bother looking. Every ball that is struck gets positive reinforcement in four-part harmony. "Good ball, pards, that is right on it!" "Kick right for him!" "Go in the damn hole!" And the ultimate: "Golf shot!" Poorly struck shots are met not with derision or gamesmanship, but with optimism befitting Tony Robbins. "Thin to win . . . that might get

there." "I've seen you make par from worse places, pards." And on the most egregious miscues, the ball that bounces down the cart path for a hundred yards, hits a stone wall, and caroms straight into the middle of the fairway: "Hey, we count the bad breaks, we count the good breaks, am I right?" The golfer having a horrible round gets his back slapped and is told it's a stupid, cruel game. The golfer having his best round of the year is told there's more where that came from, to keep it up, and "Give it to him!" is yelled at every putt, as the collective tries to will him to his lowest career round.

3. Golfers are not better humans than non-golfers. They're not even better humans than themselves once they leave the golf course. By the time they reach their cars, they start to return to their imperfect, narrow-minded, self-centered default setting. Does golf purify them for four-plus hours because they feel if they are kind to their playing partners there will be a karmic kickback by the golf gods? Maybe a little. But it's not that transactional. It is simply that they know how hard golf is, how at any given moment they could lose their nerve or the feel of their swing and suffer. Oh, how they can suffer.

4. You might ask why golfers don't then make the bigger connection to life off the course. At some level, we all know we live one phone call from being brought to our knees. We all know how we can, at any given moment, suffer. So why aren't we as kind to others in our lives as we are on the golf course? Well, we should be, but we can't make that intellectual connection on the course. Not until we figure out why the hell the ball keeps slicing right.

You're walking to your final hole, the ninth, and the group you're following is walking toward their balls. Your new swing has held up okay, with some notably ugly exceptions, but you have played strictly by the rules. You need a par to shoot 43. That's well above your handicap, but it's your first time outside with the new swing, the ground is soft, you're walking after rehabbing a back injury. Remember, it's a process! And besides, you're legit tired.

There's a wooden bench on the ninth tee and you decide a brief respite is in order. It's too early in the season for ball washers, so you decide to switch your ball out. As you lean over to reach, you see a brass plaque on the seat bench. Etched on it for the world to see is the dedication, "In loving memory of Pete, a great dad, friend, and men's club legend." It's dated five years ago. You've played here several times during that period with work friends who didn't want to come to your club. You never noticed the bench, let alone the homage to Pete. You've been so oblivious to so much. You've learned that today.

And something has shifted in five years. If you had seen the memorial plaque back then, you would have probably remarked to your group that it's telling that they say Pete was a great dad and friend, but they do not say that he was a great golfer. Shouldn't they have given him that? Or was he so bad that to write he was a good golfer would have been to besmirch his name for as long as people who knew him still roamed the course? But now, as you see the fairway is clear and it's time to hit, and you feel your knees creak and your lower back tighten as you rise off the bench, you don't cynically think that Pete getting a 4 x 6 brass paean on the 9th tee is a sad joke. You're actually weirdly jealous, even though such things are not even allowed at your club, because you know if they were, you would not be in the running. You are liked but not beloved like Pete. You decide, with not an ounce of evidence, that you would have liked Pete, and before putting on your golf glove, you polish the brass and wish him well.

Then you pull hook your drive into some hedges. Fucking Pete!

As you're lining up your shot on the ninth green, your last hole, a cart comes up behind you and parks. The cart girl. They must have decided there were enough lunatics braving the cold to make some money, so they sent the poor girl out to freeze and wait. You were about to pull the trigger when she yelled out, "Can I get you anything?" You couldn't be irritated at this breach of etiquette. She probably doesn't know, or care. Now that you looked, it was the same girl that took your money in the pro shop and gave you a ticket for the starter. She's just cold and doing her job. You held up one finger, the universal signal to wait a minute.

You missed the putt badly and swept it in. Sigh. That's 44.

When you came over to her, she said nothing and waited for you to order. You asked if she had coffee or hot chocolate, and surprisingly, she had both. She made no small talk, wasn't the least bit friendly, and as soon as you paid her, giving her a five-dollar bill for a two dollar coffee, she brusquely said, "Have a nice day," and drove off.

Maya would be appalled. Maya is the weekend cart girl at your club, a graduate student making the gig economy work for herself. During the day she's on the course bringing drinks and snacks to members. At night she runs the café at the Barnes & Noble in town. She's gorgeous, of course, an unsaid prerequisite for a cart girl, but it's not her looks that make her so popular with members. She knows everyone's name, remembers your beverage of choice, and has it ready for you when she pulls up. She'll give you a good-natured ribbing if you're playing well and acting cocky. She's got an agile mind and is quick with a retort or zinger. She knows this is your leisure time and a fun conversation with the cart girl is an example of the "customer experience" her marketing professor goes on and on about. Even on cold days like this, if you told Maya she must be freezing, she'd say, "I'm out in nature, driving around, handing out drinks, and watching you guys play a game. What's to complain about?"

And Maya knows the game. She waits until everyone has teed off before she drives away. If she's in the fairway and you're about to tee off, she'll pull over into the trees, out of your sight line. And then, even though it's not her job and is above and beyond, she'll play forecaddie and drive over to your errant ball and wave. She knows a great shot from a poor one, and will compliment you on the former and ignore the latter. Everyone at your club adores Maya, treats her with respect, and you all know she feels the same way.

After putting your clubs in your trunk and getting in your car, you realize how cold it was out there. While you wait for the heated steering wheel to warm your hands (you will never, ever buy another car without a heated steering wheel), you voice-text your Major Member-Member partner and tell him you just played nine holes in the cold because you are that dedicated to the cause. He replies instantly, asking what you shot . . . and you tell him you shot 38. (You said you would play by the rules; you didn't promise to relay the actual score.) It's not like you're recording this score in the computer. You just want to make your partner feel better. It's a victimless crime!

CHAPTER TWELVE

Maya Begs to Differ

"Would you prefer a table? We have our full menu at the bar as well."

Ten years ago, this was a no brainer. Cool people sit at the bar! There's better energy at the bar. People are happier. No married people stare vacantly at each other at the bar. They cover their sheer boredom with the sports playing on the televisions overhead, or by eavesdropping on the people seated adjacent to them.

Your wife texted you that she would be a few minutes late, so this decision was on you. You looked toward the bar, heard the music and the overheated aura, and kinda thought a nice quiet dinner would be optimal after a long day of meetings. But then you saw her on a two-top near the bar. Maya! Sitting with a friend, no doubt from school, and dressed up in a way you had never seen before. Of course! This was the end of your Friday night and the beginning of hers. You told the hostess you'd sit at the bar.

The hostess led you to a corner of the bar where two seats were available directly across from Maya's table. You walked right past her. You made direct eye contact and gave her a big smile. You didn't wave because you suddenly couldn't remember if cool people still waved, but you did give her a big, fulsome smile. You were trying to decide between saying, "Well, we meet again" and "Hey, stop stalking me," but neither seemed appropriate when she didn't seem to even recognize you. Literally no response.

Was it the fact that maybe for the first time she was seeing you without a golf hat? Or maybe it was the sport jacket and oxford shirt? Maybe she just needed a minute to assimilate.

As you pass by, still vaguely confused by the lack of recognition in her eyes, you hear a snippet of their conversation.

"It's just six more credit hours, you're overthinking it."

"No, no, it matters when you're interviewing. They want to see purpose, passion. The difference between a composable data analytics minor and a data fabric minor is night and day."

"Not in health care, all they care about is deployment costs. You can do either. This is not life or death, Maya."

Okay, that makes you feel better. Maya is distracted because she's about to cross some geek Rubicon. This isn't about you. But it is a gentle reminder that if, God forbid, you got divorced, you could never date a younger woman. How can you be in a relationship where every time they express a concern, you have to fight the urge to tell them that their concern is meaningless and that they won't even be able to recall it in a few years?

You turn back to the bar and decide to wait for the conversation to shift. Then you'll casually turn back and pretend you just noticed her, and she will not only recognize you but light up like she does when you walk over to her golf cart, affirming your unrequited but authentic secret bond. You will then offer to buy them a drink, and your loose tie to masculinity will be restored.

Then your world stops making sense. The proximity to their table becomes your worst nightmare. You can't not hear them. Your wife texts you that she's in traffic. You consider going to the restroom and sitting on the toilet for a half hour to get away from the discomfort of what you overhear. You can't move seats because there are only single seats left. You should just text your wife that there are no tables, the wait is insane, and to meet you at home. You should. But you don't. And the world falls away.

"In a couple of weeks. Don't remind me, I'm dreading it. Worst job ever."

"You shouldn't go back. You're miserable the whole goddamn golf season."

"I know, but I'm trying to make it so that I can pay off my student loans before I go on Medicare. The adult world sucks."

"Hello, I waitress at a sports bar. After ten p.m., I get my ass grabbed like it's their job! At least you don't deal with that. "

"In a way, it's worse. The pats on the shoulder, the lame innuendos delivered by sweaty, middle-aged men with their paunches hanging over their belts."

"Don't forget the flat asses. It's like these guys turn forty-five and their asses disappear."

" I shouldn't be so mean. Some of these guys are legit sweethearts, respectful, asking about school and my family. But even them . . . "

"The obligatory banter."

"Right? It's like having the same conversation over and over."

"It's exhausting."

"Exactly. You take the job because you think it's brainless. Because you can put in buds and listen to podcasts while you drive around."

"Well, at least the money is decent, right?"

"If there's enough people playing, and if they're drinking. But absolutely, some of these guys are super generous. But you know, I have to get there like an hour before my shift to load the freaking cart. I don't get tips for that."

"Lost opportunity cost!"

"Okay, I'm done complaining. No one makes me do it. I think part of the issue is I go from angry at some of them to sorry for all of them."

"Angry I get. That guy who ran you through his laundry list of what he'd do to you if he weren't married . . . "

"Oh god, I literally wanted to drive around the corner and heave into the nearest bush."

"But sorry for them? A bunch of privileged dudes killing time and the climate simultaneously? Why?"

"I dunno . . . Because I see people taking something so seriously that means absolutely nothing. Because some arbitrary number they put on a scorecard determines their whole mood for the day and defines their status. Because they stand in the sun melting and fading away, not even noticing their own fast-ap-proaching oblivion. They never seem sadder to me than when they're playing well. They're being had. And they don't even know it!"

"Hmm, well then, sistah, you are doing the Lord's work. They say mid-dle-aged men feel invisible, that women our age never see them. But you see them. You drive right up to them!"

"I see them, all right. I see right through them."

"Let's make a pact. No matter how successful we are, no matter how much money we make, we are never joining a country club. We are never learning to play golf, and we will network the old-fashioned way—online!"

"Deal. Now let's change the subject. They have their stupid Major Member-Member coming up, and after three days of that I always feel like killing myself."

You don't know how long you stood on the rim of the abyss looking down. It may have only been a few minutes, but it felt like years. You felt a hand on the back of your neck, and you don't recall ever being as grateful to see your wife. You hugged her so out of proportion to her late arrival for a routine dinner that she asked if anything was wrong. But before you could come up with a disingen-uous answer, her face changed and she moved away from you.

"Maya! How are you, sweetie? Look, honey, it's Maya! From the club!"

And Maya lit up. On cue. Just like she does when she comes to your golf cart on the weekends. Everyone loves Maya.

CHAPTER THIRTEEN

A Practice Round

I t's almost impossible to get a tee time the week of the Major Member-Member. To an outsider, the idea that you and your partner, who know every inch of the course by heart, would need a practice round in order to compete is patently absurd. You are playing sixty-three holes in three days. "Why would you burn yourself out?" ask the benighted. Even some participants scoff at the idea and just show up and play. But have any of these unenlightened ever won the tournament?

Well, actually, that happens quite often. Now that you think about it, it makes perfect sense.

But that's not you and your partner. You pay the event the respect it deserves by showing up for the practice round and dialing in your strategy. How fast are the greens? How high have they let the rough get? Crucially, what is the order off the tee? What about on the greens? Who putts first? More importantly, a practice round will get you both into competition mode and reduce the inevitable jitters you'll both be feeling.

"Dude, are you seriously sleeping in the golf cart?"

"I told you, I barely slept. I watched like a hundred episodes of *Yellowstone*. If Beth Dutton was a little crazier, I think we'd hit it off. Besides, we're not going anywhere until they blow the horn."

He had a point. You were sitting in the first fairway. The sky looked dark when you teed off, and your partner tried to tell you it wasn't worth it, that you should just go home. But you lambasted him for his lack of commitment, and just after you hit your tee shots, the skies opened, the rumbling started, and the horn blew signaling lightning in the area. Play was suspended.

Your partner fascinated you. He had a life that you wouldn't want but somehow couldn't help being envious of. He was a 5 handicap, much better than you, but he had no ego about it. He never knew how many strokes he was giving or getting, and it wasn't gamesmanship, he just didn't know. And when you played together, he would come down to the range with just a wedge, hit a half dozen balls, chat with the guys next to him and head to the first tee. When you told him about your meticulous warm-up of working your way through the bag, trying to hit a variety of trajectories and ball flights, and then simulating the playing of the first hole (driver with a fade, 6 iron to the middle of the green), he shrugged and said, "That's not a warm-up, that's a workout."

A lightning bolt flashed across the darkened sky in an intense imitation of vampire movie CGI, and the ensuing thunder was so loud it amazed you to remember that when you first got the Golf Bug, you would try to convince your partners the lightning was miles away and you were in no danger. Your partner looked at his watch and told you if it didn't blow through in twenty minutes, he was going home. He said he didn't mind dying, but doing it while swinging a veritable lightning rod in an electrical storm would be downright embarrassing.

He had a point, but even his take on death intrigued you. You were on Team Fauci during COVID-19. You washed your hands like Howard Hughes, wore a mask everywhere, and got vaxxed, then boosted, then boosted again. Your partner didn't think it was a hoax, wasn't engaged politically—he just never got around to it. Once he heard you got sick for a day or two from the vaccine, he decided to take his chances. And he got COVID-19! And he got very sick! Then he got it again! And he never even mentioned it to anyone. He wasn't at the club, and then he was back. He didn't hide it—if you asked, he'd tell you—but like his reaction when he got a horrible lie or a bad bounce, he just accepted what happened to him and didn't need any sympathy. Why hadn't that rubbed off on you after all this time playing tournaments with him?

Maybe it's just because your backgrounds are so different. He is the ultimate trust fund baby. His father owned a large liquor distributorship, which was then bought by Heublein, and with the proceeds he started buying up real estate and then building condominiums. It wasn't old money, but it was big money, and your partner has never known what it is like to be anxious about the future, or dependent on the whims of corporate restructures and moody bosses, or to have to save or borrow to reach the next social milestone of family life. He never married and has no kids. To his credit, he's not a dilettante. He's a radiology tech at the university health center, but even that profession is typical of him. Artificial intelligence will replace radiology techs as a profession in a few years. This strikes terror in the heart of his colleagues, who went into the profession thinking if nothing else, they would have stability their whole working lives. How will they pay their mortgages? Terrifying. But your partner will be thrilled. He'll be able to say he didn't quit because he was lazy or didn't have to work. The job went away. He may play more golf. But probably not.

You learn so much about a person when you sit on a golf cart for four hours and play in a three-day Major Member-Member for ten straight years. But after all this time, you have never been able to ask him what you want to know most: What do you do with all that time? All the time we all spend caring for our family, managing their expectations and needs, letting them down and being let down by them. What replaces that anguish and worry? Where does your mind go when there's nothing to fear?

The lightning has stopped but now there's a downpour. You reassure him, as one does, that this should blow over in a moment and you see some lighter clouds off in the distance that you're sure are heading your way. He rolls his eyes. And then it turns out he has a question for you. Maybe he's just killing time, or maybe it's always bothered him to play with a partner twelve years older than him.

"So when you and the old lady retire, what's the move? Florida? Carolinas?"

You give him your stock line. That you have nearly twenty years of work left, so who knows? But you and your wife have discussed it. And there is a very big part of both of you that doesn't want to become another statistic. If you live in the Northeast, with its high taxes and cost of living, you're supposed to get old enough to no longer be able to tolerate the cold, then run the numbers and realize that if you sell your house and move to Florida or South Carolina, with what you will save in property and income taxes, coupled with cashing out your Roth and 401(k) plan and your fledgling but conservative stock portfolio, you could live pretty well. You'd be a three-hours flight from your kids and whatever grandkids you might be blessed with.

But you both hate the high humidity of the Southeast. Your wife says the South is okay for a few days in the winter, but where is the culture? And even though you hear that "everyone here is from somewhere else" when you visit, you don't really believe it. You can feel the arch-conservative leanings in the zeitgeist, and you both wonder if you'll spend your golden years keeping your true feelings to yourself and changing the subject. And you never feel older than when you go there on vacation, surrounded by the gerontology groupthink—how old will you feel when you're one of them?

And your wife is a spectacular blend of idealism and pragmatism. She follows the science on climate change. When it's time for you to retire, she reasons, Florida will not be what it is today. Beaches will have eroded; flooding will have hit urban areas, and temperatures will have risen dramatically. Either the people in power will ignore this reality and the place will be uninhabitable, or the measures taken to address the problem will change the economic calculus and it will become super expensive to live there, thereby eliminating the main motivation. Additionally, she reasons, your kids will probably not stay on the east coast. They can work remotely anywhere, and they should spend their early adulthood adventuring and living in many places before they deem one to be the right fit for their family unit, however that is conceived, and it may very well not include kids. That's up to them. No, no, it's clear to your wife. When you retire, what makes the most sense is for you to move north! Maine, New Hampshire . . . maybe even Canada! Yes, being expats in Canada seems the right moral and political stance.

But you play golf. So while you agree with her in principle, it's not happening. There's work to be done on the retirement front for sure.

"What about you? You're the one who could retire any time you feel like it."

"Dude, I work four days a week. My folks have had homes in West Palm and Scottsdale my whole life. I'm already Benjamin Button."

"It's a good thing you can make birdies, because it would be so easy to hate you. You know what I would do if I were you, retirement-wise?"

"Oh Christ, here we go. Please stop raining so we cannot do this again."

"You have thirteen years before you need to qualify. If you worked at it, with your game, you could totally do it."

"I've never broken 70. Not once. On my home course."

"Right, but thirteen years! I'm not saying you wouldn't have to commit yourself. You can't tell me you have never dreamed of it."

"Literally never."

"Well, I do."

"You do? Like in the present tense? Like it's a recurring dream sequence for you? You dream about playing the senior tour?"

"You don't have to make it sound like I said I died and was resurrected on Sunday."

"Dude, billions of people believe that! Find me one that believes you could play the senior tour."

You were unwise to broach this subject. You have now opened yourself up for perpetual ridicule, and your partner will be unable to not roll this out every time you go to the first tee to play one of the nine-hole matches of the Major Member-Member. And once he gets a few cocktails in him at the post-match dinners, he's going to let the entire club membership know that they all better watch out, because his 10-handicap playing partner will be spending his golden years on TV hoisting trophies on the Champions Tour. There's no point in asking him not to discuss it. You have handed him a sure thing. Way too juicy not to use.

But while the teasing may be without mercy, it will also lack truth. You are not an anomaly. You can feel it. Oh, it may be a fleeting thought for some. For others, it's too crazy to ever say out loud, but there is a part of them, repressed by reality and reduced to absurdity by current performance data, that still lives in that liminal space. What if they set their mind to it? What if they prioritized and focused? Maybe, just maybe, it's not too late!

Dreams use bits of memory and shards of information in whatever way that serves. And in this dream, they feed their hope with facts. It's been done before! Amateurs have made their way onto the Over Fifty Champions tour! It's rare of course, but it's been done. And how do you know for a fact that you are not the only decent golfer in your forties who imagines himself bursting onto the professional circuit? Because when you Googled "How do I qualify for the Senior PGA tour," you got 109,000,000 search results. (You felt intensely indulgent when you did this because when the search string starts with "How do I qualify," the top autofill choices were "for Medicaid," "for disability," and "for food stamps." But hey, don't let them guilt-trip you into giving up your dream.) Since this is way more than the actual number of people who play golf, it's pretty clear that people Google it often and that they share their dreams with family and friends who then Google it because they think they're insane. You are clearly not the only one who dreams it; you are just the only honest one to admit it.

"Not for nothing—and remember I'm talking about *your* potential here, not mine—but it's been done! Allen Doyle won the Senior US Open and was an amateur until he was forty-six."

"Jesus, he was in the Georgia Golf Hall of Fame by then, he won every State Amateur title they had!"

"And there's Jay Sigel. Never turned pro. He worked in insurance, like me! He won nine million bucks on the Senior Tour."

"I'm sorry, do you not realize I own a smartphone? Here, his Wikipedia page says he won the US Amateur, the British Amateur, was low amateur at the Masters and the US Open, and played on nine Walker Cups. He's like the greatest amateur ever! It also says he's a senior VP at Century, so he's also way better at insurance than you."

"Well, what about Steven Alker? He never won anything and now he's dominating the Champions Tour, out of nowhere!"

"He's been on the Korn Ferry Tour forever. He was a crummy pro, but he's a pro. He would shoot 57 on our course, right now, in the middle of this storm. You are one trippy, delusional dude. Boy, can I pick partners."

"Do you see what you're doing? It's transparent, really; Psychology 101."

"What am I doing?"

"You're projecting your fears and insecurities onto me. It's easy to make fun of me, but you're the one with the talent, and the money, and fifteen years to work at it before you try to qualify. You're taking the easy way out."

"I never wanted in!"

"Do you even know how to qualify?"

"I don't care."

"There are these regional qualifying tournaments. There's a $3,000-application fee. There's seventy-eight spots. You also have to have two letters of reference from a Class A PGA tour pro or a Champion Tour Member. You don't have to win the qualifiers, you just have to be in the top twelve, although if you could finish in the top five you'd be fully exempt. And by the way, not to get in the weeds, but you could skip all of this if you got a sponsor's exemption into a Champion's tour event. Do you have any connections like that?"

"Uh, let's review: I don't know any sponsors, I don't have any letters of reference, and while I do have the three thousand, I wouldn't waste it because, returning to the premise, I don't want to do it!"

"You're selling yourself short. When you're on, your game is as good as anyone's."

"As anyone *here*. I'm a five handicap. Their caddies could beat me giving me four a side."

"But you're a five handicap now. What will you be in fifteen years?"

"Probably a ten! I'll be older, slower, fatter. I'll be telling people I play with I used to be a five and they won't believe me, just like I wouldn't believe you if you told me you used to be a five."

"That's deflecting and hurtful. You know I was never a five."

"You have no concept how good those guys are. They could roll out of bed and shoot 68 in tournament conditions. It's a joke. I know you mean well. I appreciate it on some weird level, but it's a joke."

"It's possible though, right? That's the part I love. Not for me, and maybe not for you. But there's a pathway. They made it possible."

"Yeah, I get that. That part is pretty cool."

"Because—and maybe you can't see it now—dreams get harder to come by.

You sort of run out of things to look forward to." And there, you did it again. You brought "sad" onto the golf course. Misplaced joy? More than welcome. Disproportionate anger? Bring it. But sad is as out of bounds as too many of your tee shots. You pretended to look up at the lightening clouds and replaced your mask.

Your partner has already moved on. "Let's talk about the Member-Member."

"Right! So I'm thinking I should putt first. That way I can show you the line or speed."

"That's fine."

"Unless I start draining them. Then I should go last."

"Won't happen, but also fine."

"And off the tee, here's what I'm thinking. I go first, get a ball in play, then you can bomb it."

"Totally. We do that every year, and we're officially 0 and 10, but why not."

You were about to point out that if your partner didn't bring an enthusiasm that is contagious, whatever he did bring was also contagious. But before you could, the horn blew, signaling the storm had passed and play could be resumed.

"Listen, for real, no bull. I need to know that you're all in. Do you think, do you seriously think, we can win this year?"

"Absolutely. This is our year."

"Really?"

"Nah, but I only quash one dream per person per day. I already hit my daily quota."

And with that, your partner flights a 9 iron by leaning the shaft forward and finishing low around his waist. It lands 25 feet short of the pin, skips forward and stops dead 4 feet from the flag. He wipes the turf off his club with his towel and smiles at you.

"Fuck Steven Alker."

CHAPTER FOURTEEN

The Minor Matter of the Major Member-Member Championship

From day one the energy is different at the MMM. This is not your imagination. It's the only tournament where the part-time ball kids are dressed in club colors and they meet you at your car to take your clubs. No one puts their shoes on in the parking lot at the MMM, they go to their locker. How this could possibly matter to their scores is an unknowable mystery. About a quarter of the teams have committed to matching golf outfits with coordinating hat, shirt, belt, pants and shoes. One team is in knickers and Irish flat caps. Spectacular. (You have begged your partner for years to coordinate with your look, and he said he would not only not do it, but if you happened to be wearing the same color shirt, he would either go into the pro shop and buy another or withdraw.)

You've arrived at 11:30, a full ninety minutes before the opening shot. Plenty of time for you to stretch, hit balls, talk trash, get nervous, hit balls again. Lunch is served for the participants, but you don't know how anyone can possibly eat.

You walk by the tables on the grill room deck and see that your partner has a plate hemorrhaging pasta salad, topped by a greasy cheeseburger. You ask him if he's hit any balls yet, and his response tortures you. "Pards, if you didn't bring your game here, you're not going to find it by one p.m."

The registration tables look so innocuous. The ebullient volunteers could pass for the folks who hand out numbers at a 5K run or take your donation at a school science fair. But this is very serious business. Because these ladies have in their possession the information that will determine everyone's fate: the flight sheet. For the week before the tournament, the head pro is grilled for information. Surely he knows. (He says he doesn't.) Surely it's been decided by now; the tourney starts in two days. (He says it is done the day before.) The player's committee knows, but despite taunts, bribes, and groveling that you would have thought was beneath everyone, they tell no one.

The revealing of the flights is like the Oscars. It's assumed who will win, no one has really seen the work of some of the lesser-known contenders, and just as when an Oscar is announced and they zoom in on the loser, if you are not in the flight you wanted, you pretend to be happy.

The flights are determined by the handicaps of the two team members. You combine the two handicaps and everyone in the flight has a similar total handicap. So the best players are in the A flight, the really good are in the B flight, and so forth, down to the H flight hackers. On the surface, it seems fair enough. But a veteran like you is handed the flight sheet by the mirthful volunteer and you immediately find your team and then scan the other names in your flight. Are there any former champions? Any members known to be clutch? Any choke artists? Are you playing with anyone who is a rules nazi? And since your club has twenty-seven holes and one nine is no doubt more difficult than the other two, which course are you starting on? Against whom? When do you play the best team in your flight?

Wait, what? No, no, this has to be a mistake. A computer error. Hey, it happens, do not panic—this is why you show up early, so you can catch these things. Humans have foibles; you will merely find the head pro and get this fixed. Because this can't be right!

"Nope," the head pro says while nodding, "that's right. You guys are in the A flight. Last team in. Your partner has been posting some low scores. Congrats!"

You have *always* been in the B flight. You can see from the posted handicaps that you are by far the worst player in the A flight. You can't possibly compete in the A flight! One team has the club champion paired with the kid that played Division One golf at Purdue. You wouldn't deign to play with these guys on a Saturday morning for fun, let alone in the MMM! The pro sees that you are crestfallen and tries to lift your spirits.

"Look at it this way, you'll be getting all that candy."

Candy is the strokes a higher handicap gets when playing against a better player. He's right that in a nine-hole match, someone getting a lot of candy has a real advantage. Your bogey is a par putt. On the hard holes, if you could eke out a par, that would be a net birdie with your candy. You see that several of the guys in the A flight are 1 or 2 handicaps. Even your partner gets a little bit of candy. In the B flight, he would be the best player and the one giving others candy. It's part of why you have come close but lost several key matches over the years. Maybe the pro is right, maybe this *is* a good thing.

And then you see a notation by the A flight team list. It reads, *All flights play from the standard white tees, except the A flight, which will play from the black tees.* You feel your adrenaline start to redline and your stomach to turn. Based on this notation, your plan is set in motion. You will go to the range, rub your back conspicuously, groan at an audible but not melodramatic level, and after a few swings, inform everyone within earshot that you have reinjured your back and will have to withdraw. You know that this is childish and unfair to your partner, but the notation has made the next three days impossible.

The white tees average around 6,250 yards. The black tees average just under 6,900 yards. For you that is not a workable interstice, but the length of the Great Wall of China. You drive by the black tees when you play golf. You often hit stray balls from the rough onto the black tees ahead or to the side of you, but you have never hit a ball on a peg from a black tee. Now that you think about it, you aren't even sure you know where the black tees are on some holes—that's how far back they are!

No, no. A line must be drawn. You have to have enough self-respect to withdraw. You'll be of no use to your partner, and it will be abjectly humiliating. Every par 4 you will be hitting driver, 3 wood, wedge. And some of the par 3s that are 200 yards from the white tees could be 240, even 250 from the black tees! And that's not even the worst of it. Those guys in A flight don't hit the random smother hook, the shanked wedge. They're *players*! You will have to go find your partner right now and level with him.

"Dude! Did you see? We're in the A flight! Look at us making the big time!"

"Uh, no . . . the A flight plays from the black tees. I can't do that. I'm out."

"What? Relax, you'll be fine."

"No, I won't. What's the point? I can't reach any of the holes from the black tees."

"So what? How many greens do you usually hit in nine holes? This time you'll get candy! We both will! This is a very good thing for us. Now bust out your cash, it's time to bet!"

No one carries cash anymore, except when they are playing in the MMM, because there is money to be had. Your wife thinks this three-day marathon is about bragging rights only, but that's because you didn't want to freak her out about how much money is at stake (on top of the $2,675 tournament fee that she sees on your billing statement).

- **Level one wager:** This one is easy. Because you have to show a modicum of dignity and bet on yourself. The volunteer hands you a betting sheet with all of the teams listed on it. She assumes you will bet some amount on your team. That's a given, that is, if you have even a modicum of self-belief. How can you go out and do battle for three days and not invest in yourself? This year, being the lowest seed in the A flight, you would be better served if you opened your car window on the drive in and tossed your cash away into the wind. But you and your partner have always seen this investment as the triumph of hope over reason, and besides, he is already waving a wad like Tony Soprano and peeling off fifty-dollar bills. So you have to match his three hundred with your own. (This makes you wonder how many people a soup kitchen could feed with the $600 you are wasting. Also, do they even still call them soup kitchens?)

- **Level two wager:** Here you can actually see an ROI. You get to wager on as many other teams in as many flights as you want. Since hypocrisy goes before a fall, you will definitely bet on the top team in the A flight to kick your ass. You and your partner also scan the other flights. Oh, Denny and his son are somehow in C this year? That's ridiculous, but an easy bet. They'll crush it. That's $200! Oh, look, Marty is playing with Drake again. I thought they had a falling out. No one makes more putts when it counts than Marty. That's a well spent $300 there. The Epsteins always win the D flight. That's practically stealing. $200. You're about to throw down $300 on José's team even though you don't know his partner because you have seen José shoot 75 and he's somehow able to sleep at night claiming to be a 16, but then your partner points out he had knee surgery this winter and hasn't touched a club. Good intel; sorry José. The lower flights are people you don't know so you randomly pick teams like your wife does when you hand her the March Madness basketball brackets. ("I like the way their name sounds!") By the time the volunteer has verified your picks and given you the redeemable receipt, you and your partner are $1,300 lighter.

- **Level three wager:** This one is beyond your control, the tournament-within-a-tournament flight money. Most years, every man in the eight-team flight puts in $100, and winner takes all. The winning team defrays some of their tournament expense by splitting $1,600. The custom is as follows: The top seeded team in each flight are the designated holders of the cash envelope. Once the flight is determined on Sunday, the cash is split between the two winning team members. You have never been the top seeded team, so you have never had to collect or guard the money, and you definitely have never had anyone hand you the winnings. But when Jake, three-time club champ and a guy who hits it so pure you can have your back turned to the range and know he just hit a driver from the sound it makes, comes over to collect the in-flight wager money, he tells you it is $200 a man. Then he says, as if it's no big deal and he's just running through it so there's no surprise at the end, because you know, money is money, that there's "lucky loser" money and there's a payoff for the most birdies, most sandies, and the usual "junk." Neither you nor your partner has any idea what he is saying, but you give Jake another $100 each.

When Jake said, "Any side stuff you guys do on your own during the matches is all cool, but that should be paid after each match. I won't use names, but some guys get pissy if you tell them you'll pay them tomorrow. You know?"

You shook your head like that would be an appalling rookie move but wondered if you had time to hit the ATM before you teed off.

You had fifteen minutes until the shotgun marking the beginning of match one. Perfect. You had a five-minute full body warm-up your mobility therapist had devised for you, then five minutes on the range, then five minutes on the putting green. But you saw the head pro pick up his microphone and heard the loudspeaker system kick on. Was he? No, he couldn't have been.

"Gentlemen, welcome to our annual three-day Major Member-Member, our flagship event of the season. Everyone has checked in so let's get rolling. Please hit your last shot or make your last putt and head to the golf carts so we can go over the rules."

Cortisol redlining, you have to make the call. Should you just putt? Putt for dough, right? But that's ridiculous, your putt doesn't matter if you can't get the ball in play. Go hit a few balls on the range. No, wait, that's crazy. You'll be rushing, you won't have any rhythm. Just do the mobility work and trust yourself, you know how to hit a golf ball. You were frozen in place, forced to make the Sophie's Choice of tournament golf. Why didn't you get here five hours early like you wanted to? In the end your choice was made for you because CJ, literally the nicest human in the whole club, came over to you and gave you a hug and told you, over and over, how happy he was to see you after hearing about your injury. The guy practically had tears in his eyes. "There but for the grace of God go all of us, my friend!"

It really takes some finesse to be a head pro at a country club. Job one was to not upset the members. Not when they're being demanding ("You're right, that should be ground under repair, let me speak to the superintendent"), or petty ("I know they're slow, but they are members too. I'll drive over and see if I can nudge them a little"), or cheap ("I don't set the bag storage prices, but I hear you. Would you rather take your clubs with you after your round?"). So it was important that the head pro announce the rules with enough emphasis to avoid conflict, but enough nuance so as not to have any member feel he is talking about them.

- **Rule 1:** Pace of play. It's match play. If you're out of the hole, pick up. There is no practice putting after the hole is played. Yes, it is allowed in the Ryder Cup. This isn't the Ryder Cup.

- **Rule 2:** We're playing the ball down. You can't roll it over, not even in the fairway. Here's a good rule of thumb: don't touch your ball with your hands until you're marking it on the green.

- **Rule 3:** If you hit it in a hazard, or in the fescue, take a proper drop and penalty stroke. If you think your ball might be OB, hit a provisional and save yourself the cart ride of shame back to the tee. (See rule one, pace of play.)

- **Rule 4:** Your opponents can concede putts. They don't have to. You must hear them clearly give you the putt. Once they do, don't hit the putt anyway. Pick it up.

- **Rule 5:** Each match is nine holes. You get one full point for the win, and you get tenths of a point for each hole you win by. So if you win three up you get 1.3 points on the leaderboard. Each hole therefore counts so play all nine holes even if you are getting clobbered. It is a 1.5 max drubbing.

- **Rule 6:** Verify the scores when the match is over among the foursome, sign the scorecard, and hand it in at the scorer's table. If there is a dispute, see the head pro before signing.

- **Rule 7:** The strokes (candy) for each match are on the scorecards preset on your cart. They are based on the computer index as of Monday of the tournament week.

- **Rule 8:** If you like to play with music on your cart, you must ask your opponents for permission, and must not play music if they are not comfortable.

"All right gentlemen, please proceed to your starting holes, and remember the most important rule of all—we're here to have fun."

CHAPTER FIFTEEN

Day One

There are two matches on day one. No one has ever won the championship after losing both matches on day one. Lose both matches on day one and day two is a slog. Because day two is three matches, twenty-seven holes, and an absolute grind. With the extended lunch break, it takes all day. And since every shot matters more and more as the tournament unfolds, and every putt is read and re-read, it is exhausting. The forecast, thank God, is excellent. Warm and no precipitation. Go into day two without a win and then have to sit through rain delays, and no one would blame you if you dialed 988. Day three, Sunday, is two matches in the morning. And then the flight winners are in an alternate shot playoff for the overall title. So you've heard. You've never stuck around to see the playoff.

Match One

Your introduction to the black tees starts, because of course it does, with the longest par 5 on the golf course. A dogleg right. It is doubtful that even with your best drive you can hit it far enough to take on the dogleg on your second shot. But that's not your concern at the moment. You look on the scorecard and, damn it, your team's name is on top. So you're up first. Now you deeply regret your strategy. Because you already told your partner you would go first and get a ball in play. So you can't even ask him to lead off while you gather yourself.

You tee up your ball and look down at the fairway, which looks as long as an airplane runway. When you go to take a practice swing, you can barely take the club back. You can't feel your arms. Your swing thought is "Dear Lord, please just let me make contact." Before you pull the trigger, one of your opponents' cell phones goes off. He is properly mortified, but you ask if it's the teaching pro calling with a tip and everyone laughs and you relax just a bit. You can breathe again. Then you remember your mantra, the only swing thought you're allowed: "Take the club back deep and inside, uncomfortably inside." Try not to think of anything else. You breathe deeply and swing. And then you hear it. From one of your opponents. Not loud, but not patronizing either. The simple words that give you what you want most right now—a sense that you belong.

"Good ball there."

Now let's be real. It doesn't last. You top the next shot and make bogey. In fact, you bogey the first three holes. But by the fourth tee you have already learned a few things—

- Good players make bad swings too. You're playing the second seeded team in your flight, and they are the ones with the pressure. One of your opponents was out of play on two of the first four holes.

- The black tees aren't as crazy as you thought. You have to hit driver every hole, but you always do. Only difference is now you're hitting 3 wood instead of a mid-iron for your approaches. But if you get near the green, you're pretty much where you usually are. Only now you're there in net one. Pretty cool!

- Your partner suffers from reverse impostor syndrome. He smells blood right from the start. He has never gotten strokes before. You've never seen him look at a putt from behind the ball and behind the hole before. You've never seen him appear to actually care. When he drained a 16-footer for birdie on four and pumped his fist, you told him you needed to see some valid form of identification.

And you weren't just a spectator. You hit a chunk and run with a 9 iron out of the sand on 7 and it rolled up to gimmie range. With your stroke it was a net birdie, and the match went to the last hole all square. You didn't get a stroke on 9, so you were basically out of the hole even though you were in play. One of the opponents smothered his drive, and for once you weren't the shortest ball off the tee. But his partner stepped up and nutted one. Clutch. He and your partner were both in regulation and had birdie putts. Your partner lagged up to a foot, and it was conceded. Your opponent went for the win and gunned it by the hole just over 3 feet. You looked at your partner. Concede it? But this was your new, ruthless partner, and he looked down at the ground. And your opponent never got it to the hole!

Holy crap! You won your first match! In the A flight!

Match Two

The great thing about day one is there is almost no turnaround time after the first match. As soon as you hand in your cards and the score is posted, you are handed your new scorecard and you head out to the assigned starting hole. This is done so that the matches can finish early enough to give everyone a chance to check email, return phone calls, and shower up before the happy hour.

Day one happy hour is important to attend because that is where they hand out this year's swag! You get to choose between high-end apparel, or bespoke golf shoes, or even clubs. If you putted like crap on day one, you were going right for the swag putter and putting that baby in play in the morning.

The key for you and your partner is you didn't have time to bask in your win, or second-guess it, or worry that it was pure luck. You had to just keep playing.

Your match two opponents were already on the tee. As you drove up, your partner whispered, "Check it out, he's in his head." One of your opponents was getting a lesson from his partner. He had a head cover wedged under his left armpit and he was practicing his backswing in slow motion. His partner was taking a picture of the move with his phone and showing him the evidence. As you stood on the first green, you noticed the opponent who was taking the picture for his partner was off to the side practicing his full swing with his putter. They were both in their heads.

On the third tee, already two down, one of them said to you, "I hate that they make us ride in a cart for these things. I always walk. It's how I keep my rhythm. It messes with my whole game. Why can't we walk? You know?"

You and your partner both wholeheartedly agreed (even though your partner has never walked a golf course in his life) and told him it was dead wrong of them to enforce that. "Rhythm is everything," you both said in commiserating, plaintive tones. And hey, we are cool, and don't care about tournament rules, you can walk the whole match if you want, we won't say anything to anyone.

He thanked you but said it was okay. He just wanted you to know he thought the rule was dumb and it was probably why he was playing so badly.

Absolutely, you concurred, you put a sweet move on it. I'm sure you guys would crush little ol' us every day of the week.

But not today. Today, you beat them three up. And the lowest seeds in the flight had posted 2.3 after day one! You were tied for third. It was crazy.

You stood by the leaderboard and took a pic to send to your wife, even though you knew she didn't really care. Your partner, who always abused you mercilessly whenever you posted anything about your golf game, said a bit too casually, "Hey, send that to me, would you?"

At the happy hour, it started to get a little insulting. The guys from the B flight you played with for years were a little too incredulous that you had won both your matches. "Really?" and "Seriously?" were the most common responses, but you also got a few "Jesus, how much candy were you getting?" So you turned your attention to the swag table, where you got to choose one item. Your partner immediately went for a sweet pair of wraparound Oakleys, but you were torn between a Peter Millar polo and a pink Ashworth hoodie. You decided it takes a secure guy to wear a pink hoodie and went with the polo.

Your wife had not responded to your humble brag pic of the leaderboard, and you figured she probably didn't get what it meant. So you texted her, "Look at us!!!" You threw in a face-with-open-mouth surprise emoji for emphasis. Your kids tell you your GIF and emoji game is embarrassing, but you're not sure why.

Out of the corner of your eye, you saw your partner and some other guys you didn't recognize lifting shot glasses and shouting, "LFG!!" Before you could get over there, the damage was done. You pulled your partner over to the side for a team meeting. You told him you never insisted on this when you were in the B flight, but tomorrow was a very, very big day. You don't play the club champions, who are of course currently in first place, until Sunday, but you had to go into that match at or near the lead. Keeping your hard earned day one momentum was critical! So in that spirit, you were going to have to insist on two things: No more drinking. And a ten p.m. curfew tonight. You would appreciate it if he verified this by texting you just before he turned in. Did he understand?

He nodded his head gravely and patted you on the shoulder. Then he took a shot glass off the tray of the waiter walking by, downed it, and chased it with the beer he had in his hand. Then he grinned.

"Don't freak out, pards, this is how I drank last night and look how good I played today! You need to lighten the hell up!"

Someone had to be the responsible one, so you went home a half hour later. When you walked in, the house was dark and the dog was in his crate. That meant no one was planning on being home anytime soon. You knew the kids wouldn't be home, but where was your wife and why hadn't she responded to your text? This was the Major Member-Member and she was the one who encouraged you to play! She couldn't be mad at you . . . or could she? When she picked up, you realized you were kind of hoping to get voicemail so you could impart guilt without feeling any.

"Hey, where are you?"

"I am where I told you I was going to be. We took Dee out for her work anniversary."

"Right . . . sorry . . . no, I knew . . . Did you see my pic? We're actually in this thing."

"I saw. That's great!"

"I played pretty well."

"Uh huh . . . honey she's opening gifts so . . . "

"It's loud there."

"Well, there's some game on at the bar."

Then someone said something. It sounded like a guy. Now you wanted to know what bar, but you couldn't ask because at some point she clearly told you which bar and you couldn't give her that. But whoever said whatever they said, your wife cracked up. Like really cracked up, out of proportion to whatever was said no matter how funny. *That* you couldn't let go.

"Are you drinking?"

"Yes, but look in the garage. See my car? I'm not driving. Carol is."

You wanted to tell her to stop drinking. And to be home by ten p.m. But nobody listens to reason. Why bother? She'd probably channel your partner and down a shot and a beer. So instead, you took the easy way off the phone and told her to have a good time.

You had every intention of pretending to be watching the documentary on genetic editing that you have begun a half dozen times when she came in the door, and without raising your voice, in a casual tone devoid of judgment and dripping of trust, ask her where the hell she was and with whom. But you barely made it out of the shower. You lay on the bed for a moment to regroup and fell asleep.

When you woke up it was three in the morning. She was lying next to you, and you heard no trace of the signature snoring that occurs whenever she drinks too much. You set your phone alarm for six a.m., added a reminder snooze alert, and then turned over to get a couple more hours of recovery rest.

But it wasn't going to work. You were wide awake. Day two's marathon session had already started in your mind. The three looming matches would define your destiny. You tried to close your eyes for another ninety seconds, gave up, and went to the kitchen to make coffee. You took an umbrella out of the mudroom stand and swung it deep and uncomfortably inside. You watched yourself in the hall mirror. Yep, nobody keeps an umbrella on plane like you!

CHAPTER SIXTEEN

Day Two

If you hear something a couple of times, it's okay to ignore it or at least question its validity. (The first hundred times a critic mentioned all of Aaron Sorkin's characters are witty in a way not found in nature and speak at the same passing-lane pace, he might have brushed it off and said, "There are enough dumb people in the world, why would you want to watch a movie to hear more of them?" But when every critic says it about every project? Might be time for a rewrite.) Watching golf on TV, you have heard it a million times: "He's struggling out there today, Jim, just not the same guy we saw yesterday. Swing out of sync, nothing going in. Hard to follow up a 62 with another low round!" You never really understood why this was true. Why wouldn't the guy who shot 62 feel bulletproof? Why couldn't he sustain it?

Now you understand.

It is critical in best ball match play to "ham and egg" it. That means that it's okay for you to suck on the holes where your partner is in position, and equally okay for him to suck when you are in position, but if both of you are out of the same hole at the same time, that's a death knell.

Your partner's miss is a big block right. He draws the ball and if his release point is off a touch, that ball is going straight right every time. His draw was rock solid yesterday. Everything starting right and coming back to the middle and then running out. After the fourth straight hole of yelling "fore right" to the forecaddies, his resting mellow face disappeared and he snarled to himself, "I have all of Litchfield County *left* and I block it *right?*

But that's what you have a partner for, to pick you up. And he had you. And you got it partly right. You picked up on nearly every hole since you were hitting your seventh shot to the green and your opponents were lying two and patiently waiting on the putting surface. Your constant, singular swing thought felt foreign to you, and the more you tried to find it, the more elusive it became. So you tried another swing thought, and then another.

On nearly every hole, you and your partner stayed in the cart, drove up to the green, and told your opponents that wherever the hell their balls were, you didn't know because you were in the woods trying to find your misfires. They were good, and the hole was theirs.

When your nightmare of nine holes were over, you had lost three down. As you shook their hands, they looked like they were at a wake of someone they worked with but barely knew. They genuinely felt bad for you, understood what was happening to you was painful and sad, but just under the surface they were glad it was you and not them.

Years ago, your partner made a rule about playing in the tournament together. You had just botched an easy up and down or shanked an approach or three-putted from 5 feet and apologized profusely. He said he would not play with you unless you both agreed to never apologize.

"'I'm sorry' has no place in golf. We're both trying to hit good shots. Sometimes it won't happen. I'm never going to say 'I'm sorry' *to* you so I don't expect to hear it *from* you. Okay?"

But after match three, as you were coming back from the scorer's tent, he came over to you, head bowed, and said, "Hey, I'm sorry. Really. That was embarrassing. It's my handicap that got us in this flight and I can't let that happen. I'm telling you this shit ends here. But I'm sorry."

After ten years of playing together and dealing with his cavalier mindset, you knew this wasn't just about losing a match in a flight where you two were decided underdogs to begin with. This was about the inexorable march of time. He had pounded alcohol the night before the tournament started, and when you left last night, he was on his way to needing an Uber home again. So this morning was his second hangover in a row, and while that never used to be a problem, it was now. And intuitively he knew that someday soon he would feel this way after just one night of letting loose. He wasn't feeling sorry for you because his golf game had left him, he was feeling sorry for himself because his youth was leaving too.

Knowing this, and feeling the compassion that only an older person can feel, you knew the right thing to do would be to lighten the moment, slap him on the back and tell him he had broken the rule of never saying "I'm sorry" in golf.

Instead you said, "Dude, I told you not to drink too much and to be home by ten p.m. Now we have to win both our afternoon matches."

Match Four

Your partner was on a mission. When he birdied the first two holes—the second hole the number-one handicap and set up with a sucker pin just three paces over a bunker ("Get all over it!" you yelled at his majestic 7-iron approach, and it did!)—you were duly impressed. You have never known him not to make small talk with opponents, but while he was courteous, he was taciturn and dead serious. He didn't even talk to *you* really. Even when you ebulliently lauded his latest great shot, he nodded slightly but said nothing.

Then it got ridiculous. He was getting a stroke on the longish par 5 third hole from the young stud you were playing against, a junior wealth advisor with his whole life ahead of him and a serious chip on his shoulder. The kid was a new member. Everyone was talking about him, and why not? He had effortless power and a swing to die for. A country club baby who'd been playing the game since he was four. He should give you two extra strokes just to atone for his arrogance and sinewy youth. But even though your partner was thirty yards behind him off the tee and had 247 to the pin, he pulled his 3 wood out and removed the head cover. You decided it was time for some strategy.

"Pards, you know you're getting a stroke, right? Might want to lay this up."

"Nope."

"Just saying, fescue right, water left . . . You'd be putting a lot of pressure on him if you were sitting 80 yards out in net one, you know?"

"I'm hitting the 3 wood."

"Absolutely. I like that call. It's 3 wood all day."

And he absolutely roasted it! If you had turned your back and only heard the sound of the strike, you would have known it was roasted, but you saw it all right, and it was like an airplane. It took off, then seemed to catch another gear and rise, and rise, then it peeled toward the pin and landed as softly as a sand wedge. For a brief second, as the cut spin did its magic, it looked like it was actually going to go in! But you could still see the ball. It was hard to tell from so far away, but it looked like it was stone dead. He was there in two shots and getting a stroke! On a par 5!

He said nothing in the cart driving to the green, and you weren't going to mess with his reticent mojo, but when you saw the ball was indeed within a foot from a natural double eagle . . . Holy crap!!

The stud wealth advisor laughed as they pulled up. He told your partner not to bring his putter and congratulated him on the shot. Your partner said "thanks" in the same tone you would use when someone passed you the Splenda at the diner.

He added one more birdie to his opening three and shot 32 for nine holes, getting three strokes of candy. You won five up, and you were back in contention!

One opponent was gracious. "Hello, officer, I'd like to report a murder," he said as he removed his hat.

The Stud was not having any of it. He shook your partner's hand and said, "So what do you use, Tylenol® PM?"

"Sorry?"

"Just wondering what you take at night to get to sleep knowing you're sandbagging everyone about your handicap!"

Do we ever really know anyone? Your partner's whole persona, forged over decades, was all about not sweating the small stuff and realizing it was all small stuff. Everyone dies; life is therefore meaningless, and golf is even less so—just a mindless way to whistle past the graveyard. But here in match four, nothing seemed more important to him than performing well and winning, and now that The Stud was casually questioning his integrity, nothing was more important than kicking his ass.

He dropped his putter, stepped into the guy's personal space, practically pressed his nose against his, and in a seething voice asked, "Exactly what is that supposed to mean?"

It freaked you out to see him like this, but not as badly as it freaked out The Stud. He backed up and smiled. "Easy, boss, just saying you played great. That's all. Great round. Good luck the rest of the way."

Your opponents drove off, and you knew better than to say anything about the Jekyll to Hyde transformation you had just witnessed.

Your partner took a deep breath and leaned back in the cart. He seemed to come back to himself. "I need a drink before the next match. Don't give me any grief."

"I'm having one too."

Day two is so long the club provides an extended and excellent lunch in the air-conditioned grill room between matches, a necessary respite from the sun and stress of tournament play. By this time in the proceedings the flights are taking shape, the wagered money becoming either premonition or folly, and in the din you can hear an equal amount of encouragement and gamesmanship. But not everyone is in the grill room. Mirroring the world writ large, there are the haves and the have-nots. If you are in the grill room, you have your game.

The have-nots are on the range all during lunch. They have been scraping it around all morning, and they are disgusted with themselves and wearing their partners out. With each mishit range ball, they run through their infinite scroll of swing thoughts and feels. How is it possible that what worked twenty-four hours ago does not work now? How could you go from clarity to static so fast? You're the same person, in the same body, playing the same game!

You have joined the castaways on the range. It is time for you to contribute to this team. But you have not had the courage of your original conviction. Because your singular swing thought, take it back uncomfortably inside, has stopped working. Now you are searching. And while golfers hate having a two-way miss, that would be an improvement for you. You are up to a five-way miss and count-ing. After one last foul ball into the side netting that protects the first fairway from the range, you sigh profoundly and drop your head. You hate this game.

When you look up, your partner is there. He watches you hit one more shot, winces, and seems to make a decision, but one he had been wrestling with. You were pretty sure he was going to ask you to withdraw. You couldn't blame him. But instead, he takes a small leather pouch out of his golf bag. Then he removes a small piece of foil and unwraps it. Inside was a small candy. He hands it to you and tells you to hold it under your tongue. Now, it's not that your body is exactly a temple, but you do like to have some idea of what you're ingesting.

"It's a gummy, an edible. You need to relax, and this will help. Now do it, it takes a while to kick in and we tee off in a half an hour."

"Pards, I spend half my damn week trying to convince my son not to use cannabinoids."

"So pro tip, if you call them 'cannabinoids' he will continue to ignore you. Just do it."

"I . . . I mean, I have done the research on this stuff. It can cause anxiety and depression."

"Wow, okay, we're talking one edible so that we can win match five. You won't need rehab. And by the way, how would it be possible for you to be more anxious and depressed than you are right now?"

Okay, that was fair. You placed it under your tongue but as soon as your partner left, your impulse control gave way and you chewed the rest of it. Would that make it work faster? You started to text your son to get his opinion when it occurred to you that doing so was probably proof it was already working. You had just deleted that text when a text from your wife came in.

She started benignly, saying you must be thrilled to have such glorious weather on the day with the most golf, and she said to give your partner her love, and then she segued smoothly into telling you she was going to go into NYC with some friends to do some shopping and maybe check out the new Divinity in Mayan Art exhibit at the Met that everyone was talking about. (Really? Everyone?) She closed by saying she knew that you had the big day-two dinner (a dressy, semiformal affair that she used to attend before she got sick of the unrelenting golf zeitgeist) and would be home late. So she was going to grab an early dinner with the girls in Soho, and she would text you when she was on the way home.

The edible had to be working, because this all seemed perfectly fine with you. Plus now you were rid of the latent guilt you always felt being useless the evening of day two. You were having a hard enough time being a partner without having to worry about finding the energy when you got home to be, well, a partner!

You were never one of those guys who could drink while playing golf. The guys who found the sweet spot where they maintained their hand/eye coordination but lost their nerves. Nerves make the muscles tight. Tight muscles are slow muscles. You lose club speed, and on and around the greens, you lose feel. But you, you had no sweet spot. You were either sober and tense, or drunk, mawkishly sentimental, and unable to keep your balance even when only trying to negotiate the walk to the restroom.

But now that you thought about it, you felt pretty loose right now. You didn't feel any nerves. And the last few wedges had gone pretty much where you'd aimed them. You weren't sure if the gummy was working because you hadn't been high since college, but you could feel, and had now verified with your phone's selfie camera, that you were grinning for no apparent reason. You pulled the head cover off the driver and got back to the plan. One swing thought. Bring it back uncomfortably inside. And let it go. The satisfying sound of the middle of the driver face hitting the back of the ball gave you actual justification for your grin. And you headed for the cart. Let's do this.

Match Five

You're not sure if your partner gave you the gummy he would have taken or if he just was feeling a letdown after the morning drama, but he was off. At his swing speed it doesn't take much, a millisecond early or late, for the ball to end up in the deep rough. And from there, anything outside of 125 yards is almost impossible to get to the green. But whether it's the gummy talking or the fact that you're down the middle of the fairway and on in regulation each of the first three holes, you throw his divot back at him after a woefully short approach and say, "I got you pards, it's all good."

Ben Hogan famously said you should never hit a shot in competition that you haven't practiced, but (to your knowledge) he never took edibles. You opened a lob wedge, flat as a spatula, and out of the thick rough played it like a sand shot. It stopped inches from the hole. With your stroke it was a net birdie and a hole won. A hole later, on the fringe 60 feet from the hole, for the first time in your life, you used your 3 wood and chipped it in. Natural birdie. Hole won.

One of your opponents, a guy you play with often, said he hadn't seen you choose that shot before, and your partner whispered, "You are so freaking high! Love it!"

Is this what it is like to be a low handicapper? You had no fear. You saw the shot in your mind, addressed the ball, and hit it. Simple.

On the green, the hole looked bigger than it ever had before. And you didn't need to look at the putt from behind the hole and then again behind the ball. You got in your stance, looked at the hole, and trusted yourself to put whatever stroke was necessary to make the putt.

You closed your opponents (who, full disclosure, were not in contention) out in six holes. And you only used your partner's ball on one hole. On the other hand, you were starving! You had forgotten about how hungry cannabis makes you. But given the way the scoring worked, the last three holes were still important since you got one-tenth of a full point for each hole, and by the end of match seven, that could decide the tournament.

And because you are the epitome of a human who can't stand prosperity, on the seventh hole you threw it all away. It was a par 5 and now that the match was over and your partner was freewheeling again—he blasted his drive and hybrid and was on in two shots, putting for eagle and getting a shot. You were irrelevant, and it's just as well because you went at a flag you shouldn't have with your third shot and left it in the bunker. But who cared? Your score wasn't going to count. In fact, at the green you debated whether to even play your shot, decided against it in the interests of time and your gnawing hunger, and walked up on the green to cheer everyone on and pull the flag.

Then your opponent called your partner over for a ruling on whether he got relief from an area of the rough that he thought should be ground under repair. While they talked, you figured you might as well hit your sand shot after all. You grabbed a 56-degree out of the bag and hit a pretty pedestrian bunker shot, and yelled out to your partner to play well because you were picking up. Your partner two-putted for birdie and all was right in the world.

On the last hole, your partner also hit into a greenside bunker, and now the roles were reversed because you were on in regulation and getting a stroke. Your partner has always had a completion complex when it came to golf. He never takes an X or picks it up. He plays the hole out. ("You can do what you like, I'll play golf.") And now he was nonplussed because he couldn't find his sand wedge. He rummaged through his bag as you played the hole out.

Everyone shook hands, and your partner wanted to drive back over the last few holes and see if any of the groups behind you had picked up his wedge. No way he was playing any more golf without a sand wedge! That would be crazy! And even though you were done for the day and it was very likely someone would turn it in or the maintenance people would find it before the morning match, you totally understood that he wanted it now. You'd feel the same way. So you put your putter in your bag, tried to quell your rumbling stomach, and prepared to backtrack, when you saw his wedge in your bag. He obviously put it in there by accident. Happens all the time. Problem solved! Now let's eat!

You practically strutted to the scorer's table to turn in your score. You mentioned as casually as you could that you played awesome, and the pro nodded but was too busy entering scores to give you the love you craved. He posted your 1.3 victory, and you scanned the flight to see what that did, and . . . Wait, the leaders got beat in their last match? Did that mean . . . ? Holy crap, it did! You were in the frigging lead of the A flight going into the last day! Was this real?

It was, but only for a moment. Your partner motioned you over. He had the same look your father had when you were eleven and he came back from the vet's office without your collie and said he had to speak to you. That dog was your best friend. Your partner asked you if you used his sand wedge for the shot you hit in the bunker on the par 5.

"Uh . . . oh! Yeah, I guess I did. That's why it was in my bag. Sorry, did I hit a rock and nick it?"

"It's against the rules. We're disqualified for the match. I gotta tell the pro."

"*What*? Wait, no, that's insane. We didn't even use my score that hole! What difference does it make? We crushed them. We're not disqualifying ourselves."

"Pards, that's the rule."

"It's an idiotic rule. The outcome was not affected. Look, no one else knows. We keep it to ourselves. I was lights out that match!"

"Sorry."

And then he turned and went over to the scorer's table and spoke to the head pro. Surely the head pro would tell him this was no big deal. This is a club championship, not the PGA tour. Maybe just admonish us to be more careful next time.

Now they were shaking hands. That's a good sign, right?

And then the head pro went over to the leaderboard, erased your score, and reentered it as a loss. Instead of leading the A flight from the back tees, you were now third. And your edible-aided performance meant nothing.

What had just happened? This was ridiculous. Your partner was being a sanctimonious simp! You were enraged, and it didn't help that your high was now completely gone.

He slapped you on the shoulder and his voice was playful, but he couldn't look you in the eye. And you noticed, because you were full-on glaring.

"Pards, let it go, we're still in this thing."

"I can't believe you. Seriously."

"How could you live with yourself if we buried that?"

"Oh my god, you are so unmarried. I could easily have buried it, it's an essential part of my survival kit."

"Not me . . . I'm going to shower up and go eat this fancy dinner we've already paid for. If you're going to sulk, go home."

Oh no, he wasn't getting off that easily. You were going to sulk and stay for dinner. You were going to remind him incessantly how he threw away your chance of winning, and you were going to get others on your side. You were going to spend the night proving to him that no one else in the damn club would have done anything so self-righteous and stupid. You hadn't even used your score that hole! Jesus!

You sat in the sauna and had two thoughts. First, you needed to forgive your partner. And second, you needed to find a reliable source of edibles for the rest of the golf season. You briefly thought asking your son might be both an expedient solution and a bonding opportunity.

By the time you entered the dining room for happy hour, you realized you were not a big enough person to let this go. You needed to vent and show your partner the folly of his superciliousness. But you never got the chance.

While you were waiting for a drink, two guys who normally never gave you the time of day came over and said they heard about the DQ, and they just wanted to shake your hand. They said what you did was exactly why golf was a game of honor and integrity. You told them that it was your partner's idea and that you deserved zero credit and in fact tried to talk him out of it. They moved on.

A few minutes later, the club champion came over and patted you on the shoulder and said he heard about the DQ and it was a beautiful thing. He had already told his kids about it and said it was an excellent example of why self-policing is what makes golf unique. He was actually kind of emotional, and you found yourself saying, "Well, you know, much as I want to win, had to do what's right, you know?" He nodded and offered to buy you a drink despite the full glass in your hand.

Before dinner was served, the tournament chairman asked for everyone's attention and announced that "a remarkable show of sportsmanship happened in the last match of the A flight this afternoon." After his explanation, applause broke out and everyone stood. Your partner stared at you in disbelief as you raised your hand and waved everyone off, like it was no big deal and something you do every day.

By the end of the night, you were intoxicated by both alcohol and attention, and more than once found yourself saying to your new fans, "Well, I said, 'Dude, we have to DQ,' and he fought me on it hard, because, you know, could very well cost us the tournament, but I was like, 'Hey, it's what we do when no one is looking that defines us, you know?' And it took a while, but I got him on board, but hey, anyone in this room would have done the same thing, am I right? That's golf."

As you were making your way to your car to go home, you heard your partner yell your name. You thought for sure he was angry about you taking credit for his honesty and was about to give you the dressing down you deserved for your shamelessness. But nope, he was too good a guy for that. He saw that you were unsteady, took your keys out of your hand, and said he would drive you home and pick you up in time for the matches tomorrow morning.

On the way home, you realized you hadn't checked your phone during the entire dinner. Your wife was probably out of her mind. But no, there were no texts from her or your kids. The house was dark when your partner pulled into your driveway. He told you he'd be here at seven a.m. sharp. You nodded.

"Hey, what you did today . . . was cool. I'm sorry I didn't see it at first. I'm a moron. We good?"

"All good. Just keep your hands off my sand wedge."

"It was a waste of a perfectly good edible though."

"No worries. Your son's my dealer, I'll get more."

It's too early for the kids to be home on a Saturday night, but where is your wife? Oh, right! NYC! The Divinity in Mayan Art exhibit that everyone is talking about but that you have never heard of. Her last text said she would tell you when she was driving home after dinner in Soho. It's nearly 10:30. You send her a "what's up" text with an accompanying GIF of a confused gorilla, and then you wait. Nothing. You do your stretches, pummel your golf muscles with your Theragun, and wait some more.

You should just go to sleep. Day three tomorrow. You have two remaining matches. You have to win them both to have any chance. In the penultimate match, you play the team currently in second, and your last match is against the two-time defending champs, who are ahead but not by much. Everything would have to go right for you to win. Damn sand wedge.

Your phone chirps. Your wife normally always responds to a GIF with a clever and funnier GIF of her own. But not this time. She says dinner ran late and they decided to stay over. She'll get a fresh start in the morning and be home in time to meet the landscaping guy to get an estimate. She signs off with a quick goodnight and wishes you luck in the morning. She doesn't end with her standard, "love u."

You don't know who "they" are. You don't know who she's with and you don't know where she's staying. But then again, you don't know anything about a landscaping estimate. You'll feel better if you just hear her voice. You call her and the call goes to voicemail, even though she sent that text three minutes ago. You're about to text back something cryptic and nasty, but you talk yourself out of it. That never ends well.

You lay in bed for about ninety seconds before you grab your phone and pull up Google. There is a Divinity in Mayan Art exhibit. So there's that. As with your golf game, a flicker of hope is all you need to get you through. You feel yourself falling under.

CHAPTER SEVENTEEN

Day Three

Match Six

So you know you're supposed to beware the injured athlete. Does that apply to hungover middle-aged golfers? You and your partner were a little hungover— nothing coffee and Advil® couldn't fix—but your opponents on the first tee legitimately looked like hell. Their eyes were swollen. Their skin ashen. They said they were at the club until midnight and then had decided it would be hilarious to go to a dance club and freak out the Gen Z clientele. When you asked if it had been, in fact, hilarious, they really couldn't remember. It was a blur. One of them paused midsentence and hustled over and threw up in a bush.

They barely managed to get their tee shots airborne and announced that if you really wanted to win the flight, they were okay with saying you beat them 5 up and letting them go home and sleep. When you got to your cart, your partner was having none of it.

"Listen, ignore them. They're playing us. Sid is a 5 handicap and he's going to joke and moan and cry and shoot one under. I know we can smell the alcohol on them from here, but they are faking it."

Uh . . . no. No, they weren't. That may have been their intention. And it may have worked in past years, when they were a little younger. But whether it was the mixing of liquor, their embarrassing turns around dance floors populated by people their kid's age, or the rolling in at three a.m., they were a mess.

By the second hole, they abandoned practice swings in an effort to conserve energy. They had zero feel on the greens and left putts 10 feet short or gunned them by the hole. They didn't make a par until the fourth hole. They were so bad your partner started hitting his 4 iron off of every tee. As long as one of you had a ball in play, you were going to win the hole.

At the snack shack off of the third green, Sid was in the restroom for such a long time the three of you had a discussion as to when it was appropriate to check on him. He came out, bought a beer he proceeded to chug, and did finally wake up. He made a birdie coming in and pretty much carried his partner, who pulled down his bucket hat in between shots and appeared to be napping in the cart.

But it was too late for them. You closed them out 3 and 2.

You would later hear that they won their next match 4 and 3, and Sid, by then no doubt several beers in, shot 33. So you do have to be wary of the hungover golfer, but not if you get them early!

You've so seldom been in contention on the last match of the last day of the Major Member-Member that when you and your partner walked toward the scorer's table to post your results, and there was a congregation of players standing at the board, staring at you as you approached. You had the horrific thought that something happened to your wife on her way home, and they had gathered to deliver the news.

"Here they are, the Karma Kids! Did you win? Of course you did! The karma continues! Check this out!"

The club champs had pushed their match. And the team in second place got beat handily. You were tied for first place going into your last match.

The narrative was cast. Because of your show of honor the day before, the golf gods were sending you love. And now, as destiny would have it, you and the club champs were playing each other to decide it all.

Side betting began in earnest. Would you gamble with your head and take the club champs, whose best player held the course record, or would you gamble with your heart and take the Karma Kids?

It would be another forty minutes before the match. Your partner asked you if you were going to hit balls, and you said no. You went into the locker room and checked your phone. No messages. It was nearly eleven. You knew better than to take a direct, accusatory approach. So you went obliquely. You got on the family group text, made no mention of your wife, and asked the kids how they were doing. You made a joke about their grandmother's latest mortifying Facebook post and told them you loved them. Surely this would trigger a response from their MIA mother. But five minutes later, still nothing.

Your partner walked in, looked around to see if there was anyone who might overhear, and then stood in front of you. He opened his fist and showed you the edible. He pronounced that it was "now or never."

"Okay, Morpheus, settle down. I'm not taking that. I'm not nervous."

"You know, you don't look nervous. You actually look sad. You alright?"

"Yeah, I'm good."

"Well, I'm nervous. Let's go win this goddamn thing."

And with that, he swallowed the gummy.

Final Match

You had never played with Jason, the perennial club champ. Why would he want to play with you? You had seen him on the range, of course, and marveled at the crispness of his irons, the way his 3 wood would soar in a tight draw over the 275 yard sign and roll to the edge of the netting. (He was too long to hit driver on the range; he would have pelted the houses situated behind it.) His scorecard commemorating the course record 62 he shot two years ago hangs above the bar in the grill room.

But everything you needed to know about Jason you learned when your group was called to the tee for the final, decisive match. At your club—a hold-over from bygone days that no one has corrected—if you are a doctor, they call you to the tee by announcing, "On the first tee please, Dr. Joyce." This annoys much of the new money at the club. The tech guys and ESPN executives think it's a joke—they could buy these guys three times over—but no one cares enough to do anything about it. Jason, whom you know to be a doctor of some sort, was called to the tee only by his name. Your partner has played with him and says he never lets them refer to him as Dr. Joyce.

When your group shook hands on the first tee, Jason was warm and friendly, and went out of his way to chat you up. At one level, you weren't surprised. It's long been your experience that every CEO you ever met, every person you sat next to when lucky enough to be upgraded to first class, and the biggest, fittest people in the gym, were all also the nicest and most welcoming. They had nothing to prove and wanted nothing from you, other than for you to have what they have, if that's what you wanted. When Jason set his tee down and said the exact same thing everyone says just before the match starts, "Let's have fun, boys," you could tell he really meant it. Your partner told you he was a pediatric surgeon. That seemed to fit. You could see him setting kids and their parents at their ease.

He was also a stone-cold killer.

On the first hole, with your partner in tight for par, from a "fried egg" lie in the bunker, he nearly holed out. Push. On the second hole, his partner, also a scratch player, was on the fringe in two and skulled his chip over the green. Jason said, "I got you, pards," and drained a 12-footer for the half. The key in match play is to win the holes when you have strokes, and you and your partner did your part. He made net birdie on four, and your one-swing-thought mantra was still working. You made a par/net birdie on five, but each time Jason pushed the holes with putts that never looked like they were going anywhere else but the middle of the cup. Stone-cold killer!

On the sixth hole, Jason got ridiculous. They had the tees up on the par 4. It was only playing 320 yards, but it's all carry over water. You and your partner were safely in the fairway, with both of you getting a stroke, when Jason's partner came in steep and popped it up. Splash. With the match tied and only a few holes left, Jason put the driving iron he always used on this hole back in his bag and pulled out his driver.

Jason draws every tee shot. Everyone knows that. Even if by some miracle he could drive the green, his draw spin would send it over the back and out of play. But he opened his stance, weakened his left-hand grip, and made a fierce lash with a helicopter finish to hold the clubface open. The ball reached its apex, impossibly high, before starting its buttercup fade toward the flag. It stopped 8 feet from the hole. Holy crap!

Your partner asked Jason if he wanted to try that again or just play that one, and everyone laughed. Completely intimidated, you thinned your approach over the green, wasting your stroke. But your partner is made of sterner stuff. He stuffed a wedge to gimmie distance, and Jason finally blinked. He missed the eagle putt. You were one up! You had your own stone-cold assassin!

As affable as Jason was, as garrulous as the group had been for most of the match, everyone knew what was at stake, and things grew quiet. Each team kept more to themselves. You could feel everyone focus. On the seventh tee, your partner took your cell phone and put it in his bag. There were no strokes on seven and everyone made par. No blood.

Still one up.

Number 8 was a long, uphill par 3 that always played into a breeze, the toughest of the par 3s on the course. Right was fescue, left was OB. There was a false front that repelled everything that came up short. When you pulled up and saw where the black tees were, your stomach dropped. From that far back, the hole was playing 241 yards. Yesterday it was 218 and you were short with a 3 wood you hit pretty well. You had no chance.

Your partner went first, and his 3 iron got eaten up by the wind. He was way short.

It was silly for you to even play the hole. You weren't getting a stroke. You accepted your fate and pulled the 3 wood but your partner shook his head and tapped the driver head cover. Hitting a driver on a par 3? The ultimate humiliation. Further proof you didn't belong. But you knew he was right. And who cared at this point how it looked!

Your partner walked up to the tee with you and told you to tee it down and hit that low, tumbling draw of yours. And you did! The ball landed thirty yards short and rolled onto the green, coming to rest 25 feet from the hole.

Instead of the ridicule you expected, Jason the stone-cold assassin said, **"That's the best shot I've seen in this tournament. Super smart play."**

You seriously thought about adopting a baby so you could one day send it to Jason for surgery. That's how grateful you were for his comment.

Jason's partner hit a great shot but overcooked the hook spin and ended up pin high in the first cut of rough. Doable, but no easy chip. Jason was clearly in-between clubs. For the first time in the match, he walked up to the tee with two clubs. He chose one, took a practice swing, thought better of it, and chose the other. His shot was a mirror image of his partner's. He shook his head.

"Just trying to give you the line, pards!"

In your weekly casual games, anyone off the green "brings it up," meaning they chip onto the green even if they're not away. So after your partner pitched to 6 feet, you motioned for them to go ahead and play, but Jason grimaced. He thought you were away, and in match play, the person who is away goes first. Your partner wasn't sure, and so they both walked the distance off and compared notes. Turns out they were away.

You could feel your heart pounding. It would be just like you to actually faint before hitting your putt. You were already infamous in the club for being brought away in an ambulance for your back injury last season—what if they had to call the EMTs again after you suffered heart failure? There'd be no living it down. Assuming you lived.

Jason was away, but he let his partner go first so that the better player could see the line. He read the break but left it woefully short. Eight feet. The stone-cold assassin took advantage and chipped to two and a half feet. He was above the hole, but this is Jason we're talking about here. He had been so gracious and kind to you. He probably wasn't going to miss, right? Something came over you. You were in the moment.

You smiled and said, "Pick it up, Jason. I'm not making the club champ putt that."

"You sure?"

"Hey, I gotta live with myself. That's hard enough with the life choices I've made without making you putt that."

Jason shrugged his shoulders and picked his ball up as fast as he could. You walked the 25 feet to your ball and your partner followed you. He leaned in and whispered.

"What are you doing? You don't have a stroke. He had a downhill slider for three. He could miss that! Are you insane?"

"We'll make three. If you don't make yours, I'll two-putt. I was trying to do the right thing."

Your partner rolled his eyes and went to his putt. He may have been too angry, or he may have misjudged the speed, but he hit it right through the break. He was in with four. Now you have to two-putt or you go to the ninth hole tied. There are no strokes on 9 so they have a huge advantage. Normally your partner would help you read the putt, but he stood off to the side and glared. And he was right. You screwed up. In your pathetic mind, you were still more worried about being liked and accepted than you were about the very real opportunity you had to win the tournament. You promised your wife you would quit golf—hell, you promised yourself you would quit golf. And you should have. Because here you are. Completely in over your head.

You have been a member for sixteen years. Not for nothing, but you don't know why you're taking so much time over this putt. They always have the flag where it is on Sunday. You know it breaks right-to-left then straightens out at the end. You've had this putt more times than you can count.

They say when you have to two-putt, you should try to get the putt within a 3-foot circle. Imagine a hula hoop around the hole. But that's never worked for you. It just feels like trying not to make it. You putt best from long distance when you simply try to drain the putt. So just do that and get this over with. Maybe your partner will stop seething and will birdie the next hole. (It's golf! You never know!)

Fifteen feet away, you knew you had hit it on your intended line. Ten feet away, you knew the speed was pretty good. Five feet away, you thought you had a chance. Two feet away, you saw your partner leaning backward as if he were in a limbo contest. One foot away, you heard him scream and saw Jason put his hands behind his head and his partner drop the putter he held in his hand. You didn't get to hear the sweetest sound of all, the tinny plop of the ball dropping into the hole, but you saw it disappear. It took a moment for you to realize what had happened. You made a birdie on Number 8! From the black tees! That's 241 yards! With a driver!

Wait, what now? Jason is taking off his cap and shaking your partner's hand. That's right it's coming back to you now . . . You won the hole, so you're two up with one to play. The match is over. No, the three-day Major Member-Member is over. And you're the champs!

The stone-cold assassin gave you a hug, handed you your ball and then, in a gesture that may have meant more to you than anything else that transpired during the long weekend, said, "Hey, that was fun. We have a group that tees off around eight every Saturday; we'd love to have you play with us."

Your partner waited until you were in the cart and then reminded you that you had no right conceding Jason's putt. And then he pulled your cap down over your eyes and hugged you like your mother used to when you came home for holiday break in college.

At the scorer's tent, a few dozen players, all with their parimutuel bets on the line, waited for you to pull up. Your partner coolly informed the head pro you had won 2 and 1. You got a round of applause and, to be fair, you saw a few people shake their head in disbelief. Really? You guys beat Jason?

The head pro raised his bottle of Smartwater, circled your score in red Sharpie on the leaderboard, and made a toast. "The Karma Kids are the Major Member-Member Champs!"

CHAPTER EIGHTEEN

You Have to
Protect the Field

Some people want to save whales or pandas. Your wife's mission is to save bookstores. ("Booksellers," she corrects you.) As you drove home from your Major Member-Member triumph, you remembered your trip a few months ago to the turn-of-the-century bookstore on the shoreline. The converted home, on the historical preservation registry, was built in 1689. Unlike the wide-open spaces of a Barnes & Noble, it had rooms and nooks and crannies, all lined with floor-to-ceiling bookshelves. To get a book from the top shelf, they supplied a wrought iron ladder that ran diagonally across the shelves. Your wife loved that. And there were bay windows covered by cushions where you could sit and read. You told your wife you were surprised at their branding strategy, since they sold no merch by the checkout counter. No coffee mugs or calendars, not even bookmarks. "Exactly," she beamed.

You were there to hear an author read from his latest mystery novel. This place still had authors come in and read to a live group that sipped tea or bottled water. Afterward, the author hung around to sign books and answer questions. You wanted to ask whether he knew he could sell more books if he had a YouTube channel, but everyone was in a trance of quaintness. You don't remember anything else, but you remember his response to a woman who asked him what it was like when he published his first book and saw it in a bookstore. Was it magic?

"No . . . no, it was horrible. All I could think, looking around at all the shelves, was that the last thing the world needed was one more book. I felt like I had wasted three years of my life."

People laughed, but you could tell he was not just being self-deprecating. He meant it.

As you walked into your house that night after winning the Major Member-Member, you really, really felt him. Your kids and your wife not only had no interest in golf, but they were used to you coming home from these tournaments and pouting. You created that construct, and now they were respecting it. No one asked you how it went, and you were good with that. You didn't want to discuss it.

Before you left the course, after the ball kid had cleaned your club and you got your last couple of touched knuckles and well-wishes, the guy that ran the flights and the betting handed you an envelope. The flight winnings. You had completely forgotten it was winner take all. And then he handed you a second envelope. That's right! The parimutuel betting! You counted the total in both envelopes. It came to $2,200! As if that wasn't crazy enough, he told you that this was your share and that he had already given your partner his winnings. And yet you had absolutely zero interest in bragging about your foray into professional golf and unveiling your roll of hundreds to your family. It wasn't just that you knew they wouldn't care. **You** didn't care.

All you cared about was your wife, and what, if anything, your stupid obsession with the tournament had or hadn't cost you. She seemed exhausted. And why not, she was out late in NYC and drove home this morning. Like you, she's not getting any younger. She's allowed to be tired.

You walked by the laundry room and saw that she was emptying her overnight bag of clothes and doing a load of laundry already. Why? Was there some scent or stain that would expose her? And if they'd really decided to spend the night all spur of the moment, why had she even taken an overnight bag and so many clothes?

Okay, you are an insane person. This is not about her completely innocent decision to pack a bag in case they stayed over. Your wife is a planner, you know that. This is about your pattern of neglect over a long period of time. This is about your fear that she has had enough with you, that she has accepted you cannot change, and she has begun to move on. Quitting golf was a test, and you, my friend, have failed it miserably.

Later, after you both listen to your daughter go off on a well-worn tirade about how her friend Rebecca is so disrespectful and clueless she is seriously considering blocking her this time (she won't), you are left alone together.

You ask your wife if she wants to watch a movie.

Not up for it.

You ask her how NYC was.

She says fine.

It takes all of your willpower, but you do not ask why a woman who always texts back immediately no matter the day or time was radio silent during much of her trip. You do not ask, "Alright, who is he?" like a lunatic. You nod.

She says she is going up to bed, and definitely not in the "wanna fool around" version of that statement. She reminds you that she made the salmon salad you like with the artichokes if you're still hungry, and pathetically, you see that as a sign she still loves you and it's not too late.

Upstairs an hour later, on your way to the bathroom, she is reading a book but appears to have just been crying. You ask what's up and she says the Amy Bloom memoir about her husband's dementia has gutted her. She says that losing her mind is the biggest fear she has at this point in her life. And, while on one level it makes perfect sense and some other random night in your long life together the thought wouldn't have registered, now the fact that you play no role in her biggest fear of loss has also gutted you.

"Oh," she says offhandedly, "How'd you guys end up doing? Sounded like it was going pretty good for a while."

"Uh huh . . . yeah . . . we won."

"You won what?"

"The . . . you know, the whole thing. We won the Member-Member. I'm going to go down and turn off the lights and set the alarm."

"Wait, you won the whole tournament? For the first time ever? In the A flight?"

"Yep."

"Why are you not freaking out? Or did you freak out so much earlier you're spent?"

"I didn't freak out. Then or now."

"Well, I mean, tell me about it. That's amazing!"

"Nothing to tell. It's just golf."

"Okay, who are you? You are clearly a deep fake of my husband."

"Tell me about NYC."

"Nothing to tell, just a trip to the city."

In tournament play, you make the other people in your group play by the rules because it's the only way "to protect the field." If you see a rules violation, you have to call it, even though it is often uncomfortable. But as you walked out of the bedroom and headed downstairs to close up for the night, you thought of Tim. Nicest human at the club, and a guy who can't stop coming over the top. He was playing awfully one round in last year's club qualifier and had just semi-shanked a ball into the trees. As you walked by him, he waved you over. He asked you for a ruling: was his ball OB? If it was, he would have to make the walk of shame back to the tee, would probably hit the ball in the exact same place. He looked so forlorn and tired of his own ineptitude. You looked down, and the ball was clearly out. You bent down and then pretended to pace a straight line to the white stake behind his ball. You gave him a thumbs up and walked to the green. Tim's playing partner asked you if he was still in play, and you told him he was, because you didn't have the courage to say to him what you were thinking, just as you don't have the courage to say the very same words to your wife: **"It's just easier not knowing."**

But how much longer will you be able to go on like this? At some point, you are going to have to choose to protect your field.

CHAPTER NINETEEN

Welcome to Your Intervention

You have never had make up sex with your wife. You've had made up sex, but that is only slightly less rare than make up sex, with has happened never.

Because neither of you are the type. You don't scream at each other when you're angry. When you watch movies where a couple, mid-fight, invades each other's personal space and spit flies and veins pop and they say horrifyingly mean things to each other, and then resolve the situation by clutching each other in a passionate embrace and tear just enough of their clothes off to have sex on the dining room table, you think, How is that possible?

You brood. Your wife putters aimlessly. Neither of you look at each other. You are unfailingly polite. She finds excuses to run errands that could easily wait. No matter what minor question one of your kids pose, you shrug and say, "It's up to your mom." (They could ask you if it would be okay for them to mainline fentanyl with a dirty needle and your response would be the same: "If it's okay with your mom.") If you come into the family room and turn on the TV, she will grab a book. If you walk in with a book, she will turn on the TV. She has very few hard and fast domestic rules, but one of them is to put your dirty dishes in the dishwasher, and during your silent battle, you eat when you're not hungry just so you can leave some dishes in the sink.

It is exhausting. It is childish. And you both do it. Like clockwork. Your normal running time for a medium-level argument is a week. If it runs into the weekend, someone usually apologizes. Usually you. Not because you feel you were wrong. She just has more silent treatment stamina than you. When your intern at work asked you what the key to a successful marriage is, you said, "One of you has to be emotionally aerobic, the other anaerobic, otherwise it becomes unbearable." He stared at you.

The week after the Major Member-Member and NYC was different. It wasn't a fight. You didn't brood. She didn't putter around the house. The kids ran interference, because they were never without drama, so it wasn't a sullen or fraught household energy. There really was no rancor. It was something new. Something far worse. It was apathy.

In all of your previous conflicts, love was withheld until one of you got with the program. But you couldn't withhold what you no longer felt.

Your company, due to your seniority, lets you work from home whenever you want, although they'd prefer you come in a couple of times a week to promote a collaborative environment. You went in every day that week. And your wife not only didn't ask you why you did so, you could tell she was waiting for you to leave so she could lighten up. You stayed at the office later than you normally do, because home had gotten too sad, and the irony is when you came in, she gave you that look. She assumed you ducked out early and played nine holes or at least hit balls. And why wouldn't she? That is what you did for so, so long. You brought this on yourself, buddy. Choices have consequences.

On your Friday night commute home, dreading the evening and the high probability of more passive punishment, you got your first text from her all week. It was direct. She needed you to come straight home and not stop at the club. You wanted to tell her that you were coming home, that you wanted to come home, that you had no intention of stopping to practice or play. But what was the point? And if you were going to say it, text was an inadequate delivery channel. So instead, you texted back, "Gotcha," and wondered what you were about to face.

Another laundry list of your failings? Were you going to be called out for your return to golf as your apparent reason for living? Or maybe not. Maybe you were selling her short. Maybe she was going to apologize for her puerile response to a tournament she in fact encouraged you to play in. Or no, wait! Maybe something had happened in NYC and you were about to hear a confession. If that's the case, what will you do? Are you capable of that level of forgiveness? And why assume she is even seeking forgiveness? Maybe it's not a one-off, and she's not sorry. Maybe she will deliver news, devoid of emotion, that will change your life. Maybe you have been that blind.

As you pulled into your cul de sac, your anxiety morphed into confusion. You are a car guy. Years, makes, models, you know them all and you're the go-to guy in your circle. "That's a Genesis, it's the luxury brand of Hyundai, *Car and Driver* gave it a great review in the sport SUV class." You know what all your friends drive and how much their cars cost. So when you saw your boss's Escalade in your driveway, your aunt's Prius behind it, your Member-Member Partner's Jaguar, the in-laws' Cherokee in the road—and is that your friend from Vermont's Mini Cooper? It is. Who else still has the "my kid is an honor student" bumper sticker plastered on their car a decade after the kids have graduated?

What was going on here? You pulled over 200 feet from the house. Maybe you should text your partner and find out what you're walking into here.

And then it came to you. Vivid. Like it just happened yesterday. It was actually over a year ago now. You were having a weekend gathering at your house. You were supposed to meet a guy at Taylor Rental and pick up chairs, some tables, and a tent in case it rained. Your wife had set the appointment. You had called to see what time they were open until and told your wife you were going to get the gear, but instead went to the club to play, thinking you had plenty of time. You got to the rental center five minutes too late, or (you will always believe this version of events) they closed early, but either way, you came home empty-handed. You wife, justifiably apoplectic, had said you were an "addict." There is history of substance abuse in your family, and this was the proverbial bridge too far. You told her in no uncertain terms that one cannot be clinically addicted to a game and that she was being ridiculous, to say nothing of how insulting what she said was to people who fight actual addiction every day. But she wasn't having it. She had punched her phone screen as she yelled, "Really? Really?" And she had pointed the phone like a Taser® at you as she read.

" . . . when recurrent use causes significant impairment in judgment!

" . . . when you continue the behavior despite negative consequences!

" . . . when you hide or downplay the behavior from your loved ones!

" . . . when your life has become unmanageable!

"That doesn't sound familiar? Well, let me tell you, as someone who is about to be embarrassed because her guests will have no place to sit or anything to eat, *my* life has become unmanageable because you are a golf *addict*!"

So, this was an intervention.

Like any human, your fight-or-flight instinct was, to use your son's favorite online chat acronym, being triggered HAM. The fight option was your first choice. Your partner and boss and father-in-law are in on this? They play more golf than you do! Who are these people to judge you? This isn't a damn democracy where your value judgments about how you spend your time are put to a vote! You wanted to confront their hypocrisy head-on and then throw them out of your house. And they can take their ringleader, your wife, and the kids too if they're in on this, along with them!

Then your flight instinct stepped in to rebut. Turn your car around and get out. Text your wife that you know what she's up to and you will not indulge her little Lifetime movie fantasy. Then invite her to a neutral site where you can discuss this calmly, as you have always been able to. You know she had good intentions, you're not mad, but you are absolutely not an addict, and you can make a go-forward plan together. You will even suggest an objective third party, a marriage counselor of her choosing, to help you learn better communication and coping skills. But you will not leave that neutral site without making it clear the counseling sessions will also include a goddamn minute-by-minute recounting of her NYC trip!

But whether it was guilt, or exhaustion, or your lifelong tendency to go to any lengths to not disappoint people, you found yourself walking to the door.

You will take the heat. You will listen. You will not get defensive or angry. Unless someone suggests they have a bed for you somewhere and they have thoughtfully packed your essentials. Is there even such a thing as a golf rehab center? (If not, the thought races through your mind, you may have finally found the start-up idea that you can go to the private equity people in your company with and begin your ascent to mogul-ness.) Okay, you're ready. Open the door and take your medicine.

You understood the assembled probably didn't have much more experience with interventions than you did, but they all seemed way too happy when you walked in. They yelled, "Surprise!" which also seemed inappropriate, and some of them had pointy paper hats on. Your wife hugged you, and the commotion freaked out your psycho dog, who popped one of the balloons that lined the doorway to your family room, and everyone laughed. A huge cake was on the dining room table and the number 48 was suspended from the chandelier above it.

"Happy birthday, honey!"

"But it's not my birthday for like three weeks!"

"Hence the surprise element! Plus your birthday falls on a holiday this year."

"And none of us would have shown up. We're not kidding!"

More ruthless teasing ensued. Gag gifts were opened. Some thoughtful ones too. Your mom made the kind of speech she lived for, codifying her image as a badass by wondering how someone as young as her could have a forty-eight-year-old child and where was it written that parents are supposed to die before their children. People mingled, mostly in the kitchen, ate and drank, and in what felt like moments but was actually hours later, you and your wife were cleaning up. She made it easy by serving everything with paper plates and plastic utensils. When you came back from taking the trash bags to the garbage cans in the garage, she was putting the leash on the psycho dog. You followed her out, and you both stood there silently while you waited for the dog to do his business.

You take your wife's hand. "I wanted to send everyone home. I mean, I was glad they came, and it was great, but I just wanted to send them home so we could have sex."

"On a Friday?"

"So I was thinking, we should take up pickleball. We can get lessons, join a league. I mean, everyone is doing it."

"What? I'm a tennis player. We don't play pickleball. I can still run, thank you very much! Pickleball . . . Jesus."

"Okay, not pickleball then, something else. You pick. Something we can join together."

"Like what?"

"I dunno. We could join a cult. I don't care, I prefer something non-Satanic, but I'm open. Just something we can start together."

"What is going on with you? Why have you been so weird lately?"

"So, when I pulled up tonight and saw the cars, there was this brief moment where I thought you had staged an intervention . . . like a golf intervention."

"Is that even a thing?"

"I don't think so."

"Okay, well it wasn't, it was a birthday party, because you are loved."

"Right. But if it was an intervention, if there was that level of concern . . . I mean, they don't work, they never work . . . until the addict has bottomed out, right? I mean, that's what they always say, right? No one can help the addict until the addict wants help, until the addict has finally lost something so precious that they hit rock bottom and choose to get better."

"Yes, I suppose that is what they say, but it wasn't an intervention. That's in your head. I wouldn't do that to you, not in that way."

"Okay, but if it was, and if you would . . . I just need you to know . . . "

"What? What, baby?"

"I've bottomed out."

CHAPTER TWENTY

Burn the Boats

Are you ready to quit golf this time? Really ready?

Then burn the boats.

You first heard the phrase from your CEO, who fancied himself a cross between Tony Robbins and Colin Powell. He kept trying to make the insurance business analogous to war, and no annual meeting was complete without him wearing out Sun Tzu quotes. But you had to admit, the "burn the boats" reference did make sense to you, the idea that the way an army could be assured of victory was to burn the boats they'd sailed in on and destroy the bridges behind them. Soldiers without options were more likely to meet their objectives.

It turns out ol' Sun Tzu probably plagiarized the idea from Alexander the Great, who, seven hundred years earlier, had his men burn their boats upon their arrival in Persia, where they were greatly outnumbered. If what you are doing is not irrevocable, you're not committed. And the Macedonians did in fact win!

But while it's not clear who really came up with the idea and who was plagiarizing whom, since the use of writing three thousand years ago was not widespread, Homer's *Odyssey* not only gives us the best example of burning the boats, it illustrates the real beauty of the concept: when you burn the boats you are forced to innovate!

The Sirens of Greek mythology were fetching ladies, their songs so alluring boats would crash into the reefs and sailors would perish. Everyone knew this, and when Odysseus was returning to Aeaea for Elpinor's funeral rites, there was no way through except to sail directly by the sirens. (Long before Marvel, Homer knew how to challenge a hero to make for a good story.) Odysseus, being a disrupter and a bit of a prima donna, decided he wanted to hear the sirens, but it would also be nice to live through it. What to do?

With only one way forward, he was forced to innovate. So the sailors stopped their ears with beeswax—all but our boy Odysseus, that is, who instructed his men to tie him to the mast and not to untie him no matter how much he begged. And while he was nearly driven mad by the song of the sirens, he and the crew survived.

Homer, Sun Tzu, and Alexander the Great all understood how hard it is for mankind to resist something appealing. Something that feeds a part of you while simultaneously eviscerating the whole of you.

Your father never went to college. You're sure he never read Homer or *The Art of War* or Greek history. You're pretty sure he never saw Tony Robbins. But you sure remember his advice when you asked him, when you were wobbling about whether to get engaged to your now wife or whether you should just keep dating and "see what happens." He asked you if you were committed to her or involved with her. You said you didn't get the difference. He shrugged and said, "If you look at a plate of ham and eggs, the chicken is involved, the pig is committed."

He might as well have said, "Burn the boats!" *But how to do it?*

- **Step one: sell your golf clubs.** Your wife recommended Facebook Marketplace as the fastest way to dispose of your clubs. But you soon got lost in a dizzying array of tap instructions: tap "Sell," tap "Items," tap "Add photos/video," tap "List in more places." You tapped out, and then inspiration hit. You would have an old-school yard sale!

- Saturday mornings used to be the universal yard sale day. There was a whole sub-cult of yard sale aficionados who saw every Saturday as a treasure hunt. And while it usually ended with a piece of junk or two in a basement, every Saturday held the unspoken promise of a lost Jackson Pollock painting or a first edition Melville that the sucker selling it was too dumb to know he was giving away.

- The sheer genius of your yard sale would be your recognition that the world of contemporary commerce belonged to the specialist, not the generalist. You had one item to sell, a set of practically new golf clubs. Then you would upsell them your golf bag, your golf shoes, training aids, boxes of tees, golf gloves, and the set of Speed Sticks that gave you tendonitis but no increase in MPH.

- You picked the date and informed your wife she needed to get her car out of the garage and not be home the following Saturday morning so you could stage the venue properly—you envisioned setting up your garage as a hitting bay—only for her to issue the latest in a long line of marital vetoes. No one did yard sales in your neighborhood! It would be mortifying! People would think you had run into financial trouble! And she didn't want strangers "traipsing" through *her* garage.

- The contradiction between her lauding you for selling the clubs and then impeding the sales process didn't seem to occur to her. In any marriage, you have to pick the battles big enough to matter, small enough to win. Was this worth it? Considering you were counting on her to actually make the signage required to attract customers, probably not.

  o Then you remembered Dwayne, the IT contractor your company brought in to work on the new HRIS initiative. A great guy. It's hard to assimilate into a culture when you know you only have a six-month assignment, but everyone loved Dwayne. When he told you he also played golf, you invited him to be your partner in a charity scramble event. He was a garden variety 19 handicapper, but he loved the game, which made you love him even more. But his clubs were atrocious. His irons were the OG Pings, handed down from his father, the grooves nearly nonexistent. His driver, the square-shaped Nike Sasquatch from the late '90s, was right out of the Smithsonian!

You never thought you'd see one again. His putter was a Zebra mallet, last used by Nick Price back in the damn day. Atrocious!

○ So you called Dwayne. Did he want your clubs? Yep, all of them. Nope, you don't want a dime. There is no catch, Dwayne. Well, one catch: you need to come get them right now. Before you lose your nerve.

- **Now you needed to delete your digital golf footprint!** For you that meant Golf Genius had to go. It was how you added your scores to maintain your handicap, how you scheduled tee times and kept score while playing. Even when you weren't playing in a tournament, you could track how your friends were doing. ("Whoa, Seth tripled 12 after shooting 37 on the front! That's soul crushing. I wonder if he pulled it into the heavy rough and never found the ball . . . Oh shoot, I'm supposed to be on a Teams call!")

- You also deleted Golf Now, since you were no longer going to be booking golf trips at iconic venues. And ShotTracer, since there would be no more golf trajectories or shot shapes to be assessed. Same with Imagine Golf, which was supposed to help you with the mental aspect of your game, but while it promised it would instill confidence, you found the user interface clunky and weren't even confident about how to use it. Motocaddy was also gone, since no golf meant no GPS required.

- And finally, you called Xfinity and asked the delightful customer service rep how you could block or delete the digital supervillain, Golf Channel, from your cable mix. When she told you that was no problem, it would just take a moment, you were stunned. You thought there might be some red tape, a chance to reflect on this momentous decision. You just wanted to gather info as to your choices. Was a TV channel really even part of your digital footprint? Does watching golf even count as an infraction if you have quit playing golf? Were you getting ridiculous? Absurdly literal-minded? You were about to ask her if this was reversible, or was that impossible, or possible but painful, like a vasectomy? But you were on hold and she was gone, lost in the ether. When she came back, she thanked you for holding and told you it was all set, you could no longer access Golf Channel. She expected you to say, "Thanks and have a nice day," but you told her that you hoped in the fullness of time you could come to forgive her.

- Now the hard part: quit your country club. You had been a member for nearly two decades. At first you just had two requirements: a high-quality golf course and a place you could play a round in less than four hours. You were raising two kids and had to maximize your time. Your club didn't have tee times, so you could just walk up and play. In the beginning, you rarely used the restaurant. Hell, you barely used the locker room. You changed your shoes in the parking lot and left as soon as your group putted out.

- But then you got to know the other members. And the kids started using the pool. And your wife joined committees and helped stage events and parties and cooking classes. Soon you had "your people": likeminded parents with kids of roughly the same age living in roughly the same neighborhoods and playing to roughly the same handicap. The restaurant became the go-to place for dinner on weekends. The Super Bowl, the Final Four, and of course the golf majors, were all experienced together on the big screen in the pub.

- You reminded your wife that quitting the club might very well shift the zeitgeist—you would not only lose these rituals, you might lose the connection to your people if you burn this very big boat. She wasn't having it. "If that happens, they're not really friends. If all we have in common with them is the game you play and the status it conveys on us, then we're better off without them and finding new friends."

- You nodded, but for not the first time, it was clear to you that if the two of you ever got divorced, after a proper period of grieving, your wife would get on with it. You would be devastated. She would redirect. You once asked her if she thought you were soulmates, and she simply said that she hoped you would be together forever, but soulmates? "There's no such thing," she said, and her face looked like it did when you had to tell the kids the truth about Santa so they wouldn't get made fun of in school.

- You had to officially resign, and if you didn't do it today, another month would start and you'd get billed for your procrastination. You pulled into the club lot, for the first time ever with no clubs in the trunk, and walked into the business office to see Daria, the longtime manager and keeper of the flame. She'd been there forever.

- Daria, once the Tiger Woods–effect wore off and membership started dropping a decade ago, came up with a strategy that served the club well. You could be a 1) full member, with privileges for all facilities at all times; 2) a social member, with no golf, tennis, or pool privileges but you get to eat and drink in the restaurant and go to events; 3) a golf-only member, where you can play but only at certain times, and only once all the full members were tended to; or 4) just an individual member for golf or racquets or pool, which meant you could use the facilities but couldn't bring in guests or family members. Awkward!

- The price points reflected the various levels of membership. The point was to take some of the elitist sting out of the club but still convey status. In a bold move, they even reduced the initiation fee from $20K to $7,500. It irritated some of the older members, but you weren't one of them. The more paying members you had, the less your assessments would be. As long as the golf course wasn't crowded, you didn't care who got in or what they paid.

- Daria waved you into her office—relatively tiny given her clout—and you prepared for the sell. She'd try to get you to stay on as a social member, or encourage you to incrementally quit the game by becoming a golf-only member, as if you could handle the humiliation if one of your friends asked you to play and you had to say, "I can't go out until noon on a Saturday, I'm a golf-only member now." Failing that, you knew her backup plan would be to suggest you "freeze" your membership for a year. There's no penalty to do it and you can get reinstated without a new application or initiation fee. That one was going to be tough to resist; you had been thinking a lot about that option. But no! Burn the boats!

- You took a deep breath and told Daria you had decided to give up golf and pursue other endeavors more conducive to your family's interests and would be resigning effective immediately.

- There. You did it. It was now out in the universe!

- Then you sat back and waited for Daria to change your mind. But she nodded and said that sounded great. She pulled out a piece of paper from her desk drawer and asked you to sign it, and while you did so, she said you shouldn't have bothered yourself by driving over, they now use DocuSign, so she could have emailed you the form. She said to give your lovely wife her best and told you to have a good summer. Then she not-so-furtively looked at her watch and kind of coughed.

- You were in your car sixty seconds later wondering what had just happened. As you pulled out of the parking lot for what you presumed would be the last time—no, no, it *would* be the last time—you passed Hal taking his clubs out of his trunk. Fair-skinned Hal sprayed himself down with SPF 50 sunscreen, as he always did, and then he saw you and motioned for you to roll down the window.

- You knew the drill. He would assume you'd just finished and ask you what you shot, or ask you if he could talk you into another quick nine. You thought of one of the district managers, Anna Bell, with whom you'd worked for years before she moved to the Sun Belt and tried her hand at buying a Smoothie King franchise. She had been to rehab many times and finally gotten sober. It was a heroic effort, and you always felt for her when you would be at a conference or dinner meeting and someone who didn't know and was only being polite would offer her a drink. She could have said "no thanks," but that would mean they would ask her again shortly. She could have said "I'm an alcoholic," and that would have been gutsy but invited judgment. It always impressed you that she would say, simply and firmly, "I don't drink." She allowed you to fill in the narrative. She didn't care what you thought.

- So why not start now, with Hal? You rolled down the window, and when Hal asked you how you played, you said, "I don't play golf anymore. Great to see you, Hal." And you rolled up the window, pulled right out of the parking lot to head home, and in so doing had to drive the length of the par 5 third hole near the road. And for the first time in twenty years, you didn't turn your head at the light to see who was on the hole or how far they had hit their drives. You kept your eyes on the road, on what might lay in front of you, and when the light turned green, you fought the urge to look in the rearview mirror and see who had hit the green.

CHAPTER TWENTY-ONE

A Grace Period (If Not a Period of Grace)

When you had something that filled your time and the space between your ears and then you quit cold turkey, there is a grace period. You have bought into a new narrative. There is no regret or remorse. A new era has begun for you. Your story does not end with your golf skills inevitably diminishing. It turns out you will not be witness to a sad decline. Your swing will not shorten, you will never play the forward tees, you will never hit a shot and ask your partner where it went, your narrowing macular capacity in stark contrast to your widening shot pattern disbursement.

The first two weeks are easy. You feel energized by all you have salvaged. You never again have to face first-tee jitters that one day would have led to ulcers. You will never again hate yourself for missing a 2-foot putt, and you will never again mistake an angina attack for your reaction upon showing up to play a match and finding the range is closed and you have to play with no warm-up.

In your grace period, you pass your first big test with no problem. The unstated rule in your house for as long as anyone can recall has been that, four times a year, when golf's majors are played, you watch the final thirty-six holes. It would be outrageous for your family to expect you to participate in any activity on Sunday afternoon as the leaders made their way to the back nine. This year, of all years to choose to quit golf, your favorite player, Rory McIlroy, is in the lead of the US Open after fifty-four holes. He is being chased by young upstarts, including the winner of the US Amateur, doing his best Bobby Jones imitation, and grizzled veterans who will probably have no other chance to win golf's biggest prize. The list also includes LIV traitors, who would love nothing more than to validate their tour at the expense of Rory, their biggest critic. Drama! Suspense! Golf at its highest level! Couch potato nirvana!

You didn't watch a single hole.

This was due in part to your new resolve, and to a sarcastic comment your son had made. You decided you needed your family's support if you were going to truly quit. You knew that once you said it out loud to people who would then notice if you were to backslide, thereby introducing the element of shame, you would have a better chance of staying strong. When you made the announcement during dinner, they smirked. They didn't believe you, and why should they? But you didn't need them to believe you, you needed them to hold you accountable.

You told them that the hard part was going to be filling the time, especially the time you would previously have spent making yourself a drink or snack and sitting down to watch golf. That's when your son said it. "I have one word for you: RESUME. Click on the damn RESUME button."

You have Netflix and Hulu and HBO Max and Paramount+ and Amazon Prime and probably some others. Here is your pattern. Someone recommends you watch a show ("You would *love* it!") and so you do, and they are right! But they all have multiple seasons and each season is eight episodes, and the episodes are all an hour long. Putting aside your need to watch golf and your flagging energy at the end of a workday, you are not a binge watcher. You cannot watch a full season of *Outer Banks* or *Stranger Things* in one sitting, even though as a communications professional you admire the cunning. When streaming first came out and an episode ended, you had to hit the BACK button, find the next episode and hit PLAY. But now one episode ends and you are about to get up and reengage with the real world when the whirling circle appears unbidden, accompanied by a countdown message. "Next episode starts in 15 seconds." Oh, might as well watch the next episode! Eight episodes later, you realize you haven't showered or eaten, and you're not really sure if it's still Saturday. So you would fall in love with *You* or *Emily in Paris* or *Ozark*, watch an episode, maybe two if your wife was with you, and then switch to Golf Channel or ESPN Plus and get caught up on what really mattered. Your wife liked to point out that you could binge watch golf with no problem.

And so, while for all you knew Rory and his chasers were locked up in the greatest US Open battle since Francis Ouimet in 1913, you made it your mission to go to all of your shows that you had started and hit RESUME. There was something about that prompt and what you were attempting to do with your life that seemed symmetrical and true. Resumption! Rory would have to win without you.

Grace periods wear off and habits are hard to break. When you broke for lunch at work, you found yourself making half swings with just your hands in the elevator. Just a smooth wedge swing. The only other guy in the elevator could have let it go, but instead he said, "You never miss a shot in here, right?" You knew that if you didn't find some purpose to take up the time you had devoted to golf, you would fall back in. You'd be buying new clubs in no time.

But what? It seemed logical for you to revisit the things you were unable to do with your wife because of your golf schedule. She had wanted to take cooking classes together. And there was that wine tasting club she had to join. Then she had suggested the two of you take graduate school classes at night. She reasoned that now that grades didn't matter and you weren't chasing a degree and there was no price to pay for failure, it would be a pure experience. Learning for learning's sake! But you were unmoved. In your darkest days, when everything around you was falling apart, you found solace by reminding yourself that at least you no longer had homework to do. You're done with school.

This time it was your daughter who bailed you out. You asked her what she thought you should do with your newfound free time, and she said simply, *"Well, it's been a minute since you did something for someone else. Not judging."*

She had a fair, hurtful point. Everything you were considering had some built-in benefit to you. In some ways, everything you had ever done had a built-in benefit for you. Sure, you worked to take care of your family, but even that was about you at some level, wasn't it? It felt good to be needed, to be depended on, to have power in your little fiefdom. What about altruism? Had you ever done anything that was strictly selfless? You remembered being flabbergasted when you heard about a guy on the underwriting team who had donated a kidney. Anonymously! He never knew who he had helped, and he made it a point, actually signed papers making it impossible for them to track him down and thank him. This was so alien to you. You weren't sure you were capable of donating an organ, even one you had a spare of, but you sure as hell knew if you did you would want recognition, copious attention, and you wouldn't say no to a cash prize.

Okay, volunteering it is!

You wouldn't think it would be hard to volunteer, but after filling out your application for the United Way (yes you had a car, yes you were a citizen, yes you were okay with a background check, yes you had five to ten hours a week to give), you heard nothing for a week. So you called and, after suffering through John Denver Muzak®, you punched the zero button, and when that didn't work you repeated "representative" a dozen times before a human came on the line. But she was awesome. Would you like to work with young people on climate activism? (Hmm, maybe, but why should they be subjected to your cynicism? They would learn soon enough that the world is burning and they would be wearing hazmat suits to go outside by the time they're your age. Why ruin it for them now?) How about volunteering to read to senior citizens in hospice care? (That seemed easy enough but could be depressing. And what would you read to them? It would be cruel to read a novel if they might never know how it ends. Essays? Blogs for the ones on feeding tubes? Didn't sound like your style.) And then, just as she was getting slightly irritated, she nailed it. "How do you feel about animals?"

It is well known in your house that it is your psycho dog's world and you all just live in it. Both you and your wife have made it clear that you love your dog more than you love your kids, and your kids told you the feeling was mutual. Your dog is nearly nine now, and you know the day is coming that you will all be broken people. It seems to all of you that life spans should be the complete opposite of what they are. Dogs should live well into their eighties and humans should be put down in their mid-teens. So animal volunteering would be your new purpose in life. It would make you forget you'd ever played golf.

When your spouse heard about your idea, she immediately tried to get you to reconsider the "cow cuddling" you spent several golf-worthy weekends doing in upstate NY. It was just what it sounds like. You drive to a farm, are led out to the unwitting cows, and, uh . . . hug them. You are encouraged to really get in there, to put your arms around them, to lay your face on them, and you're instructed to match their breathing. They have higher body temperatures than humans, and their heart rates are slower, and this is supposed to reduce a human's anxiety. Cows are sort of like dogs—they're curious, they know their names. But after you pay your $75 (per person, per hour), you're told it's potluck. The animals are not confined, they can take to you or walk away from you as they like. You can't force them to interact because . . . cows! Of course your wife was in heaven. Her cow allowed her to brush it and pet it, and you probably imagined it but you think you heard purring. She could have stayed there all day. You and your cow had that awkward moment. Are you going in for a hug too soon? Should you just bump knuckles? You ended up giving it a kind of pat down, like a TSA worker who keeps asking you if you're sure there's nothing in your pockets. Then your cow moved off like this was a cocktail party and you were not conversation-worthy.

But while there's no denying the therapeutic benefits of cow cuddling (your wife always comes armed with data points, and she showed you the documented oxytocin release from cow cuddling, to which you replied that you could also get an oxytocin release from oxy and you didn't need to drive three hours to find a dealer) it still was about what *you* got from *them*! You wanted to help animals who weren't some farmer's side hustle. You wanted to do something that you got nothing out of. For once in your whole damn selfish life!

The problem was, your desire for purpose was no match for the cosmic inhumanity of having to actually show up for volunteering. The Animal Rescue Foundation had plenty of need for an injury transport specialist. Someone hits a deer, or (sweet Jesus, your worst nightmare) a dog or cat in the street, and you pick up the bodies, and if they are alive you bring them in. But they're mostly not. It's an important job, but you simply didn't have the heart for it. There were plenty of "animal daycare" support jobs that turned out to be cleaning the muck out of stables or yards or cages. You knew that you would do that for a short time and suddenly shooting 60 for nine holes would seem like two weeks in Club Med.

Then you remembered that your neighbor's daughter worked for Wagging Tails, a pet sitting service. People who are at work for long periods of time or who don't want to kennel their pets while they're away on vacation hire them to visit their pets. Play with them, walk them, feed them, clean the litter box. Easy, right? You'd get to play with pets and wander around people's houses when they weren't home. Sanctioned voyeurism! You wondered if the Abbotts used Wagging Tails; you'd love to get a look at their medicine cabinets. Those people are wacky!

But when you did your Zoom interview with the Wagging Tails owners, you could tell they had made a decision not to hire you in the first ninety seconds. At first you thought they were worried that you'd want a lot of money due to your age, and you assured them you wanted to volunteer, you didn't need to be paid. Then it was clear that it was simply due to your age. This was a kid's job. They never said it out loud, but you knew it wasn't meant to be when one of them said, "We have a few more interviews, but we'll make a decision soon. If you don't hear from us, it probably means we went with someone else." They had competitors but you figured they all had the same business model. For a brief shining moment, you thought about starting your own pet sitting business, hiring a battery of middle-aged people, and driving their businesses into the ground, but the moment passed. Apparently your umbrage was no match for the hassle of forming an LLC.

So you knew you wanted to be an animal volunteer, but you were going at it all wrong. You were reading volunteer job postings and seeing if anything piqued your interest. But these postings were advertisements, not affidavits. You didn't know what was true, and worse, you didn't know your own truth. What do you have to offer these organizations? It was time for a character inventory.

You opened your iPad's Notes application and decided to brainstorm. Just free-associate. You'd been an adult for nearly thirty years now—what were your essential qualities?

- You are relentless. Everyone who has played golf with you calls you a "grinder" and it's a compliment. If you can find a way to help animals, and its right for you, you'll work your butt off. You've gotten where you are because, unlike most people, you don't rest until you're tired. Ask the kids on the club's driving range who had to keep bringing you baskets of balls.

- You like making things happen. Some people make things happen, some let things happen, and some wake up and wonder, "What happened?" You have no tolerance for anyone who says "That won't work" without 1) a better plan, or 2) even trying.

- There is a thin line between being tenacious and stalking someone; you have crossed that line. But that's okay, you apologized, and it's better to be forgiven than forgotten.

- You have a great memory. This makes you hard to argue with, since you remember exactly what the other person said, but it also helps you win, because you don't run out of ammunition to use in a debate or at the end of a deal you are trying to close.

- You're considered "the Fixer" at work because you were brought up working the phones. You don't hide behind email or text, and you are skilled at practicing "disruptive honesty." Social media has made people passive, so your approach, which once was considered indecorous and even obstreperous, has now made you invaluable. You're the shock comic of insurance.

- You've been labeled a control freak by so many people, friends and family alike, over such a long period of time, that you have made peace with it. (Sort of. You're a control freak but it's not your fault you happen to know what's best for everyone all the time.)

You figured you'd better stop while you were behind. Reviewing your list, it occurs to you that you should not only not volunteer to work with animals, but that you should probably find a better home for your own dog. You are the anti–St. Francis of Assisi. It was hard to see how your skill set could make you helpful to humans, let alone innocent creatures. You were heaving a deep sigh, lamenting your flawed, useless character, when you realized your wife was standing over your shoulder reading your list.

"If you're making a dating profile, this isn't going to be helpful. You'd better include a really old picture."

Once you explained the idea behind your brainstorming exercise, her gaze softened. She found the good in you even when you offered clear evidence to the contrary. Thank God. Then her eyes got really wide. She got her own brainstorm, and started furiously scrolling through her phone.

"Watch this video. Watch it to the end, even though it's heartbreaking. It's the *perfect* cause for you!"

The puppy mill video was 2:46 of an emotional ride. First it shocked you, then it was so agonizing it was hard to watch, and then it outraged you. How could this be going on? How could you not have known? Something had to be done. Then it asked you to step up. With time, or money. Or both. You had both.

Puppy mills are commercial dog breeders that put profits ahead of the wellness of the animals. If you've bought a puppy from a pet store or an online breeder, you can almost guarantee they came from a puppy mill. The females are forced to continually breed, giving birth to several litters a year, until they are no longer physically capable and then they are discarded, sometimes literally ditched on the side of the road or worse, put to death. Before then they are kept in horrific conditions. Overcrowded, filthy spaces, kept in small cages and often not given enough food. There is almost no veterinary care. They are never allowed to exercise.

You had to stop the video when an undercover journalist "took a tour" and surreptitiously recorded it with her iPhone. A nonstop cacophony of stressed out, barking dogs. Urine and feces everywhere. Over time the damage to the dogs' psyches is so deep that it keeps them in perpetual fight-or-flight mode.

Those who survive and are sold often have had no normal relationship with their mothers or littermates, and have no social or survival skills. So their owners have buyer's remorse and return them to animal shelters, where they often barely last a week. A close up of one puppy's dead, shell-shocked eyes gutted you. The puppy wasn't even imploring the journalist for help. It didn't know what help was. It just wanted to die. The cessation of pain.

When you looked up, your wife did two kind things. She didn't mention your weepy eyes, and she brought your dog over to you. Your happy, healthy, loved dog who was all those things by the luck of the draw.

Your search for purpose was over. There are two million puppies sold from puppy mills each year. It has to stop, and you made it your personal mission to see that. You were all in! When you took up golf, you asked the teaching pro how many balls you had to hit in order to become a scratch player. He shrugged. Thousands? Deadpanned, you told him that his answer was in the form of a question, and if he didn't know, who would? And you did hit thousands. You never became a scratch player, but you got better than he thought you could. Maybe you couldn't get from two million puppies a year to zero, but you were all in. And you were going to get closer than anyone would have thought possible. This was your sweet spot!

It took a week of prep and research, and then you mobilized.

In 2017, California became the first state to prohibit the sale of commercially raised puppies, kittens, and rabbits. Your goal was to get your state to follow suit, and then move on to other states.

Working the phones was your bread and butter. You started in sales and had no fear of rejection or cold calling. In the age of texting, this was a superpower. You called every newspaper, TV station, and radio show. Did they know about the abuse of puppies? Wouldn't they love to post a story or do a segment that would get a visceral emotional response from their audience? You called twice a day, before you started work and before you left. You followed up your voice-mails with emails and sent them LinkedIn invitations. Once they accepted, you sent them an InMail with an accompanying article about the horrors of puppy mills.

You became a lone lobbyist. You called every state legislator, not just in your district but in the whole state. You befriended their gatekeeping assistants. If they didn't call back within a day, your next message was ablaze with faux outrage. You were a taxpayer! A voter! You demanded to see the rep/senator. Then you remembered a guy at the club (your old club, back when you were a golfer, a few days ago) was the property manager of the capitol building. You got five minutes with the governor that you turned into twenty minutes. The governor, you saw on TV, has a golden retriever he likes to score points with during campaigns. You shook his hand and asked him, "Where'd you get your golden?"

Within a few months you got assurances that in the next legislative session they would sponsor a bill to strengthen and enforce the existing Animal Welfare Act. When you got that call, it was as thrilling as anything you had ever experienced as an adult. More thrilling than getting chosen to represent your company at a global conference in Barcelona, more thrilling than when you paid off your fifteen-year mortgage and felt the immense pride of living up to your commitment as your family's provider, and yes, even more thrilling than the putt that won the Major Member-Member. Because while this was by you, it was not for you.

The next arm of your outreach was social media. Seeing you skip dinner to hassle thought leaders during their dinners inspired your kids. Your daughter, maven of Insta and Reddit and TikTok started a "Stop Puppy Mills" campaign online. She made a graphic that looked like a billboard that read "It's a puppy, not a sweater" featuring the cutest damn puppy ever, and asked people to stop buying puppies online and to share and like and repost to their hearts content. She got tens of thousands of clicks.

Meanwhile, your wife, the practical one, knew money talks. She started a GoFundMe page to hire a professional lobbyist. In no time she had a fundraiser at the library, which she turned into a 5K race with your daughter's billboard graphic on T-shirts you could buy for $20.

And your son was not to be outdone. Flea markets are overlooked places where puppy mill puppies are sold under the radar. The first time out, your son offered money to any of his friends who would show up at a flea market and protest the sale of puppies. Your wife armed them with signs and you alerted the media, who by now were sick of hearing from you and dispatched reporters before you were even done talking. By the second flea market the kids wouldn't take money and they brought their friends and their friend's friends. A few times you had to remind them that if they got belligerent or used the flea market as an excuse to party, they would hurt the cause and the puppies. Did they always listen? Come on, they're teenagers. But by the middle of the summer, your son said ABC News had interviewed him and they were covering the protests! A couple of weeks later you got an email from a guy at Georgetown who was thinking of making a documentary about puppy mills and heard about your activism.

The summer flew by. In a good way. Not the usual longing, the weight of concealing your awareness that your life was drifting, your days running into each other, indistinguishable. For years you have felt two contradictory, overarching feelings each summer: "My days are empty and meaningless," and "I'm sad I don't have more of them." This year you never felt enervated or distracted. You had a lightness about you, even when you hit some temporary roadblock with your puppy mill campaign. The miracle of purpose was that even the setbacks were sweet, preferable to days designed only for entertainment and sensory satiety.

Who knew when the legislation would be passed? Who knew if your tenacity would run its course? What if every puppy mill was closed? Would you find another cause? Would anything ever move you like the puppies?

Too soon to know. But you knew that you'd passed the ultimate test.

Jeff was the kind of guy who knew everyone. If you needed something done around the house, he knew a guy. Need tickets? Call this guy. Jeff took a lot of pride in his connections. You hadn't talked to him in a long time, and when you heard his voice, the first thing you thought was that you should have called Jeff at the outset. He would know someone who could help with the puppy mill cause! Jeff was also a golfer, and a good one. He didn't know you had quit the game.

"Buddy, you sitting down? What are you doing next Saturday? No, shut the hell up, I'll tell you what you're doing next Saturday. You are playing Winged Foot with me in a best ball tournament. Winged Foot, dude! I *told* you someday I'd get us out on that freaking track. Winged Foot! You know I'm going to hit my tee shot on 18 farther left than Phil did when he choked in '06. Buckle up, buddy! We're going to have ourselves a day!"

Out of respect you let him finish. He was so happy and once upon a time, you would have been profusely thanking him and then texting every golfer you knew about your windfall. But Saturday mornings had become a new kind of sacred time for you. If you didn't have a fundraiser or an event, you used the time to set up a call sheet or send out an email campaign. In fact, the Saturday of Winged Foot, you had set up a meeting with a podcast company that would record, edit, and distribute a podcast for you. You wanted to launch the stop the puppy mills podcast by Labor Day. You needed to find animal rights experts for guests and sponsors; you needed to estimate the cost and figure out the reach and ROI. None of this was worth explaining to Jeff.

"Aw, Jeffie, thank you for thinking of me. I don't play anymore, dude. I don't even have clubs."

"What? Well don't worry, it's Winged Foot, their worst rentals are better than your clubs. You'll be fine."

"I can't do it. I've got something."

"I'm sorry, did part of the call drop? Winged Foot! Please put down the phone, take a look at your bucket list, and right there at the top is, oh look— Winged Foot! So do *not* tell me you can't play!"

You were getting annoyed. And that wasn't fair or kind. Jeff didn't know what he didn't know. You had moved on, and he hadn't. That didn't make you better than him. But that's exactly how it felt. And that made you annoyed with yourself. Should you have tried to explain? No. Just end this.

"You're right, Jeff, I can play. I just don't want to. I gotta go."

"Wait, wait a sec! Look, I know we haven't kept up with each other. Are you okay? Did something happen and I'm being an insensitive jerk? Are you in a wheelchair?"

A wheelchair. That's the only thing a hardcore golfer could imagine would keep you from accepting an invitation to play Winged Foot. (If you said yes, Jeff would suggest you ride around in the cart and watch him play Winged Foot.) Suddenly it occurred to you that of all people, Jeff would understand what happened to you. Jeff had an epic scandal a few years ago, when he left his wife and young kids and took up with, and then married, a girl with two kids who had been in the country a month from Albania. She worked at the Starbucks he frequented. It was all anyone could talk about for most of that year. When you played golf with Jeff, you didn't bring it up. You thought the course should be the one place he could go to escape the drama. But he brought it up himself one day. He was at an inflection point and needed to talk about it. You asked him the question—the only question, really—why?

"Nobody leaves a situation that is bad for them without having a better situation to go to first. No one is that strong . . . at least I wasn't."

And you weren't either.

"No, no, I'm fine, it's all good. Enjoy the round, and tell me how it goes."

You knew he wouldn't tell you how Winged Foot was, and that was for the better. Because you really didn't care.

CHAPTER TWENTY-TWO

Exiled in Elba

Bandon Dunes is gorgeous. The new Mecca of golf with the best links golf this side of Scotland. Five of the top one hundred golf courses in the country. Coastal landscapes and natural dunes and even forests. And everyone there shares a common language, purpose, and devotion. Everyone walks, no one complains, and everyone is happy regardless of their score or how long it took to get to remote Oregon.

At least that's what you have gathered. You're not there. You're in Tuscany with your wife, the Krausses, and the Pattersons. But while you have tried earnestly to untether yourself from golf, you can't block everyone you know, and you have to check email.

You have completely forgotten that this is the week of the big Bandon Dunes trip. And even if you weren't consumed by the vineyards and olive groves and cypress trees in the little towns of northern Italy; even if you weren't busy eating bowls of pappa al pomodoro or drinking Chianti at every stop in the wine region; even if you weren't blown away by the rugged cliffs and clear water and endless osterias of the Amalfi Coast, you know for a fact you wouldn't have been sneaking away to check your phone to see if anyone in the group had broken 80 on Bandon trails.

Because you don't belong anymore. At first you assumed you would be able to keep an honorary status—once a golfer always a golfer. You thought it was like your friend Dave, an ex-Marine who has been out of the service for thirty years but still refers to himself as a Marine in the present tense. (With all the accompanying swagger. You were with him once in the baggage claim area when a kid in a Navy uniform happened to be waiting at the same carousel. Dave introduced himself as a Marine and said, "Navy, huh? You're the guys who give us a ride to the fight. Appreciate you.")

But you can't seem to make it matter. Their concerns are not your concerns anymore. You read the posts and emails full of stories, gamesmanship, and shot-by-shot depictions of birdies made or rounds ruined. Once breathless reads for you, they don't even hold your attention to the end of the email anymore. You already know how every story ends!

It occurs to you that maybe it is easy to be disengaged when you are seeing the Leaning Tower of Pisa or Da Vinci's *Annunciation* or Michelangelo's *David*. (You insisted on a guided tour, and here's where going on all those golf trips helped you. The Pattersons wanted to "freewheel" the trip and be spontaneous, much like when you played Pinehurst and some guys wanted to eschew caddies and read the greens themselves. Nope. These guys see this place all day every day, you're paying for them to enhance your experience and shoot a damn score. You told the Pattersons you were not going to spend your precious vacation time driving aimlessly around Italy.) But you know your decision is deeper than just a temporary distraction. You have left golf, and much more importantly, it has left you.

But only you knew this. And you understood your wife's anxiety. She was on high alert. Were you genuinely engaged? Were you listening to the tour guide? Enjoying yourself as much as you appeared to be? Or was this trip a down payment? Leverage that you would cash in when you got back home and told her fall golf was your favorite time to play and you were thinking of putting your toes back in the water. It's a tactic you were absolutely capable of way back, like five minutes ago. This had to be what it was like once an addict came out of rehab. She saw you looking detoxed, healthy, alert. The person she once knew had been returned to her! But for how long? She had been fooled so many times.

So who could blame her for the abject fear in her eyes when at breakfast, Dean Patterson pointed his phone at you and told you the Marco Simone golf course, the site of the Ryder Cup, was not only open to the public but a mere two-hour train ride from where you were staying? You and high handicapper Krausse should make a half day of it and let the girls have some time to themselves. Krausse said he was game, as long as he got mulligans. His wife said sure. Your wife was as still as the statues you'd been seeing. And you said it would be great if they went, and if the girls hung out together, because you wanted to do something on your own—you wanted to take a cruise over to the island of Elba.

"Elba . . . Why do I know that name?"

Napoleon, after pretty much dominating Europe from 1799 to 1810, à la Tiger Woods at the turn of this century, wore out his welcome and was forced to abdicate his throne and was exiled to the island of Elba. Ten months later, again channeling his inner Tiger, he escaped and mounted a comeback. It didn't work out, and he was exiled again for good, this time to the remote island of St. Helena.

How had you forgotten that your first love, your first obsession really, was history? Your dad was obsessed with World War II, which got you obsessed. The more you knew, the more you had to talk about, the more he wanted to spend time with you, so you wanted to know more. Of course, your first obsession was your dad's approval; your second was golf's approval. Both proved fleeting.

Napoleon would always be remembered as a tyrant out to rule the world, and of course he was. His height and his flaws (he may have died of venereal disease) become stereotypical fodder, but during his reign he championed reforms that the Western world now takes for granted—voting rights, judiciary systems, and religious tolerance. So you were here at Elba to reconnect with your love of history.

But also because you too are in exile. You have chosen to cut yourself off from a large part of your identity. The pro bono puppy work is satisfying and has served you well, but it's not going to be enough. Golf got deep—how will you replace the spectrum of experience it brought you? You've reconnected with your family; you are present and focused at work; you give back and you think you're a pretty decent human, as humans go. But a part of you has been cut off. It seems preposterous to say out loud that no longer playing a game has somehow left you unsure of who you are or what to do. You want to stay open to whatever is next, but it is scary to have no idea what that might be.

One day Napoleon literally ruled the world. The next he was on a boat to Elba. He lived not in a castle but in the Villa dei Mulini, so he could view the sea and watch for invaders. It is now a national museum, and you are standing on the steps. You assumed Napoleon was despondent at Elba. He had been disgraced and lost everything. In today's world he would have been on suicide watch, given meds and counseled to prioritize his mental health. If he had, someone would have called him brave.

But in exile, if he didn't thrive, he certainly wasn't despondent. He personally designed and managed renovations on his digs, including adding a theater. He played cards every night: solitaire and whist and blackjack. He attended public dances and horse races. He wrote his memoirs. And in due time, plotted his escape and his return to the throne. Like Tiger at Augusta in 2019, he had a brief return to power. And like Tiger, while his reign didn't last, it had to be immensely satisfying.

To the world, Napoleon had been exiled. To Napoleon, he had downsized and moved to a warmer climate near the beach, as one does.

It's all in how you look at it. Your exile will end. You know that now. How and when and in what fashion? Well, that's to be decided. And that's okay.

When you got off the boat, your wife was waiting for you on the pier. She had been shopping and was holding up a bunch of bags. She gave a shrug and a smirk that said, "See what happens when you go off without me?" She seemed kind of hot to you. Was she getting hotter, or was it Italy? She gave you a big hug.

Hugs. That's the thing you will miss the most about quitting golf. Golf is sanctioned hugging for grown-ass men. You hug when you see someone on the range. You hug on the first tee. Roll in a 50-foot putt and come over here and gimmie some! Hug it out on the 18th green after removing your caps. Get one last squeeze when you pick up the check in the grill room and head home.

You will truly miss the golf hugs, and yet now that you have really and truly given up golf, your wife hugs you differently. At least, they feel different, but you know from all your time as a golfer that "feel may not be real." So you're probably wrong and your wife hugs you the same way she has always hugged you, and always will. A guy you used to golf with would hit a bad shot that would hit a tree and bounce back into the fairway and say, "You don't get what you deserve in life. Thank God." And now, you understand.

Epilogue

"You can't say that anymore."

"I just meant it's unusually warm for October."

"Then say that."

You used the term Indian summer, and you never will again. You should know better. Because you have quit golf, and you know that remnants linger long after they have lost their original meaning.

But it is a beautiful evening. Crazy warm. You shouldn't waste it. This is a one-off. Your wife says she has a summer craving for ice cream. Your kids are home, which never happens, and they say they're up for getting ice cream with you, which also never happens. What year is this?

It turns out the new ice cream place near the town hall also features a miniature golf course. Once you have your ice cream, your son issues a boys against girls challenge (which he crudely refers to as "the Cs against the Cs," and your wife smacks him). At first you weren't sure if this was a violation of the new world order, but you thought it was probably a healthy sign if you could just goof around, like you did when you played mini golf before actual golf.

You knew him even though you had never seen him before in your life. There was a backup on the 4th tee, and he was there with his wife and another couple. They were all laughing, but he was watching the group in front of him intently. Did they go straight at the hole or did they try to bank it off the side board? While trying to decipher how best to play the hole, he was checking his full swing grip with his putter, and then he started to practice full swings, even holding his pose and checking his angles. He had a scorecard in his back pocket, and as soon as they holed out, he asked everyone for their score, and he corrected his wife—she made a four, not a three, since she had to take a penalty stroke for that ball that went off the course onto the walkway. She rolled her eyes. On the next hole, he told his buddy that he was not allowed to move the ball from the side board. "Sorry, dude, play it as it lays is kinda the whole idea."

You were actually kind of amused, but you tried to keep concentrating on your own family. After a while he left, probably, you thought, to go get a drink or an ice cream. But then he came back with his actual Odyssey putter from the golf clubs in his car. Now you were fully, disproportionately aggravated.

On the next tee back up, he apologized for the delay and said, "We'd let you through but there's no place to go." You nodded, not realizing it would give him license to say what he really wanted to say.

"I shot 80 this afternoon. Lipped out an eight footer for 79."

"Here?"

"What? No, on an actual damn golf course. I'm just screwing around here, probably going to mess up my stroke. You play?"

"Uh, I used to."

"Were you any good?"

Not that you were going to engage with him, but it's a good question. Were you? For all you gave to the game, for all you gave up for the game, were you any good? It turns out memories are kind to us. Maybe they have to be for us to survive our choices. Your parents have been divorced forever now, and it was as ugly a divorce as has ever been. For a few years they would not show up to events if the other was present. Then they were able to be in the same room but wouldn't acknowledge each other. Now they go to events in order to see each other. You remember your good shots. The clutch putts, the lucky breaks. You were not good, you played golf swing more than you played golf, and you always played in a state of ambient fear. But that's not how you will remember it.

"I was okay."

"Well, I'm obsessed. I only took it up three years ago and, like I said, I shot 80 today, and I'm going to get a lot better than that. I'm willing to put in the hard yards. I have plans for this game!"

You were no longer aggravated with this guy. You wanted to take him over to the picnic tables near the parking lot, sit him down, and try and save him. But he wouldn't listen. Whenever an older person tries to share their experience with a younger person on the same path, the young person may listen politely. They may nod, they may even express thanks for sharing. But what they are thinking is, "I'm not you, and it's not my fault you got old."

The wind was picking up, the kids were getting restless and were tapping at their phones, the ice cream was gone, and the big family moment had passed. So you turned in your colored balls and rubber headed putters to the kid at the counter and headed home before turning to the back nine.

"Hey, Dad, did you see that guy playing with his actual putter? What a clown!"

You turned to your wife, leaned in, and whispered, "Remind you of anyone you know?"

She squeezed your free hand tightly.

"No, not at all."

About the Author

DANNY CAHILL is the last guy to talk to about work-life balance. As a headhunter, he has built Hobson's Associates into one of the country's largest privately held search firms. His coaching and training company, According to Danny, is the largest in the staffing industry. His motivational speaking and career coaching earned him the industry's highest honor, the NAPS Lifetime Achievement award. In his writing life, as a playwright, he has had works produced off-Broadway and won both the Maxwell Anderson and CAB theater awards. He is the author of the popular memoir, *Aging Disgracefully*, and *Harper's Rules*, which won an Axiom award. He attributes his success, fledgling as it is, to a systematic, consistent, and disciplined . . . neglect of loved ones.